Student Activity

College English and Communication

and

Eighth Edition

Glencoe McGraw-Hill

New York, New York   Columbus, Ohio   Chicago, Illinois   Peoria, Illinois   Woodland Hills, California

Glencoe/McGraw-Hill

A Division of The **McGraw·Hill** *Companies*

Printed in the United States of America.

Send all inquiries to:

Glencoe/McGraw-Hill
21600 Oxnard Street, Suite 500
Woodland Hills, CA 91367

ISBN 0-07-828271-3 (Student Edition)
ISBN 0-07-828272-1 (Instructor's Annotated Edition)

1 2 3 4 5 6 7 8 9   024   07 06 05 04 03 02

Table of Contents

Contents *(continued)*

Contents *(continued)*

Notes to the Student

Developing the skills presented in your *College English and Communication* text requires practice. Reading and studying the text is an effective beginning, but to master those skills you need to apply them—you must improve your use of language; listen and speak with confidence; prepare memos, letters, and reports; write, edit, and proofread correspondence. Remember that no matter what you want to accomplish and what specific skills you have, to succeed in business you need effective communication skills.

College English and Communication, Eighth Edition, offers you several formats for practicing those communication skills. Within the text, each section has Practical Application and Editing Practice activities; many sections also have Critical Thinking activities.

In addition to the opportunities within the text, *College English and Communication, Eighth Edition* also provides many additional practice situations in this *Activity Workbook for College English and Communication, Eighth Edition.* Use your developing communication skills and the references you have available as you continue your study of *College English and Communication.*

Remember that communication skills are not separate units to be studied and practiced individually and then stored away so that you can study another skill. Listening, speaking, reading, and writing are integrated skills. Two or three or even all four may be used in a single application. In the *Activity Workbook for College English and Communication, Eighth Edition,* you will use the building-block approach: Each succeeding chapter builds on those that came before. You will be asked to use all that you have learned—not only the skills in the current chapter—to complete the activities.

The *Activity Workbook for College English and Communication, Eighth Edition,* is organized and labeled to match the text. The workbook offers extensive and varied additional practice including short-answer, true/false, multiple choice, and narrative formats.

Communicating in Everyday Life. Chapter 1 of the text offers an introduction to the communication process—applied both to your personal life and to your business life. Chapter 1 in the activity workbook asks you to apply principles in the text to simulated business situations and to your own experiences.

Interpreting Communication. Chapter 2 introduces the basics of nonverbal communication, including basics of listening and reading documents. The focus is on improving listening skills and on developing awareness of the importance of nonverbal communication.

Global, Electronic, and Ethical Communication. Chapter 3 introduces some of the technologies used to communicate globally and focuses on factors dealing with cultural diversity, ethics, and nondiscriminatory language in communication. Chapter 9 examines in detail the considerations for communicating electronically. Corresponding exercises in the activity workbook provide opportunities to apply the concepts covered in these chapters to realistic workplace situations.

Grammar, Punctuation, and Style. Chapters 4, 5, and 6 in the text provide a thorough discussion of the principles of grammar, punctuation, and style. These chapters in the activity workbook give intensive application of these principles using business situations for the examples.

The Craft of Writing. Chapters 7 and 8 in the text and the workbook uses a building-block approach in presenting the techniques for writing messages—moving from word choice and spelling to structuring phrases and clauses, writing sentences, and building paragraphs. Chapter 7 also will give you an understanding of revising, editing, and proofreading and the importance of these processes in producing error-free communications. Developing your skills in proofreading and editing is not easy. First, you need to be able to spot a possible error. Next, you must decide if the situation really is an error. Finally, you must know how to correct the problem if an error exists. Another challenge is to find a better way to explain something. The workbook activities for Chapter 8 include practice in locating errors—first by category and then by document. You also have opportunities to rewrite messages for improvement.

E-mails, Memos, and Letters. Chapter 9 helps you work with letters, emphasizing the importance of reading in researching and retaining information and in writing and revising correspondence. The text and the workbook focus on reading strategies, vocabulary power, retention and comprehension, and note taking.

Specific Communication Situations. Chapter 10 addresses specific situations requiring unique methods of communication. These include the persuasive document, claim and adjustment messages, letters for the purposes of public relations, communications of a social-business nature, and form letters and templates.

Preparing and Writing Reports. Chapter 11 guides you through a number of other business communications—informal reports, formal reports, minutes of meetings, and news releases. Included in the Chapter 11 workbook activities are opportunities to explore the technology resources available to report writers.

Working with Technology. Chapter 12 discusses the ways technology affects communication. The accompanying workbook activities provide exercises for exploring the impact technology has had on business communication.

Customer Service Communication. Chapter 13 discusses the importance of customer service communication in business. The accompanying workbook activities provide realistic business situations for practice in customer service communication.

Oral Communication. Chapter 14 of the text presents guidelines to help you speak effectively in one-to-one and group situations. Chapter 14 of the activity workbook guides you through specific skills to help you improve your listening and speaking abilities—listening strategies, nonverbal cues, pronunciation and enunciation, organization, effective use of words, telephone techniques, and development of an oral presentation.

Communication and Your Career. In Chapters 15 and 16 of both the text and the activity workbook, you will apply all the communication skills you've developed in preparing for the job search, making your interviews more effective, and advancing in your career.

By a thorough study of your *College English and Communication, Eighth Edition,* text and a careful application of the text principles to completing the exercises in the *Activity Workbook for College English and Communication, Eighth Edition,* you can develop the proficiency in writing, listening, speaking, and reading that you will need for career success.

CHAPTER 1 Communicating in Everyday Life

Section 1.1 Elements of Communication

A. Purposes of Communication

Directions: On the lines provided, write the most likely purpose of each of the following sentences—to inquire, to inform, to persuade, or to establish goodwill.

1. What is the address of your company's Web site?

   _____

2. The Web site address has changed because we have a new server.

   _____

3. Thank you for inquiring about our new online banking system.

   _____

4. Paying your bills online will save you time and money.

   _____

5. How do I open an online account?

   _____

6. The Foundation's generous donation of equipment to Elm Park School is greatly appreciated.

   _____

7. Workshops on Web searches are held every Thursday at 7 p.m. at the Springfield Public Library.

   _____

8. If you purchase a new cell phone today, you will receive 500 minutes of free calling time.

   _____

9. Is this a good time to invest in technology stocks?

   _____

10. Click the Resources icon for more information about current employment opportunities.

    _____

B. Giving Feedback

Directions: For each of the following situations, describe the type(s) of feedback the receiver should give. Indicate whether the feedback should be oral, written, or nonverbal, or a combination of these.

1. You are meeting with your supervisor to discuss a sales report you are to compile for a meeting next week. Your supervisor is explaining what information is needed and how it should be presented. However, your supervisor has not been clear on several points. What feedback would you give your supervisor to show that you need clarification on the instructions?

_____

_____

_____

2. A co-worker leaves a message on your voice mail. The co-worker asks you to provide monthly sales figures for the last six months. What feedback would you give your co-worker?

_____

_____

_____

3. At the health clinic where you work, a patient asks you a question about tests that the doctor has ordered for the patient. What feedback would you give this patient?

_____

_____

_____

4. You work in the order department at a major electronics company. A customer asks you to make some changes to an order that she phoned in yesterday. The customer asks to receive confirmation that the order has been changed. What feedback should you give the customer?

_____

_____

_____

5. A co-worker who is also a friend of yours asks you to review a memo he wrote and to comment on the writing style. What feedback should you give your co-worker?

_____

_____

_____

C. Identify and Respond to Needs of the Receiver

Directions: Based on the following situations, identify which need of the receiver (esteem, physical, security, social, self-actualization) is not being met. Describe what could be done to meet that need.

1. Attendees at a one-day conference have not eaten since the 7:30 a.m. breakfast, and the noon luncheon program starts with an hour-long keynote speech.

    _____

    _____

    _____

    _____

    _____

2. A new staff member is continually left to look after the office while the other staff members go to lunch together.

    _____

    _____

    _____

    _____

    _____

3. A salesperson who frequently travels by car is hesitant to travel in unfamiliar surroundings, especially at night.

    _____

    _____

    _____

    _____

    _____

4. The hardest working employee in the department has been passed over several times for recognition as employee of the month.

    _____

    _____

    _____

    _____

    _____

D. Analyzing Communication

Directions: In each of the following situations, identify the type of feedback the receiver would most likely give (oral, written, or nonverbal). In addition, explain your interpretation of the message.

1. At 2:45 p.m., Donna Ortega tells Mike, the summer intern, to stop what he is doing and make 20 copies of the agenda for the departmental meeting. The agenda is two double-sided pages. The meeting will take place at 3:00 p.m.

   _____

   _____

   _____

   _____

   _____

   _____

2. Jenna, a clerk in an electronics store, is setting up new displays before the store opens at 10 a.m. At 9:55 a.m., a man knocks on the store's plate-glass window to get Jenna's attention. Then he points to his watch.

   _____

   _____

   _____

   _____

   _____

   _____

3. Jon Talbot, a software designer, receives an E-mail about a meeting to discuss the schedule for the development of new product. The meeting will take place on Thursday afternoon, Jon's day off.

   _____

   _____

   _____

   _____

   _____

   _____

E. Taking the Receiver's Background Into Account

Directions: In each of the following messages, determine the most appropriate way to communicate the message based on the receiver's background and the nature of the message.

1. You are a librarian, and you are working with a person who wants to research his family history. The person has never used the Internet before, and you must clearly explain all the steps to be followed in detail.

    _____

    _____

    _____

    _____

    _____

    _____

2. A friend has asked you to help her buy a computer. She insists that she wants a very simple system, perhaps a word-processor with E-mail capacity. You think your friend should learn to use a full-powered computer system.

    _____

    _____

    _____

    _____

    _____

    _____

    _____

F. Eliminating Barriers to Communication

Directions: For each of the following situations, identify any barriers to communication (physical, emotional, or language). List suggestions for overcoming or dealing with the barriers.

1. A training session is taking place in a room where the temperature is very warm.

    _____

    _____

    _____

    _____

    _____

continued ➡

2. An employee is having a difficult time concentrating on work because there is a rumor going around the office that employees are going to be laid off due to an upcoming merger with another company.

_____

_____

_____

_____

3. A potential customer receives a sales letter that contains several misspelled words.

_____

_____

_____

_____

G. Responsibilities of the Sender and the Receiver

1. Briefly describe a situation in your life where miscommunication occurred, and describe how the miscommunication could have been avoided.

_____

_____

_____

_____

2. Describe a situation on the job where it would be important to maintain goodwill, and explain how you would accomplish this.

_____

_____

_____

_____

3. Describe a situation on the job where it would be important to maintain confidentiality, and explain how you would accomplish this.

_____

_____

_____

_____

Section 1.2 The Communication Skills: Listening, Speaking, Reading, and Writing

A. An Interrelationship of Communication Skills

Directions: The four communication skills—listening, speaking, reading, and writing—are interconnected. In each of the following examples, one of the communication skills is featured. Explain how one or more of the other skills might be used in the situation to reinforce the primary skill.

1. Listening to a co-worker's concerns about completing an important project on time.

_____

_____

_____

2. Speaking to a customer about the differences between two computer products.

_____

_____

_____

3. Writing a report about the advantages and disadvantages of using E-mail to communicate messages.

_____

_____

_____

4. Reading several books on conducting a job search to determine the best strategies to use.

_____

_____

_____

5. Listening to your supervisor explain the preparations being made for an upcoming meeting with clients from Japan.

_____

_____

_____

B. Reading and Writing

Directions: Below are ten activities that require reading skills or writing skills. On the lines
provided, write the skill that you would primarily use to complete each activity.

1. Looking up a word in the dictionary _____

2. Completing an application form _____

3. Setting up a new E-mail account _____

4. Preparing a digital presentation _____

5. Reviewing notes on your personal digital assistant _____

6. Receiving an E-mail _____

7. Designing a Web page _____

8. Preparing a memo for a meeting _____

9. Researching frequently asked questions on a Web site _____

10. Learning to use a new DVD player _____

C. Effective Communication

Directions: Indicate the communication skill or skills you would be most likely to use for
each of the following situations and explain why you would use them.

1. Researching material for a speech.

_____

_____

_____

_____

_____

2. Attending a sales presentation.

_____

_____

_____

_____

_____

_____

3. Giving a friend directions to your new house.

_____
_____
_____
_____
_____

4. Explaining an assignment to a classmate.

_____
_____
_____
_____
_____

5. Helping a family member cope with a personal problem.

_____
_____
_____
_____
_____

D. Using the Four Communications Skills on the Job

Directions: Imagine that you work in the Human Resources department of a software development company. Write a paragraph that explains how you might use each of the four communication skills on the job.

_____
_____
_____
_____
_____
_____
_____
_____
_____
_____

E. Combining the Communication Skills in Your Social, Educational, and Professional Lives

Directions: For each of the following situations, write one paragraph that explains how you would use a combination of communication skills to communicate.

1. Communicating with a colleague who works in a different part of the United States.

_____

_____

_____

_____

_____

_____

_____

2. Communicating with a supervisor about an upcoming professional conference that you would like to attend.

_____

_____

_____

_____

_____

_____

_____

_____

3. Communicating with a co-worker about a digital presentation the two of you will give during a staff meeting.

_____

_____

_____

_____

_____

_____

_____

_____

F. Sensitivity in Communication

Directions: Sensitivity is the key to all effective communication. In the space provided next to each of the following phrases, write *S* if the phrase reflects sensitivity in business situations or *I* if it reflects insensitivity.

1. Considering who will be hearing or reading what you have to say _____

2. Considering the needs of your audience _____

3. Interrupting a speaker _____

4. Changing the subject of discussion suddenly _____

5. Keeping your emotions under control _____

6. Using facial expressions and gestures to express a negative reaction to what the speaker is saying _____

7. Giving credit for others' contributions _____

8. Giving incomplete information _____

9. Being punctual _____

10. Speaking in an almost inaudible voice _____

11. Giving a speaker your undivided attention and interest _____

12. Reading a handout while someone is speaking _____

13. Taking into consideration what your audience already knows about the subject _____

14. Thinking about what your audience is interested in hearing _____

15. Not doing your fair share of work _____

16. Keeping your mind focused on the speaker's topic _____

17. Reading to gain background information before listening to a presentation _____

18. Not reading your company's employment manual _____

Section 1.3 Communicating in the Business Environment

A. Using the Correct Tone

Directions: For each of the following communication situations, determine whether the tone should be formal or informal.

1. Inform a friend about an upcoming career day at your college.   _____

2. Discuss with your supervisor an idea for improving sales.   _____

3. Write instructions for the company procedures manual on the proper way to format letters.   _____

4. Give a presentation to the human relations committee at your company.   _____

5. Discuss weekend plans with a co-worker.   _____

6. Write a letter to your senator describing your view on funding for education.   _____

7. Present your findings on the cost efficiency of new computer equipment to your supervisor.   _____

8. Inform staff members about plans for a new break room.   _____

9. Write a letter responding to a customer's request.   _____

10. Explain to your employer the reasons you decided to purchase a more expensive type of copy paper.   _____

B. Components of Business Communication

Directions: Indicate whether each of the following examples describes an external or an internal form of business communication.

1. A memo from the sales manager to all salespeople in the office.   _____

2. A staff meeting on ideas for decorating the new office.   _____

3. A sales letter sent to prospective clients.   _____

4. A telemarketing survey of local citizens.   _____

5. A retreat for employees of the company to develop teamwork skills.   _____

6. A newspaper ad for a paralegal position.   _____

7. A sales pitch to a group of potential clients.   _____

8. An office manager giving employees directions for dealing with problem clients.   _____

9. A memo from human resources about the new health care package.   _____

10. A brochure explaining the new class offerings sent to current students.   _____

C. Flow of Communication Within an Organization

Directions: In a paragraph, describe how the tone of upward communication might differ from that of lateral or downward communication.

_____

_____

_____

_____

_____

_____

_____

_____

_____

_____

_____

_____

_____

_____

_____

_____

D. Upward, Lateral, and Downward Communication

Directions: Describe the upward, lateral, and downward communication that might occur in each of the following situations.

1. The president of a company in Houston holds a videoconference with vice presidents in three other cities.

_____

_____

_____

_____

2. A college instructor holds a real-time, online discussion with her students.

_____

_____

_____

_____

3. A staff member sends an E-mail to all the people on the production team, whose members include both managers and staff employees.

_____

_____

_____

_____

4. An experienced computer technician explains software upgrades to a newly hired technician.

_____

_____

_____

_____

5. An unemployed person visits a company's Web site, clicks the "Contact Us" button, and writes a message requesting information about a job.

_____

_____

_____

_____

E. Applying the Six Cs of Business Communication

Directions: Describe how you would apply the six Cs of communication to each of the following situations.

1. Setting up a sales appointment with a client.

_____

_____

_____

_____

_____

2. Arranging for repair work to be done to the electrical wiring in your office.

_____

_____

_____

_____

_____

3. Giving a new worker instructions on sending out mail.

_____

_____

_____

_____

_____

4. Writing a status report to your supervisor about an ongoing project you are working on.

_____

_____

_____

_____

_____

continued ➡

5. Answering a telephone call from a patient about test results.

_____

_____

_____

_____

_____

_____

F. Editing to Meet the Six Cs of Communication

Directions: Edit the following paragraph to reflect the six Cs of communication. The edited
paragraph should be clear, complete, concise, consistent, correct, and courteous.

    I am writing this letter to inform you that the shipment you ordered
will be mailed to the address you requested on or before Wednesday. We
could not get the shipment mailed any earlier due to processing
problems at our plant. I hope this does not inconvenience you because
we need your business and look forward to doing business with you in
the future. If you have any questions or concerns about this shipment
wait until next Tuesday to call so I have a chance to recover from the
weekend.

_____

_____

_____

_____

_____

_____

_____

_____

_____

_____

_____

_____

_____

_____

CHAPTER 2 Interpreting Communication

Section 2.1 The Basics of Nonverbal Communication

A. Identifying Forms of Communication

Directions: Each situation below involves either verbal or nonverbal communication. On the line provided, write *V* if the communication is verbal, or *N* if the communication is nonverbal.

1. A baby is hungry and so it cries. _____

2. A co-worker, opening her office and finding birthday balloons, laughs out loud. _____

3. Watching the clock run down, a basketball coach yells, "Foul! Foul!" _____

4. A summer intern is standing by the jammed photocopier with a look of anguish on his face. _____

5. The potential employee enters the room, shakes your hand, sits down, and smiles warmly. _____

6. A delivery person gets on the elevator with a pile of packages in his arms. You ask, "What floor?" _____

7. In the cafeteria, a co-worker puts coins in the vending machine and then pounds on the glass with his fist and jiggles the coin-return button. _____

8. During a meeting, your supervisor checks her watch. _____

9. A co-worker stands at the mailroom window, tapping her foot impatiently. _____

10. The conference room telephone rings, and your team leader asks, "Can you please answer that?" _____

B. Identifying the Message Behind Nonverbal Communication

Directions: The situations below involve nonverbal communication. Read each situation and then, on the lines provided, write the message that you think is being conveyed.

1. You have been invited by a business acquaintance to a lunch. You show up in your best suit. Your acquaintance is wearing jeans, boots, and a T-shirt.

_____

_____

_____

_____

2. You give a co-worker a copy of your report and ask him to read it. He hands it back to you, and you ask, "Well?" Your co-worker shrugs.

_____

_____

_____

_____

3. A colleague comes out of the conference room where the company's departmental managers are meeting. Your colleague sighs and frowns as she walks away from the closed door.

_____

_____

_____

_____

4. You meet a former co-worker at the grocery store. You smile and move toward him, extending your hand. The former co-worker does not make eye contact or extend his own hand.

_____

_____

_____

_____

5. In the cafeteria, you carry your lunch to a table where two co-workers are sitting. They are sitting close, their heads together, and they do not look up when you approach.

_____

_____

_____

_____

C. Categorizing Nonverbal Communication

Directions: Read the following situations. Then, on the line provided, identify the category of nonverbal communication that is illustrated by the situation. Write *P* for paralanguage, *K* for kinesics, *E* for environment, *T* for touch, and *S* for space.

1. You are giving a presentation to your colleagues on Internet searching strategies. Before the meeting, you make sure all the chairs are facing the projection screen. You adjust the blinds so the room will be dim, and you check the thermostat because the room is a bit warm.   _____

2. You enter a meeting room a few minutes before the staff meeting. Your supervisor is sitting at the far end of the room. As you sit down, your supervisor slides a sheet of paper across the table toward you and asks, "Would you please make copies of the schedule?"   _____

3. You are having lunch in order to celebrate a colleague's recent promotion. Everyone is chatting and enjoying their meals. At some point, your manager clears her throat to get everyone's attention.   _____

4. You have been attending a two-day conference. You have asked a speaker at the conference to talk to you after the last session. The speaker finds you in the hotel lobby, slumps down in a chair, loosens his tie, and stifles a yawn.   _____

5. You and a co-worker have been struggling to make a deadline. You E-mail the last file just before 5 p.m. on Friday. Your co-worker turns to you and raises his palms for you to slap.   _____

D. Identifying Conflicting Signals

Directions: Each of the situations below involves conflicting signals or messages. On the lines provided, identify the messages that are in conflict.

1. A patient visits a doctor about some unusual symptoms. The doctor enters the room with a serious look on her face. She says, "Everything is going to be fine."

_____

_____

_____

_____

2. A co-worker has been working around the clock to make a key deadline. The afternoon the project is due, her computer crashes. Your co-worker begins to laugh out loud. She says, "This is just perfect."

_____

_____

_____

_____

3. At a conference you see a writer whose work you admire. He is sitting in the row ahead of you. You tap him on the shoulder, introduce yourself, and tell him how much you admire his work. He turns in his seat and extends his hand, but his handshake is weak, and he does not make eye contact. The writer says in a whispered voice, "Oh, thank you very much. I always enjoy meeting my readers."

_____

_____

_____

_____

4. You call a technology hotline for help with your new computer. The person who takes your call mumbles into the phone, "May I help you?" You explain your problem and the tech expert solves it for you. Then he says, "Thank you for calling Helpline. We appreciate your call," and hangs up before you can say goodbye.

_____

_____

_____

_____

Section 2.2 Learning the Basics of Listening

A. Active and Passive Listening

Directions: Read each of the following situations. Then, place a check mark in the appropriate column to indicate which kind of listening should be done.

	Active Listening	Passive Listening
1. voice-mail message from a colleague	○	○
2. yoga class instruction	○	○
3. political science lecture	○	○
4. emergency weather bulletin	○	○
5. song on your MP3 player while doing your taxes	○	○
6. conversation with friends	○	○
7. instructions on searching Lexis-Nexis	○	○
8. explanation of a new job task	○	○
9. fire drill procedures	○	○
10. medical instructions from your pharmacist	○	○

B. External and Internal Noise in the Classroom

Directions: List five sources of *external* noise that may interfere with listening while you are taking this class.

1. _____
2. _____
3. _____
4. _____
5. _____

Directions: List five sources of *internal* noise that may interfere with listening while you are taking this class.

1. _____
2. _____
3. _____
4. _____
5. _____

C. Dealing with External and Internal Noise in a Critical Situation

Directions: Reread the section "Improving Your Listening Skills" on page 47 in your text-book. List any external and internal noises that could affect your listening to the flight attendant's safety speech. You may include those mentioned in the text and others that might possibly be present in such a situation.

External Noise

1. _____
2. _____
3. _____
4. _____
5. _____

Internal Noise

1. _____
2. _____
3. _____
4. _____
5. _____

D. Thinking Clearly

Directions: A good listener can weigh ideas to determine whether the ideas are facts or opinion or to determine whether more information is needed to make a decision. Below are ten statements. In the space to the right of each, write the letter of one of the following choices:

F Fact *The statement is a fact that can be supported.*

O Opinion *The statement is an opinion.*

? Undecided *More information is needed to make a decision.*

1. Deeana's Web page has the most creative graphics. _____

2. Admissions to the university have increased by 10 percent this year. _____

3. Becker Insurance offers a 10 percent reduction in premium payments if you have not received traffic tickets in the last four years. _____

4. You will love reading Stephen Sutherland's online novel. _____

5. The videogame *Aliens from Beyond* will keep you engaged on every level. _____

6. Buying a hybrid car will be the best choice for you. _____

7. Professor Hartman teaches an online writing course during the summer. _____

8. Installing *Megaboost* software will increase the memory capacity of your out-of-date computer. _____

9. Five hundred people have visited the new Web site since last Tuesday. _____

10. I believe that Kristina Nguyen is the best candidate for the job. _____

E. Distinguishing Soundalikes

Directions: Choose the word from the pair in the parentheses that correctly completes each sentence. Write the word in the space provided.

1. Completing his degree took longer (than, then) Gregory expected because he was working full time. _____

2. Before the members left, they set the date for the next (board, bored) meeting. _____

3. It was not an easy (feat, feet) to convince the department manager to allow each staff member use of a laser printer. _____

4. Returning to work after six weeks' maternity leave, Megan was careful not to (overdue, overdo) it. _____

5. Jen was thrilled to win (forth, fourth) place in the company sponsored triathlon. _____

6. Both Ken and Mercedes displayed (tack, tact) during the intense negotiations. _____

7. Writing an E-mail in all capital letters is a (minor, miner) offense in most online chat rooms. _____

8. Regina did a (great, grate) job as leader of the workshop. _____

Student _____ Class _____ Instructor _____

Date Assigned _____ Date Completed _____

F. Paraphrasing the Message

Directions: When you paraphrase, you restate an idea in your own words. Read each statement of an idea. Then, on the lines provided, paraphrase the idea.

1. Many people in the business world spend more time listening than they do speaking, reading, or writing. At meetings and during telephone and conference calls, people must rely on their skill of active listening.

   _____

   _____

   _____

2. Active listening is what you do when you need to remember the information you hear. It requires concentration and mental preparation. Otherwise, distractions will interfere with the process of communication.

   _____

   _____

   _____

3. Passive listening is not acceptable in the workplace environment. If you are attending a meeting, you need to be engaged, both as a listener and as a speaker. The point of meetings is to share information and work together to form goals.

   _____

   _____

   _____

4. There are several strategies for being an effective active listener. One is to take notes. Another is to think about how the information you are hearing affects you or your work.

   _____

   _____

   _____

5. Another strategy for being an active listener is to speak. Ask questions to confirm what you think you heard. Your questions give the speaker important feedback. He or she will realize whether his or her speaking has been effective.

   _____

   _____

   _____

G. Overcoming Listening Barriers

Directions: Read the following workplace situation. Then answer the questions about the situation.

Ben Epstein works as a designer for a computer shopper's guide. His job duties include designing promotional pieces for new products that will be advertised in the guide. Ally Duarte, the marketing manager, is responsible for writing the copy for the promotional pieces. Last week, Ally E-mailed Ben the copy for several new product promotions and asked that he complete the designs in three days. However, Ally had not given Ben all the information he needed. In a replying E-mail, Ben set up a meeting for that afternoon to discuss the promotional pieces.

The meeting did not begin well. Ben was upset about the short time frame Ally had given him to complete the designs. Ally was working on the department budget for next year and was only half listening to Ben. When Ally did speak, she first commented on how the design staff always made mistakes and missed deadlines. Surprised by her comment, Ben was ready to interrupt Ally with an angry reply.

1. What internal noise is affecting Ben's listening? What internal noise is affecting Ally's listening?

    _____

    _____

    _____

    _____

2. How could Ben manage his internal noise? How could Ally manage hers?

    _____

    _____

    _____

    _____

3. How should Ben respond to Ally's comment about the design staff making errors and missing deadlines?

    _____

    _____

    _____

    _____

Section 2.3 Listening in Casual and Business Settings

A. Identifying Good Listening Habits

Directions: Read the following sentences. If good listening habits are indicated, place a check mark in the *Yes* column. If good listening habits are *not* indicated, place a check mark in the *No* column.

	YES	NO
1. An active listener interrupts a speaker who talks too slowly in order to give the speaker feedback.	○	○
2. One way to screen out distractions is to close your eyes.	○	○
3. Concentrate on what the speaker is saying by listening for ideas and feelings as well as listening for factual information.	○	○
4. Pay attention to such nonverbal signals as gestures, posture, and facial expressions.	○	○
5. Try to decide in advance whether it is worthwhile to listen to the speaker.	○	○
6. Keep your eyes on the speaker as much as possible.	○	○
7. Avoid doing another activity—such as reading a newspaper—while trying to listen.	○	○
8. Stop listening if you do not agree with what the speaker is saying.	○	○
9. Wait until a speaker has finished before asking for clarification of a point you missed, unless the speaker specifies otherwise.	○	○
10. Listen carefully even if you dislike the speaker's appearance or mannerisms.	○	○
11. If the speaker is uninteresting, let your mind wander to subjects that interest you.	○	○
12. Continue to listen even if a great deal of effort is required to understand what the speaker is saying.	○	○
13. Avoid eye contact with the speaker if you think the speaker is shy.	○	○

B. Keep a Listening Journal

Directions: During the next two days, keep a journal of listening situations in which you are a conversation participant or a listener. Include a variety of listening situations such as casual conversations, committee meetings, class lectures, telephone calls, and so on. Write your descriptions on the lines provided, and underline either *active* or *passive* for the type of listening you did.

Listening Situation 1 *(Active /Passive)*: _____

_____

_____

External Noise Present: _____

Internal Noise Present: _____

Effective as a listener *(Circle one)*   Poor   Good   Excellent

Reasons for Rating: _____

_____

_____

Ways to Improve as a Listener in the Above Situation: *(Complete if the rating was poor or good.)*

_____

_____

_____

Listening Situation 2 *(Active /Passive)*: _____

_____

_____

External Noise Present: _____

Internal Noise Present: _____

Effective as a listener *(Circle one)*   Poor   Good   Excellent

Reasons for Rating: _____

_____

_____

Ways to Improve as a Listener in the Above Situation: *(Complete if the rating was poor or good.)*

_____

_____

_____

C. Team Listening

For this activity the class will be divided into teams of four students. You and your team members should agree to watch the same specific evening newscast and take notes on the items covered in the newscast. Type your notes and give copies to all team members. Meet with team members to compare notes. Using the best set, merge additional notes from the other team members to form one final copy. Submit this final copy to your instructor.

Directions: Answer the following questions. Explain your answers as needed.

1. Were the notes you took adequate? Why or why not?

_____

_____

_____

_____

2. What important points did you overlook that your team members included? What important points did you include that your team members overlooked?

_____

_____

_____

_____

3. How did keying the notes help you remember the content of the newscast?

_____

_____

_____

_____

4. How did discussing the notes with your team members help you remember the content of the newscast?

_____

_____

_____

_____

D. Recalling Key Points

Directions: To review what you learned about listening in Section 2.3 of your textbook, add the appropriate terms to complete the following sentences.

1. Being _____ and showing _____ are two attributes of good listeners.

2. You can use _____ and _____ to convey your interest in what the speaker is saying.

3. One way to determine your listening objectives is to find out the expected _____.

4. A good listener will ignore the speaker's _____ and concentrate on his or her _____.

5. Note taking is not a substitute for _____ listening.

6. To improve your listening retention, review your notes within _____ hours.

7. Highlight only _____ in your notes.

E. Synonyms

Directions: Circle the letter of the word closest in meaning to the indicated word.

1. incriminate
   a. vindicate   **b.** accuse   **c.** defend   **d.** prejudge

2. propitious
   a. proper   **b.** steep   **c.** evil   **d.** favorable

3. obtuse
   a. sharp   **b.** discerning   **c.** wide   **d.** dull-witted

4. constrain
   a. stress   **b.** compel   **c.** contract   **d.** injure

5. aperture
   a. summit   **b.** overture   **c.** closure   **d.** gap

6. mitigate
   a. moderate   **b.** increase   **c.** aggravate   **d.** move

F. Antonyms

Directions: Circle the letters of the two words in each group that are antonyms (opposite in meaning).

1. **a.** well-read
   b. transitory
   c. momentary
   d. illiterate

2. **a.** caution
   b. temerity
   c. upheaval
   d. density

3. **a.** adequate
   b. mundane
   c. spiritual
   d. satisfactory

4. **a.** revoke
   b. invoke
   c. approve
   d. take

5. **a.** responsively
   b. avidly
   c. radically
   d. conservatively

Section 2.4 Reading Business Documents

A. Adjust Your Reading Rate to Your Purpose

Directions: For each of the following situations, decide if you should read for specific data, for retention or analysis, or for checking or copying.

1. Proofreading a production spread sheet you just printed out. _____

2. Reading the online manual for a new software program. _____

3. Reading an online journal to learn about a new product. _____

4. Looking up a company's telephone number using the Yellow Pages. _____

5. Reading the instructions for your new personal digital assistant. _____

6. Verifying that the information entered into the computer screen matches the original hard copy. _____

7. Searching for a specific person's name in an online newspaper article. _____

8. Reviewing bank statements for accuracy. _____

9. Reading a Web page for information about submitting a résumé. _____

10. Looking up a topic in a multimedia encyclopedia. _____

B. Previewing Reading Material

Directions: Review the steps for previewing reading material on p. 63 of your textbook. Then, preview the excerpt from the article below and answer the questions.

MANAGING DIVERSITY IN E-BUSINESS

In today's global economy, E-businesses need to address the interests and needs of diverse groups if they are going to attract and retain both qualified employees and loyal customers. Managing diversity includes recognizing and understanding differences in gender, culture, ethnic background, age, and physical abilities.

> *"Managing Diversity is an important issue for E-business."*

The First Step: Accommodation

To attract and retain a diverse work- force, E-businesses must recognize and accommodate differences in employees' lifestyles and cultures. For example, the increase in the workforce of the number of women who are the heads of households has led businesses to offer a variety of flexible work schedules for employees. The influx of workers who are practicing Muslims has caused many companies to provide time off and even facilities for religious practices.

1. What title and headings did you find in the article?

_____
_____
_____

2. What was the first paragraph about?

_____
_____
_____

3. What was the first sentence of the second paragraph about?

_____
_____
_____

4. Were there any illustrations or quotations to help you figure out what the article was about?

_____
_____
_____

C. Checking for Accuracy

Directions: Compare the items in **List A** with the items in **List B**. Write *match* if the items in both columns match. Write *do not match* if the items do not match.

List A	List B	
1. Personal Digital Assistant	Pesonal Digitl Assistant	_____
2. http://www.exclamation point.com/index	http//www.exclamation point.com/index	_____
3. broadband Internet access	braodband Internet access	_____
4. Human Resources Department	Human Resorces Department	_____
5. McIlvaine Software Development	MCIlvaine Software Development	_____
6. Confirm your password now.	Confirm your password now.	_____
7. 600,743,983.32	600,743,938.32	_____
8. August 28, 2002	August 28, 2002	_____
9. Account #3489-345	Account 3489-345	_____
10. Phone # 1-800-555-3852	Phone # 1-800-555-3852	_____

D. Improving Reading Comprehension

Directions: Read the following passage. Take notes on the passage, making sure to identify the main idea and supporting points in each paragraph. Write your notes on the lines provided.

   Managers of small- to medium-sized companies that are planning to expand their computer networks are faced with a new question—whether or not to invest in wireless networks. Until recently, computers that were part of a network were literally wired by means of cables through a hub or switch to a common server. Wireless networks do essentially the same thing, except without the cables; each computer sends out its information in the form of radio waves. Wireless networks will change the way even small companies network their computers.

   There are distinct advantages and disadvantages to wireless networks. One advantage is very simple. A wireless network means foregoing putting holes in the walls to run cables into every office. One disadvantage is that the wireless technology is new and imperfect. The frequencies of the signals emitted by wireless computers can be disrupted by other wireless devices, such as telephones.

continued ➨

PARAGRAPH 1
Main Idea

_____

_____

_____

_____

_____

Supporting Points

_____

_____

_____

_____

_____

_____

_____

_____

PARAGRAPH 2
Main Idea

_____

_____

_____

_____

Supporting Points

_____

_____

_____

_____

_____

_____

_____

_____

E. Selecting Reading Strategies

Directions: For each of the following situations, determine what reading strategies you should use to comprehend and retain information.

1. You are a summer intern at a local accounting firm whose computers are becoming out-of-date. Your supervisor has asked you to research an in-expensive way to upgrade the existing office computers. You must read several print and online articles about computer upgrades, compare the information, and write a report for your supervisor. What reading strategies would you use to comprehend and retain the information?

2. As an online customer-service representative for Woodbine Software Company, your job is to answer software-related questions submitted by customers through the company's Web site. Today you received a 12-page description of the latest software packages released by the company. This software will be shipped to customers in two days, so you must familiarize yourself quickly with the information. What reading strategies would you use to comprehend and retain the information?

F. Achieving Variety in Word Usage

Directions: It is easy to develop the habit of using the same word over and over. In the following expressions, use substitutions for the much overused words "check" and "nice."

1. check the date _____

2. check the account balance _____

3. check the appendices _____

4. check the itinerary _____

5. check the dictionary _____

6. nice person _____

7. nice time _____

8. nice weather _____

9. nice work _____

10. nice outfit _____

G. Identifying Ideas

Directions: Read the following passage and make an outline that lists the main idea and supporting points in the passage. Write your outline on the lines provided.

THE JOB SEARCH

When conducting a job search the important thing to remember is that you are selling a product—yourself—to prospective employers. Making yourself marketable involves preparing a résumé, writing a letter of application, and preparing for an interview.

One of the first things you should do before looking for a job is prepare a professional-looking résumé. A résumé includes information such as your name, address, education experience, previous work experience, honors, and references. Often your résumé is the only information an employer has to evaluate you before the first interview. For this reason, it is extremely important that your résumé be complete yet concise.

Another item you need when applying for most jobs is a letter of application. This letter tells the employer in which job you are interested, highlights some of your best qualities, and encourages the employer to contact you for an interview. The first paragraph of your application letter is especially important because it must grab the employer's attention and invite him or her to read further. The body of your letter must highlight your best qualities and provide supporting examples. The closing must convince the employer to call you for an interview.

When interviewing, be sure to dress professionally. First impressions can be lasting impressions, and you want to make a positive first impression with the employer. Address the employer in a courteous and professional manner. In response to the employer's questions, give concise, honest answers that highlight your strengths and abilities. After the interview, send a follow-up letter that thanks the employer for talking with you and highlights your assets.

Throughout the job search, remember to present your product—yourself—in the best possible light. Whether you are preparing your résumé, writing a letter of application, or interviewing for a job, be concise yet thorough. Always maintain a positive attitude. Remember: The job you apply for may just become yours.

_____

_____

_____

_____

_____

_____

_____

_____

_____

_____

_____

_____

_____

_____

_____

_____

_____

_____

_____

_____

_____

_____

H. Taking Notes

Directions: Read the following passage. Take notes on the passage using the tips for taking notes found on page 67 of your textbook.

Few business owners can afford to overlook the importance of building and maintaining a Web site that will attract and keep customers' interest. Web sites for businesses should do two things—keep the online visitor's needs in mind, and present a favorable image of the organization.

When planning each section or page in your Web site, think about the overall effect you want to have on your visitors. The Web site as a whole should be clearly organized and thoughtfully mapped out. Also, the graphics should be attractive but not overwhelming. After all, not everyone has a state-of-the art computer. Your graphics may be works of art, but they will not be appreciated if your visitor cannot wait for them to download. Another way to promote goodwill is to offer your visitor something fun, such as a quiz or a puzzle, on the opening page of your Web site. This will keep your visitor interested.

Web sites have a big impact on what people think about an organization. Your message and how you present it makes an impression on the people who visit your Web site. Take advantage of the opportunity afforded by the Internet to create a favorable view of your organization.

continued ➥➤

Student _____ Class _____ Instructor _____

Date Assigned _____ Date Completed _____

_____
_____
_____
_____
_____
_____
_____
_____
_____
_____
_____
_____
_____
_____
_____

I. Using Secondary Sources

Directions: Select two topics from the following list that you might like to research. For
each topic, locate three secondary sources. Take notes from each source using
the guidelines for note cards found on page 65 of your textbook.

application service providers (ASPs)　　　videoconferencing　　　wireless networks
Personal Digital Assistants (PDAs)　　　firewall security　　　extranet

_____
_____
_____
_____
_____
_____
_____
_____
_____
_____
_____
_____

J. Reading an Outline

Directions: Below is an outline prepared by a student who read an article in an online business journal. Read the outline and then use the information in it to answer the questions that follow.

I. What is telecommuting?
   A. People work off-site
   B. People work own hours without supervision

II. Goals of telecommuting
   A. Reduction of traffic and pollution
   B. Efficiency
   C. Lower costs

III. Realities of telecommuting
   A. Off-site workers lack motivation
   B. Supervisors doubt workers' dedication
   C. Lack of boundaries—workers working all the time

1. What is the topic of the article from which the outline was drawn?

   _____

   _____

   _____

2. What is the focus of the first section of the article?

   _____

   _____

   _____

3. What is the focus of the third section of the article?

   _____

   _____

   _____

4. What conclusions do you think the article reaches?

   _____

   _____

   _____

CHAPTER **3** Communicating Globally

Section 3.1 Domestic and International Communication

A. Taking Cultural Differences and Customs Into Account

Directions: List the guideline that should be followed to improve communication when working with people from different cultural, religious, and ethnic groups.

1. Before a business trip to Quebec City, Rick rented a recent French film to brush up on his accent and develop his limited vocabulary. While on the trip, he used some slang he heard in the film. Later, he discovered that his language was offensive to his French-Canadian colleagues.

_____

_____

2. A software development company had an annual awards luncheon and invited several clients. The organizer of the event was surprised when several of the clients would not eat. She discovered later that the clients were Muslims who fasted daily during Ramadan, the ninth month of the Muslim calendar.

_____

_____

3. Terry was talking with a potential client over lunch at a highly recommended Mexican restaurant. Their server was a Mexican woman who had been slow in delivering the check to the table. Terry made a joke about the server having taken a siesta.

_____

_____

4. In Middle Eastern countries it is considered impolite to cross one's legs while sitting or to show the bottom of one's shoe to another person. Janelle, an American businessperson, unaware of etiquette, visits with an executive in Egypt. When he asks her to take a seat, she immediately sits, crosses her legs, and inadvertently points the bottom of her shoe at her host.

_____

_____

B. Domestic Communication

Directions: Throughout the United States, cultural and religious groups speak traditional languages and follow traditional practices. Look at the following list of groups below and select one. On the lines below, jot down what you know about the language, customs, or practices of the group you selected.

- Chinese quarters, or Chinatowns, in New York City, San Francisco, and other large cities
- Hasidic Jewish neighborhoods in New York City and other large cities
- Vietnamese communities in Minnesota, Wisconsin, and Texas
- Amish settlements in the Midwest and Pennsylvania
- West Indian communities in New York City
- Polish neighborhoods in Chicago
- Native American communities in the Southwest and Northwest
- Hispanic neighborhoods in Miami and in cities in southern California and southern Texas

_____

_____

_____

_____

_____

_____

_____

_____

_____

_____

_____

_____

C. Calculating Time Differences

Directions: Consult a time zone map and use the information to calculate the times in the questions below.

1. It is 3:00 p.m. in New York City. What time is it in
   Dallas, Texas?   _____

2. It is 4 a.m. in Sydney, Australia. What time is it in Chicago?   _____

3. It is noon in Beijing. What time is it in Los Angeles?   _____

4. It is 9:00 a.m. in Anchorage, Alaska. What time is it in London, England? _____

5. It is 5:00 p.m. in Mumbai (Bombay), India. What time is it in Cairo, Egypt? _____

D. Using Appropriate Language

Directions: Each of the following items violates one of the guidelines for using English in communicating with people in other countries. Revise each of the items to reflect sensitivity.

1. A traffic jam caused me to be late for my flight.

_____

2. The negotiations ended on a bad note.

_____

3. We need to decide now while the iron is hot.

_____

4. The meeting will begin in a little while.

_____

5. Because she was late to the meeting, she missed the boat during negotiations.

_____

6. At sales meetings, we show a neat little presentation.

_____

7. Be sure to remember your PIN for the ATM.

_____

8. Jack LePelletier is our company's computer guru.

_____

9. The meeting was a disaster because my machine crashed during the presentation.

_____

10. You'll need to pull an overnighter to get the program ready for the presentation.

_____

E. Revising to Use Straightforward Language

Directions: Rewrite the following business messages intended for recipients in other countries. Be sure to replace clichés, slang, trendy terms, and abbreviations with straightforward language.

1. The new laser printer goes wicked fast, and we are putting it to good use.
_____
_____

2. The sum total result is that we nailed the new account.
_____
_____

3. We expect the company's president to be kicked out after the takeover.
_____
_____

4. The IRS is auditing our business, which throws a wrench in our schedule.
_____
_____

5. The great thing is that I can download my PDA files right onto my Mac.
_____
_____

F. Researching Information for an Overseas Trip

Directions: Make a list of the types of information to research before taking a business trip overseas. Write your answers in the spaces provided.

1. _____
_____

2. _____
_____

3. _____
_____

4. _____
_____

G. Demonstrating Knowledge of Other Cultures and Customs

Directions: Explain what you would do in each of the following situations based on your knowledge of other cultures and customs.

1. You have arrived for a business meeting with clients in Mumbai, India. As a woman, you notice that the male clients are reluctant to shake your hand. Instead, they press their palms together and bow slightly.

_____

_____

_____

_____

2. A videoconference with clients in Brazil has been scheduled for the last Thursday in November.

_____

_____

_____

_____

H. Rewriting for Clarity

Directions: Rewrite each of the following figures of speech and clichés to use clearer wording. Write your answers in the spaces provided.

1. You should practice what you preach.

_____

_____

2. We have an early morning meeting, so I'm going to hit the sack now.

_____

_____

3. This is a once-in-a-lifetime opportunity.

_____

_____

4. We hope to score big time with this new product.

_____

_____

continued ➡

Section 3.2 Ethics and Professional Courtesy in Business Communication

A. Demonstrating Ethical Behavior

Directions: The situations below describe situations involving ethical decisions. Read each situation. Then, on the lines provided, identify the behavior as ethical or unethical, and explain why.

1. Miles is unhappy at his job. One day, during his lunch hour, he interviews for another job. The interviewer does not offer Miles the job, but at his next evaluation session with his current supervisor, Miles plans to say that he has been interviewed for another job that pays more money.

_____

_____

_____

2. Melanie works in the Human Resources department and receives a call asking about the employment record of a former employee. It is company policy only to confirm that a person worked at the company. Melanie knows that the employee was fired for stealing equipment. She tells the caller that the employee worked at the company for three years and two months.

_____

_____

_____

3. Brett just bought a new home computer that he plans to use when he quits his job to work freelance. Brett needs to load his new computer with the programs that he currently uses at work. His company's software license agreement allows workers to load their home computers with the software as long as it will be used for company work. Brett checks out copies of the software and loads them onto his computer. The next day, Brett submits his resignation.

_____

_____

_____

4. The president of an online business needs more funds to keep the company solvent. He has a meeting with potential investors, but they will not provide the funds he needs unless he agrees to lay off a certain number of his employees. The previous week, the president had a meeting in which he assured his staff that he would do his best to avoid letting people go. Nevertheless, the president agrees to the lay-offs.

_____

_____

_____

5. The manager of a small architectural firm receives a call about the work of a former employee. The manager remembers that Anna was under a great deal of stress from taking care of an elderly parent while trying to make her start at the firm. She often asked others to cover for her and missed key deadlines. Finally, Anna resigned. The manager tells the caller, "Anna was under a great deal of stress during her time here. I think under different circumstances her performance would improve."

_____

_____

_____

B. Making Introductions

Directions: Describe what you would say when making introductions in each of the following situations. Write your answers in the space provided.

1. Introducing Lara Tillney, a new production assistant, to your department manager, Mike Robbins.

_____

_____

2. Introducing Lara Tillney, a new member of the production staff, to her co-worker in production, Lindsay Feldstone.

_____

_____

3. Introducing the vice president of your firm, Alicia Guerrero, to a potential client, Mr. Amala.

_____

_____

C. Acknowledging Invitations and Thoughtful Actions

Directions: Read each of the situations below. Decide whether the person in each situation acted appropriately or inappropriately. On the line provided, write *A* for appropriately or *I* for inappropriately.

1. You have been invited to the wedding reception of a co-worker but have no interest in attending. You throw away the invitation without responding.   _____

2. After spending months planning a successful business meeting, your supervisor tells you to take an unofficial day off. You tell everyone around you how great your supervisor is.   _____

continued ➡

3. Your grandparent died and your co-workers sent flowers to the memorial service. You send your co-workers a short thank-you note.   _____

4. You receive a set of tickets to the local opera company from a potential client. You send a thank-you note expressing your appreciation for the gift.   _____

5. Your department manager sends an E-mail asking you to lunch on Thursday, but you must use the time to go to your son's school play. You call and explain your situation.   _____

D. Code of Ethics

Directions: Write a code of ethics for business communications using what you have learned in Section 3.2. Use Exhibit 3.4 on page 86 of your textbook as a guide.

_____

_____

_____

_____

_____

_____

_____

_____

_____

_____

_____

_____

_____

_____

_____

_____

_____

_____

E. Selecting the Best Sentence

Directions: In each of the following pairs of sentences, one sentence is more specific. Select that sentence, and write its identifying letter on the line provided.

1. (a) Ms. Grabedian is a person with sound business principles.
   (b) Ms. Grabedian is a person who knows what's right. _____

2. (a) Our Human Resources staff keeps its mouth shut.
   (b) Our Human Resources staff understands and maintains confidentiality. _____

3. (a) An ethical person sticks with the facts.
   (b) An ethical person states facts instead of opinions. _____

4. (a) Ethical business communicators use objective language and verifiable information.
   (b) Ethical business communicators go with what they know. _____

5. (a) Confidential information should be released to authorized people only.
   (b) Confidential information should be kept secret from all but a few people. _____

6. (a) Professional courtesy means being polite.
   (b) Professional courtesy involves good manners and appropriate behavior. _____

7. (a) Deliberately withholding information is unethical.
   (b) Deliberately withholding information is not right. _____

8. (a) Ethics involves working toward the good of all rather than the good of some.
   (b) Ethics involves working toward the good of all rather than the good of a specialized group. _____

9. (a) A code of ethics for a business states rules to follow.
   (b) A code of ethics for a business states the goals in terms of how the business operates. _____

10. (a) An RSVP notation on an invitation tells you to reply.
    (b) An RSVP notation on an invitation tells you to whom and by when to reply. _____

Section 3.3 Nondiscriminatory Language

A. Avoiding Discrimination in Communication

Directions: Rewrite each of the following sentences replacing gender-specific words with gender-neutral words.

1. The secretary completed the tasks efficiently.

_____

_____

2. The work of housewives benefits the entire economy.

_____

_____

3. The chairman of the board called the meeting to order.

_____

_____

4. The nanny took the children for a walk.

_____

_____

5. The old man at the door offered us a shopping cart.

_____

_____

Directions: Rewrite each of the following sentences to use nondiscriminatory language. You may omit or replace words as needed.

1. The Mexican American student was graduated with honors.

_____

_____

2. My African American doctor explained the procedure.

_____

_____

3. Old people are learning to use computers, too.

_____

_____

4. The paraplegic woman uses a motorized wheelchair.

_____

_____

5. She teaches students who are hyperactive.

_____

_____

Directions: Rewrite each of the following sentences to eliminate stereotypes.

1. People who are overweight are lazy.

_____

_____

2. Unwed mothers who drop out of high school never get anywhere.

_____

_____

3. Staff members like working with Mrs. Lawson because she babies them.

_____

_____

4. Doctors will take you for every cent you've got before they'll cure you.

_____

_____

5. New Yorkers are rude.

_____

_____

B. Avoiding Discriminatory Actions

Directions: Explain how you could improve the communication in the following situations.

1. A student who is deaf but who is trained in lip reading visits her advisor during office hours. In answering her questions, the advisor speaks loudly. He also continues talking while turning his face away from her as he looks for her files.

_____

_____

_____

_____

_____

2. A client who uses a motorized wheelchair comes to your office for a meeting. Your new office assistant makes the comment that "the chair is really cool" and that it must be great for racing around.

_____

_____

_____

_____

_____

3. A traveler who is visually impaired asks for assistance at the information booth at the train station. The person at the desk explains how to get to the library by saying, "Go out these red doors here and turn left. Go up about five blocks. It will be a brick building on your right."

_____

_____

_____

_____

_____

CHAPTER 4 Exploring Language Elements

Section 4.1 The Parts of Speech

A. Identifying Parts of Speech

Directions: Identify the words in parentheses in the following sentences. Use the following abbreviations: *N* (noun), *P* (pronoun), *V* (verb), *Adj* (adjective), *Adv* (adverb), *Prep* (preposition), *C* (conjunction), *I* (interjection).

1. (We) have interviewed (six) candidates (for) the position. _____

2. Several (of) my co-workers (commute) to work at least 12 miles one way. _____

3. All (full-time) employees are eligible (for) the dental plan. _____

4. Ms. Carsey is the (chairperson) for the (all-day) seminar. _____

5. Teresa is (scheduled) to visit many of (the) sales representatives (during) the next three weeks. _____

6. If (you) have a (question), please call Larry Sleva. _____

7. (Congratulations!) Completing your degree is (quite) an accomplishment. _____

8. (Craig Lawrence) manages the (branch) offices (in) Modesto and San Jose. _____

9. The (committee) will review the materials (and) submit (its) report (at) the next meeting. _____

10. Most of (our) employees have access (to) the Internet. _____

11. (I) was selected to be a member of the jury. _____

12. Joan Miller (toured) the inventory warehouse (during) (her) visit to Tucscon. _____

13. (Our) office manager (holds) a (weekly) status meeting for our department. _____

continued ➡

14. (Every) business person should (have) a style manual
(for) reference.   _____

15. Harry (or) Meg will contact (you) (soon) with information
(about) the contract.   _____

16. Within the next (few) days, we should (receive) (several)
bids (for) the project.   _____

17. (Congratulations!) Completing your degree is (quite)
an accomplishment.   _____

18. (By) October, we will have (completed) the registration
process for (new) customers.   _____

19. Automated bank tellers will be (installed) at all our
(branch) banks.   _____

20. The enrollment period for the employee health (and)
retirement plan is (always) in September.   _____

B. Knowing Your Subjects

Directions: On the line provided, write the *simple subject* or the *compound subject* from
each of the following sentences.

1. Erika was an original partner of the dot-com.

_____

2. By September 10, we will have completed the entire project.

_____

3. Everyone in Human Resources has signed up for the company blood drive.

_____

4. Alex and Casey are the most recently hired programmers.

_____

5. Two to three years' experience as a Web master is a requirement for the job.

_____

6. Is Jacob aware of the changes we made to the password program?

_____

7. Courtney and Austin are leading the meeting.

_____

8. Marc, Lydia, and Harrison will attend the seminar.

_____

9. The new firewall software will be installed on all the computers this weekend.

_____

10. I am responsible for purchasing new flat panel LCD monitors for the computers in our department.

_____

11. All the staff members must take a training course in the new encryption software.

_____

12. The top sales representative in each region will receive a 15 percent bonus.

_____

13. You should apply for your passport at least two months before your trip abroad.

_____

14. Michaela's expertise in designing digital presentations makes her a popular speaker.

_____

15. Have you discussed these procedures with your project manager?

_____

16. Toni and Nick are both experienced presenters.

_____

17. Excellent opportunities for creative programming are available in this company.

_____

18. The Internet and the World Wide Web are two essential resources for consumers.

_____

19. For consumers, the Internet and the World Wide Web are essential resources.

_____

continued ➡

20. Only Amy or Lewis is authorized to upgrade the software.

_____

21. In the production department library are the design plans for all our products.

_____

22. Maria, Nikki, and Claire have volunteered for the personality profiling seminar.

_____

23. To whom should this overnight package be delivered?

_____

24. Revising your E-mail messages is easier when you use the grammar checker function

_____

25. Devon and Jonah are on the executive search committee.

_____

C. Identifying Predicates

Directions: On the line provided, write the *simple predicate* from each of the
following sentences..

1. Matt and Chris explained how the new firewall program works.

_____

2. A new dot-com startup has rented the office space next to ours.

_____

3. Advertising on the World Wide Web is necessary for any business.

_____

4. Ms. Cho will arrive on Monday for the production meeting.

_____

5. Bianca called the clients about the change in the time of the meeting.

_____

6. Staff members may enroll in the health maintenance organization after six months of employment.

   _____

7. Paul used his personal digital assistant to check the time of his flight.

   _____

8. The data is stored in our digital archive.

   _____

9. Lena will participate in the videoconference today.

   _____

10. Both Jason and Alexis recommended the new videogame.

    _____

D. Writing Sentences

Directions: On the lines provided, write the type of sentence indicated for each item.

1. Declarative (makes a statement)

   _____

   _____

2. Interrogative (asks a question)

   _____

   _____

3. Imperative (states a command or request)

   _____

   _____

4. Exclamatory (expresses strong feeling)

   _____

   _____

E. Identifying Clauses

Directions: Identify each of the following groups of words as *independent clauses* (sentences) or as *dependent clauses* incorrectly treated as sentences. Use the abbreviation *I* for independent clause and *D* for dependent clause.

1. Sending E-mail messages.   _____

2. Using the company's intranet, we can keep information secure.   _____

3. When we heard news of the buy-out.   _____

4. To attract more visitors to our Web site.   _____

5. E-businesses should use colorful graphics on their Web sites.   _____

6. Click the Human Resources icon for more information.   _____

7. Once we have studied the design specifications.   _____

8. We will hold a meeting to discuss costs.   _____

9. Working off-site, you can work the hours you choose.   _____

10. Before we agree to the plan.   _____

11. Whenever an issue is raised in a meeting.   _____

12. The new personal digital assistants are now in stock.   _____

13. Thank you for inquiring about our company.   _____

14. Your call is important to us.   _____

15. Both the production manager and the staff.   _____

F. Using Phrases

Directions: In each sentence, identify the type of phrase described in parentheses. Write the phrase on the line provided.

1. Use the spreadsheet program to organize the production schedule. (infinitive phrase)

_____

2. The product's specifications will be approved by the end of the month. (verb phrase)

_____

3. Most of the inventory has already been sold. (prepositional phrase)

_____

4. Ask Marina if she knows how to change the password. (infinitive phrase)

_____

5. Mr. Ganz has asked me to write the report. (verb phrase)

_____

G. Sentences or Fragments?

Directions: Which of the following are complete sentences and which are fragments? At the right, circle *S* to indicate a complete sentence and *F* to indicate a fragment (incomplete sentence).

1. Melissa, our travel agent, made the arrangements for our trip.   **S**   **F**

2. As you probably read in the company newsletter.   **S**   **F**

3. If you plan to enroll in the database course.   **S**   **F**

4. You and I will be in charge of the recycling committee.   **S**   **F**

5. Two inventory analysts have reviewed the problem with our system.   **S**   **F**

6. In response to your request for tuition reimbursement.   **S**   **F**

7. So that we may better serve our customers.   **S**   **F**

8. Greg made the announcement at our last status meeting.   **S**   **F**

9. Molly specified the type of desktop publishing software to order.   **S**   **F**

10. Since the profit-sharing plan was started two years ago.   **S**   **F**

Section 4.2 The Sentence

A. Changing Fragments to Sentences

Directions: Each of the following fragments is a dependent clause. For each fragment, add an independent clause to make the item a complete sentence. Write your answers on the lines provided.

1. While Keeley prints out the report,

   _____

2. Because we completed the work ahead of schedule,

   _____

3. Unless you fax us your résumé,

   _____

4. When you receive approval for the trip,

   _____

5. Before you interview for a position,

   _____

B. Proofreading Practice

Directions: Read the following paragraph from an E-mail. Underline any spelling errors, and write your corrections on the spaces provided.

Beginning April 2, we will install a new fingerprint-activated   _____

security system in the office. The instalation should be complted   _____

by the end of the month. As part of the new system, all staff   _____

members will have to submit fingerprint samples to the securty   _____

office. The new system will provide a more secure working   _____

envirnment, particularly in the evenings and on the wekends.   _____

Entraces will lock and unlock automatically each day during   _____

working hours. Please read and print out the atached file, which   _____

contains the instructions for using the nwe system.   _____

Section 4.3 Verbs

A. Principal Parts

Directions: On the lines provided, write the past tense, the past participle, and the present participle for each of the following verbs.

PRESENT	PAST	PAST PARTICIPLE	PRESENT PARTICIPLE
1. prepare	_____	_____	_____
2. listen	_____	_____	_____
3. enjoy	_____	_____	_____
4. call	_____	_____	_____
5. need	_____	_____	_____
6. drop	_____	_____	_____
7. enter	_____	_____	_____
8. start	_____	_____	_____
9. greet	_____	_____	_____
10. try	_____	_____	_____
11. attend	_____	_____	_____
12. occur	_____	_____	_____
13. die	_____	_____	_____
14. fill	_____	_____	_____
15. type	_____	_____	_____

B. Writing Skill

Directions: For each of the following verbs, write a sentence using the form of the verb described in parentheses.

1. offer (present perfect)

_____

_____

2. present (past)

_____

_____

3. check (present)

_____

_____

4. try (present progressive)

_____

_____

5. fix (past)

_____

_____

6. agree (present perfect)

_____

_____

7. install (future)

_____

_____

8. consider (past)

_____

_____

9. finish (present perfect)

_____

_____

10. travel (past)

_____

_____

C. Identifying Verb Tenses

Directions: In the sentences below, underline the verbs or verb phrases. Then, on the line provided, write the tense of the verb or verb phrase. Choose your tense from the following list: present, past, future, present perfect, past perfect, future perfect, present progressive, past progressive, and future progressive.

1. Had you already seen the latest version of my Web page? _____

2. Lately, I have had problems connecting to the server. _____

3. Jocelyn E-mails her clients about changes in the schedule. _____

4. By December we will have met all the deadlines. _____

5. Claire responded immediately to her pager. _____

6. Ross is putting the finishing touches on the project tonight. _____

7. Will Mina go to the software conference in Seattle? _____

8. No, she was planning to attend via videoconference instead. _____

9. Alexis will be presiding over the departmental meeting. _____

10. The photocopier is being repaired. _____

11. Use the laser printer instead. _____

12. Has the invoice for the new laser printer been paid? _____

13. Regular attendance of all meetings is required. _____

14. He did not agree with the budget figures? _____

15. Write your objections in a memo. _____

D. Principal Parts

Directions: On the lines provided, write the past tense, the past participle, and the present participle for each of the following verbs.

PRESENT	PAST	PAST PARTICIPLE	PRESENT PARTICIPLE
1. grow	_____	_____	_____
2. go	_____	_____	_____
3. give	_____	_____	_____
4. forget	_____	_____	_____
5. fly	_____	_____	_____
6. fall	_____	_____	_____
7. eat	_____	_____	_____
8. drive	_____	_____	_____
9. do	_____	_____	_____
10. come	_____	_____	_____
11. choose	_____	_____	_____
12. bring	_____	_____	_____
13. break	_____	_____	_____
14. begin	_____	_____	_____
15. am	_____	_____	_____
16. know	_____	_____	_____
17. lay	_____	_____	_____

PRESENT	PAST	PAST PARTICIPLE	PRESENT PARTICIPLE
18. leave	_____	_____	_____
19. lie	_____	_____	_____
20 pay	_____	_____	_____
21. rise	_____	_____	_____
22. see	_____	_____	_____
23. send	_____	_____	_____
24. sit	_____	_____	_____
25. speak	_____	_____	_____
26. stand	_____	_____	_____
27. take	_____	_____	_____
28. tell	_____	_____	_____
29. wear	_____	_____	_____
30. write	_____	_____	_____

E. Finding Errors

Directions: Underline any irregular verb errors in the following sentences, and write your corrections on the lines provided. Write *OK* for any sentence that has no error.

1. Has Monica began entering the data into the database? _____

2. If the price of the dot-com shares raises any further, we should buy more shares. _____

3. The lunch order I placed for the staff was ate within ten minutes. _____

4. Please lie the manual on the desk next to the printer. _____

continued ➡

5. Had we knew about the delay, we would have cancelled our order. _____

6. He has been using a typewriter for years and refuses to try a computer. _____

7. Miko and Danny have went to the spreadsheet training session. _____

8. With careful planning and good sales, we have growed our company over just a few years. _____

9. Have you drove one of those hybrid cars? _____

10. If my computer was upgraded, it would have more room in its memory for additional software. _____

11. Our sales have fell since the economic downturn. _____

12. Job turnover has dropped dramatically since the economic downturn as people have chose to stay put in their jobs. _____

13. She makes it sound as if it was possible to finish this project this week. _____

14. Deniece has went to the mail room to pick up the overnight mail. _____

15. I have forgot my password again. _____

F. Choosing the Correct Verb

Directions: On the line provided, write the verb in the parentheses that correctly completes each sentence.

1. The patient should (lie, lay) on his back for a few days. _____

2. The manual for the new copier should be (laying, lying) on the second shelf. _____

3. The design samples were (sitting, setting) on the table. _____

4. Please (set, sit) the climate control for a cooler temperature. _____

5. Just (lay, lie) the printouts on the floor; I have no room on my desk.

_____

6. After flying across the country, Lena was exhausted and (lay, lied) down for half an hour.

_____

7. In most cultures, it is polite to (rise, raise) to your feet and greet a visitor.

_____

8. After the presentation will you please (raise, rise) the window blinds so we can see better?

_____

9. The final printouts are just (sitting, setting) in my outbox waiting to be sent by overnight mail.

_____

10. To fit the entire text on the page, you should (set, sit) wider margins.

_____

11. Due to changes in federal law, we have (raised, risen) the minimum wage.

_____

12. (Lay, Lie) the two designs side-by-side on the table so we can compare them.

_____

13. Remember to (raise, rise) that point at the next meeting.

_____

14. New fiber optic cables have been (lain, laid) in our offices.

_____

15. These hard copies have (laid, lain) for months in the file cabinet.

_____

16. Please (sit, set) the CD-ROM writer next to the printer.

_____

17. Do you know where Jon has (laid, lain) the blank CD-ROMs?

_____

18. If I (was, were) you, I would make a copy of the file before sending it.

_____

19. We have (sat, set) around long enough; let's get back to work.

_____

20. I will (sit, set) the new LCD monitor here until you tell me where it should go.

_____

G. Transitive, Intransitive, or "Being"?

Directions: Underline the verb or the verb phrase in each of the following sentences. Then, at the right, write *T* if the verb is transitive, *I* if the verb is intransitive, or *B* if the verb is a "being" verb.

1. Miko will assist us with the digital presentation. _____

2. Karinna was interviewed by a member of the staff. _____

3. She has had several interviews with top companies. _____

4. Luis has been a software designer here for three years. _____

5. I filed my taxes electronically this year. _____

6. Stewart has argued in favor of installing a wireless network. _____

7. With online banking, my bank is open every day of the week. _____

8. Griffin's consulting firm has become a great success. _____

9. I would suggest that you call him. _____

10. Her contract expires in January. _____

11. I asked a financial planner for some advice. _____

12. The system shut down last night due to a power failure. _____

13. Our policy for dealing with broken contracts has not changed. _____

14. My cell phone rang during the meeting. _____

15. Of all the programmers, only Nurjani has a Ph.D. _____

16. Did Mimi return all the copies of the contract? _____

17. I am confident in your abilities to finish the project on time and under budget. _____

18. Antony just bought his personal digital assistant. _____

19. Tomorrow, Zack will fax the updated schedule. _____

20. Next week, I will be on a leave of absence. _____

Section 4.4 Predicate Agreement

A. Singular or Plural Verbs or Pronouns?

Directions: Circle *S* if a singular verb or pronoun would correctly complete a sentence.
Circle *P* if a plural would be correct.

1. All summer interns _____ been informed of the
   change in assignments.   **S**   **P**

2. Do you know if he and Jorge _____ planning to
   attend the conference?   **S**   **P**

3. As reported in the online newsletter, the company
   _____ planning to buy its nearest competitor.   **S**   **P**

4. The designers _____ familiar with the latest
   software.   **S**   **P**

5. Where _____ the original copy of the contract?   **S**   **P**

6. The Human Resources department _____ noted a
   record number of job applicants this year.   **S**   **P**

7. The month of June _____ the highest number,
   due to recent college graduations.   **S**   **P**

8. Staff researchers _____ consulting the online
   archives.   **S**   **P**

9. Geena and Rob _____ responsible for entering the
   data into the database.   **S**   **P**

10. Ask Nat if he wants to place _____ order for the
    new software.   **S**   **P**

11. Did you know that over 500 people _____ visited
    our Web site this month?   **S**   **P**

12. Our manager, as well as her two assistants, _____
    compiling the figures for the yearly sales report.   **S**   **P**

13. The consultant _____ planning to submit a design
    in early May.   **S**   **P**

continued ➡

14. Does Angel _____ access to the building on weekends?   **S**   **P**

15. Give Rikki _____ own keycard so she can get into the building on Saturday.   **S**   **P**

16. Nearly two-thirds of our staff _____ been through the orientation.   **S**   **P**

17. Our most dependable paper recycling service _____ Maxwell Recycling.   **S**   **P**

18. If either Sal or Jenna calls, please give _____ this message.   **S**   **P**

19. Or tell Sal and Jenna to check _____ voice mail.   **S**   **P**

20. _____ Robyn contacted the warehouse?   **S**   **P**

21. Call the suppliers to inform _____ of the change in the order.   **S**   **P**

22. Both of the videogames _____ popular this year.   **S**   **P**

23. Scan in the images and then insert _____ into the document.   **S**   **P**

24. Does Anna know when _____ flight is?   **S**   **P**

25. Most people in the field _____ enthusiastic about the product.   **S**   **P**

B. Selecting the Correct Verb

Directions: For each of the following sentences, choose the correct verb in the parentheses. Write your answers on the lines provided.

1. Miri and Sabrina (is, are) planning to update the production schedule.

_____

2. The committee (is, are) responsible for setting the agenda.

_____

3. Tyler (has, have) developed a new procedure for handling the problem.

_____

4. Stephanie (downloads, download) most of the software from the Internet.

_____

5. The consultant explained that (there is, there are) plenty of other companies who can help us with this project.

_____

6. According to Dana, the criteria for the decision (is, are) sound.

_____

7. One half of the proceeds from the sale of the compact disc (has, have) been donated to charity.

_____

8. A number of recent graduates (has, have) applied for work here.

_____

9. There (is, are) several ways to approach the problem.

_____

10. None of the solutions (seems, seem) quite right.

_____

11. Suppose he or his assistant (want, wants) to check for messages while out of the office.

_____

12. Our office is one of those organizations that (has, have) frequent staff meetings.

_____

13. I wish the new software (was, were) easier to install.

_____

14. Jesse is one programmer who (has, have) been here since the company started.

_____

15. Neither Lise nor her assistant (checks, check) the documents for errors.

_____

continued ➡

16. (Is, Are) the original specifications for the Greiner project attached to the latest draft of the site plans?

    _____

17. The designer and the editor (disagree, disagrees) on how much print should appear on the page.

    _____

18. (There is, There are) only one way to resolve the dispute.

    _____

19. The number of Web site designers seeking new jobs (have, has) increased this year.

    _____

20. The members of the committee (is, are) debating the proposal to limit the amount of required overtime.

    _____

C. Predicate Agreement with Compound Subjects

Directions: Circle *S* if a singular verb would correctly complete a sentence. Circle *P* if a plural verb would be correct.

1. Knowledge of Microsoft Word and proficiency with Pagemaker _____ required for this job.   S   P

2. Neither the printer nor the CD-ROM player _____ plugged in.   S   P

3. Both of these ink jet printers _____ suitable for your home office.   S   P

4. Neither Bryce nor Caren _____ interested in learning to use the presentation software.   S   P

5. All the new interns and managers _____ required to go to orientation.   S   P

6. According to Toni, child care and medical coverage _____ topics of great interest at the orientation.   S   P

7. Each assistant and department manager _____ received an upgraded version of their Internet browser.   **S**   **P**

8. Neither Juan nor Peggy _____ attended the personality profile workshop.   **S**   **P**

9. Presenting to large groups and traveling overnight _____ required for this job position.   **S**   **P**

10. Neither the editor nor the proofreader _____ received the most up-to-date copy of the style changes.   **S**   **P**

11. Either underscoring or italics _____ used to indicate the title of a book or newspaper.   **S**   **P**

12. My spouse and I _____ interested in learning to trade stock online.   **S**   **P**

13. If either the budget or the number of staff for the project _____ increased, we will be able to complete the project.   **S**   **P**

14. All the designers and copywriters _____ agreed to the terms of the new contract.   **S**   **P**

15. Neither the first nor the third week of the month _____ a good time for a staff meeting.   **S**   **P**

D. Proofreading for Agreement Errors

Directions: Rewrite the following sentences, correcting the errors in agreement.

1. Is the files ready to be E-mailed to the client?

_____

_____

2. Antony, our technology expert who handles all the computers in three departments, are not able to fix the problem.

_____

_____

continued ➡

3. Do you know whether there are another person who can take a look at the problem?

_____

_____

4. The goal of making all three deadlines are not likely to happen if our computers don't work.

_____

_____

5. The reason Victoria can't attend the meetings are that she is leaving for a conference in Dallas.

_____

_____

6. In Dallas, is there telephones she can use to conference call with us, then?

_____

_____

7. Every person is responsible for submitting their own invoices on this project.

_____

_____

8. The head of the marketing department, as well as two assistants, are coming to the meeting this afternoon.

_____

_____

9. Of course, each employee may contribute additional funds to their own retirement accounts.

_____

_____

10. Evan is one of those supervisors who expect to meet with his staff members at least once a week.

_____

_____

11. Our videoconference with the satellite offices in Hong Kong and Amsterdam are scheduled for tomorrow at 2 p.m. our time.

_____

_____

12. Every employee is expected to do their part to promote a stress-free work environment.

_____

_____

13. The original contract, as well as two copies, were mailed to the freelancer.

_____

_____

14. There is only two people who have access to these files.

_____

_____

15. In the newspaper today is two stories about the increasing popularity of telecommuting.

_____

_____

16. Has Michael and his team prepared the draft of the proposal?

_____

_____

E. Editing Practice

Directions: Underline any errors in the following sentences, and write your corrections on the lines provided. Write *OK* for any sentence that has no error.

1. Nearly two-thirds of the staff members has volunteered for
the fund raiser.   _____

2. A travel agent and an airline reservations representative has
recommended this Web site.   _____

3. Neither Ms. Pao's nor Mr. Kosta's assistant know where the
missing computer cables are.   _____

4. On the conference table is the questionnaires that were
completed by the staff.   _____

5. You and Thahn may request a list of compatible software
programs from the Technology Department.   _____

6. Half of the order for the new LCD monitors have been filled.   _____

continued ➡

7. Do you know if everyone has submitted their updated personal information forms to Human Resources? _____

8. Call Marissa and tell her that there is two software consultants waiting to see her. _____

9. Here's more Web sites you should check before you write your report. _____

10. We asked each staff member to give us their opinion about the new software package. _____

11. Here are the list of the names of the five leading Internet providers in our area. _____

12. Several recommended computer dealers are mentioned in the online newsletter. _____

13. The major distinction between our product and our closest competitor's are described in the report. _____

14. On my desk is three copies of the contract. _____

15. Ms. Ikawa asked Sean and his assistants, if he would like to switch offices. _____

16. At the front desk, copies of the customer comment form is available. _____

17. Heather and Lewis claims to be happy in their new jobs. _____

18. Is there any new job opportunities at your firm? _____

19. In my opinion, the facts that form the basis for your argument is out of date. _____

20. As you know, every employee have the right to an annual evaluation. _____

21. Ashley is one of those people who won't turn off his or her cell phone during a meeting. _____

22. Neither Kelley nor Daniel are interested in using the old software for this project. _____

23. The number of consultants budgeted for this project are
subject to change.   _____

24. A number of you has expressed concern about the change in
the schedule.   _____

25. The data in her report was correct and up-to-date.   _____

F. Proofreading Application

Directions: There are six errors in the following passage. Underline the errors, then
rewrite the passage on the lines provided, correcting the errors.

There is many companies today that could benefit from using
Web-based application service providers (ASPs). Both large and small
companies could improve its productivity by allowing an ASP to provide
services such as payroll or voice communications. Small companies that
do not have the resources for constant upgrading or the staff for data
entry benefits from using an ASP. One reason that ASPs appeal to some
businesses are that all the data is stored off-site. No data is subjected to
dangers such as local power outages or system crashes. Of course, every
business has their own priorities. For some, however, using an ASP may
be one of those expenses that save money in the end!

_____

_____

_____

_____

_____

_____

_____

_____

_____

_____

_____

_____

_____

CHAPTER 5 Mastering Nouns and Pronouns

Section 5.1 Nouns: Plural Forms

A. Supplying Plurals

Directions: In the space provided, write the plural of each of the following nouns.

1. company _____
2. physics _____
3. life _____
4. crisis _____
5. key _____
6. fax _____
7. lunch _____
8. analysis _____
9. tomato _____
10. sister-in-law _____
11. Scully _____
12. Ms. _____
13. 2000 _____

14. glitch _____
15. motto _____
16. child _____
17. vice president _____
18. agenda _____
19. sheaf _____
20. criterion _____
21. chief of staff _____
22. memorandum _____
23. handful _____
24. proof _____
25. salary _____
26. notary public _____

continued ➡

27. Dr. _____

28. deer _____

29. scissors _____

30. half _____

31. Nguyen _____

32. class _____

33. attorney _____

34. Culross _____

35. video _____

36. bulletin board _____

37. proceeds _____

38. category _____

39. PDA _____

40. Gomez _____

41. woman _____

42. I.O.U. _____

43. service _____

44. timetable _____

45. money _____

46. Lipinski _____

47. belief _____

48. Levy _____

49. x-ray _____

50. staff _____

51. veto _____

52. brush _____

53. A and B _____

54. Mr. _____

55. datum _____

56. schedule _____

57. CD _____

58. Schwartz _____

59. portfolio _____

60. alumnus _____

B. Supplying Singulars

Directions: In the space provided, write the singular form of each of the following nouns.

1. diagnoses _____
2. appendices _____
3. odds _____
4. tomatoes _____
5. knives _____
6. men _____
7. curriculum _____
8. geese _____
9. bunches _____
10. employees _____
11. bases _____
12. cargoes _____
13. aircraft _____
14. chiefs _____
15. policies _____

16. utilities _____
17. series _____
18. syntheses _____
19. shelves _____
20. vetoes _____
21. CEOs _____
22. ratios _____
23. decisions _____
24. the Salters _____
25. the Mmes. Stuart _____
26. flights _____
27. attorneys general _____
28. curriculums _____
29. plaintiffs _____
30. lengths _____

C. Proofreading for Plural Errors

Directions: Underline the incorrect plurals in the sentences below. Then write the correct plural form on the line. If the plural is correct, write *OK* on the line.

1. Please fax two copies of the contract to the Peters.

_____

2. Shelby, the computer expert, took a look at the network problems and made some diagnosis.

_____

3. The appendix for the report contained helpful information.

_____

4. Check the online bulletin board for information about the upcoming seminars.

_____

5. At this law firm, there is one legal assistant for every two attorney.

_____

6. Two notary public share an office at the local library.

_____

7. Were both the Voss at the shareholders' meeting?

_____

8. Our printer paper and office supply are purchased wholesale.

_____

9. Most everyone who works here is the kind of person who got all A's in college.

_____

10. When you proofread the document, make sure that all the page numbers appear in parenthesis.

_____

11. The Miss Underwoods took the news of their father's death badly.

_____

12. Back in the early 1990's, the idea of buying and selling stocks online seemed incredible.

_____

13. Her legal partners are actually her sister-in-laws.

_____

14. When the completed survey are tallied, we will have the necessary information for the proposal.

_____

15. Both of the promotional videos will be filmed on site.

_____

16. Before we begin this project, let's get our priority straight.

_____

17. This software package meets all the criterion.

_____

18. Lani and Austin are in their early fortys.

_____

19. The proceeds from the fundraiser will be used to buy computer equipment for local schools.

_____

20. The designers brought in their portfolio for us to review.

_____

21. Needless to say, we discussed all the alternatives with both our generals manager.

_____

22. I ordered three dozens ink jet cartridges for you.

_____

23. According to one set of statistic, more and more people are shopping online.

_____

24. The company gala will feature music, including a concerto for two piano.

_____

25. There are actually several URL that will provide the information you need.

_____

D. Using Plurals Correctly

Directions: On the lines provided, rewrite the following sentences, using the correct plural forms. There may be more than one error in plural form in each sentence.

1. All the editor in chief attended the Internet search seminar.

   _____

   _____

   _____

2. The new media center has facilitys for watching DVD's.

   _____

   _____

   _____

3. I ordered two dozens pairs of contact lens over the Internet.

   _____

   _____

   _____

4. The agendums for the staff meeting were distributed via E-mail.

   _____

   _____

   _____

5. The Murrayes and the Dunbars used their digital cameras to take photoes of the event.

   _____

   _____

   _____

6. Of the 12 CPA's in our firm, 11 filed taxs online this year.

   _____

   _____

   _____

7. All the children in the day-care center have parents who worked in different companys in the 1990's.

_____

_____

_____

8. The decision to use two APS's to handle payroll and track shipments was based on several specific criterium.

_____

_____

_____

9. The artists presented us with two possible logoes to choose for our new line of videos and DVD's.

_____

_____

_____

10. Two Thursdayes a month, several alumnus meet and share their lunch.

_____

_____

_____

E. Editing for Accuracy

Directions: Underline the ten errors in the use of plurals in the following paragraph from an E-mail. Write your corrections on the lines provided.

Beginning May 10th, the Technology Support staff will offer _____

two consecutive serieses of workshops on emerging technologys. _____

As we move further into the 2000's, the knowledge and use of _____

new equipment are the two keyes to our growth among our _____

competing industrys. The classes will be informative and fun, _____

featuring videoes and useful statistic. You will also receive a _____

handbook to keep on your shelfs and receive PIN's that will _____

allow you to navigate helpful URL's.

Student _____ Class _____ Instructor _____

Date Assigned _____ Date Completed _____

Section 5.2 Nouns and Pronouns: Possessive Forms

A. Possessive Case of Nouns

Directions: In the space provided, write the correct possessive form of the nouns in parentheses.

1. (Cassie) notebook computer   _____

2. Marc (Stamas) Web site   _____

3. our (supervisor) office   _____

4. the (Baskis) account   _____

5. three (week) vacation   _____

6. her (trainer) encouragement   _____

7. (Dallas) airport   _____

8. the (manager) meeting   _____

9. his (sister-in-law) telephone number   _____

10. our (children) birthdays   _____

11. (Seth and Tara) digital camera   _____

12. the (attorney general) opinions   _____

13. my (advisor) recommendations   _____

14. Ms. (Martinez) request   _____

15. both (witnesses) testimony   _____

16. the (doctor) diagnosis   _____

17. the (vice president) promotion   _____

18. all sales (representatives) commissions   _____

19. (Ross) portfolio _____

20. the (company) health plan _____

21. a (consultant) fees _____

22. several (consultants) suggestions _____

23. both (women) idea _____

24. one (year) time _____

25. the (association) members _____

26. the (computer) cables _____

27. several (scientists) findings _____

28. (Ito and Tracey) online businesses _____

29. the (Surgeon General) recommendation _____

30. one (editor) decisions _____

B. Possessive Case of Nouns and Pronouns

Directions: On the line at the right, write the correct possessive form of each word in parentheses.

1. While the company's sales have increased, (it) costs have also increased. _____

2. (Ani DeNova) resignation came as a surprise to us. _____

3. Our (supervisor) management style is to use a team approach to solving problems. _____

4. Can you tell me (who) fax this is? _____

5. (Kim and Deena) Web site receives many hits per day. _____

6. The (Schauss) airline reservations can be confirmed online. _____

continued ➡

7. Ramesh is the person (who) hard work won the contract for our company. _____

8. Each (programmer) cubicle will be equipped with a LCD monitor. _____

9. (They) reasons for voting against the proposal are clear. _____

10. Both (Minh and Dale) children work at the hospital. _____

11. Your technology stocks have done quite well despite last (year) disastrous showing. _____

12. The (Marx) new house was designed by a local architect. _____

13. My project is tedious but (your) seems more interesting. _____

14. Ellen (Sykes) presentation is next on the agenda. _____

15. An (employer) hiring policy must be fair. _____

16. According to the media, the Senate will announce (it) decision today. _____

17. Members of the (men) and (women) soccer teams must pass physicals first. _____

18. Our manager approved (Erik) traveling to New York. _____

19. I have only one (hour) more work to do. _____

20. What do you think of (Ling) rising so quickly in the company? _____

21. (Everett & Chavez) stock price has risen dramatically since the announcement of the buyout. _____

22. Of all the presentations, Ms. (Matthews) was the most informative. _____

23. If this business does well, success will be (their). _____

24. Is this printout (your)? _____

25. (Jian) film was produced with only digital technology. _____

C. Proofreading for Possessive Errors

Directions: Underline any possessive errors in the following sentences, and write your corrections on the lines provided. Write *OK* for any sentence that has no error.

1. After one year online, Lucia's and Danny's business is doing better than anyone expected.   _____

2. Both of Marcia projects are ahead of schedule.   _____

3. Most of the employees have completed their assignments.   _____

4. I think that the personal digital assistant is her's.   _____

5. All staff members should submit they're reports to me.   _____

6. Patrick edits everybody's else reports.   _____

7. Several applicant's résumés have been sent to Human Resources.   _____

8. Each employees' workstation has an Internet connection.   _____

9. Both of the managers congratulated us on our presentation.   _____

10. Unfortunately, we do not know whose responsible for this excellent suggestion.   _____

11. The companys' annual financial report is available online.   _____

12. One of you're assistant's time sheets is incomplete.   _____

13. Jasons' suggestion for purchasing DVD players is a good one.   _____

14. Why are they delaying there decision?   _____

15. The responsibility for completing projects on schedule is strictly your's.   _____

continued ➡

16. The accountants are checking they're figures again. _____

17. Who's presentation should go first? _____

18. As you requested, we are examining you're proposal more closely. _____

19. Whose going to make the suggestion at the meeting? _____

20. The insurance investigator said that the Walshes claim was valid. _____

D. Editing for Accuracy

Directions: Rewrite the following sentences, correcting any errors in possessive forms.

1. Mr. Ferrellys' speech was the keynote address at the conference.

_____

_____

2. Katie said that the responsibility for meeting the deadline was our's.

_____

_____

3. As of the beginning of May, the company had exceeded it's sales projections.

_____

_____

4. Do you think its necessary to get more bids for this project?

_____

_____

5. Have you seen Ms. Closs' presentation?

_____

_____

6. Tell him theirs no way he can miss this deadline.

_____

_____

7. Can I say that your planning to hold a meeting?

_____

_____

8. In a few years time, no one will be amazed by wireless computing.

_____

_____

9. You're training as a Web master was the reason we hired you.

_____

_____

10. Look for snapshots of the company picnic on Nancy's and Duncan's Web site.

_____

_____

E. Proofreading for Errors

Directions: Underline any errors in the following paragraphs, and write your corrections on the lines provided.

We need to help all our employee's use there time more
efficiently. One way to make better use of our time is to
understand each others jobs so that we can work as a team.
Therefore, any employee whose interested may register for team-
building sessions during work hours. If your interested in finding
out more about the sessions offered and how to register for
them, call Debbie Payne in the Human Resources Department, or
ask for Debbies' assistant, Clara Farrell.

The sessions will be held each Tuesday and Thursday in
Septmber. A session lasts too hours. Participants will be divided
into teams and given tasks to accomplish. At the end of a session,
each team will assess it's performance.

_____

_____

_____

_____

_____

_____

_____

_____

_____

_____

_____

Section 5.3 Pronouns: Nominative and Objective Forms

A. Nominative Case or Objective Case?

Directions: Circle *N* if the nominative form of a pronoun would correctly complete a sentence. Circle *O* if the objective form would be correct.

1. Do you know whether it was _____ who prepared this report?   **N**   **O**

2. We would prefer to have John, rather than _____ lead the meeting.   **N**   **O**

3. Two manager trainees, Eva and _____, could not attend yesterday's seminar.   **N**   **O**

4. _____ will you recommend for the new position.   **N**   **O**

5. In Bryan's opinion, the new sales manager will be Tom, Nina, or _____.   **N**   **O**

6. As you know, it was _____ who developed the Internet site for our company.   **N**   **O**

7. To _____ does this personal digital assistant belong?   **N**   **O**

8. Alex, _____ is my manager, will also have to approve the budget.   **N**   **O**

9. The most ingenious programmer here at QuickLinx Communications is _____.   **N**   **O**

10. After the meeting, _____ E-mailed the results to the staff.   **N**   **O**

11. Mari is as much an expert in Web page design as _____.   **N**   **O**

12. Give Clara and _____ all the proof pages.   **N**   **O**

13. With _____ are you attending the dinner?   **N**   **O**

14. If I were _____, then I would certainly ask for a raise.   **N**   **O**

15. Did both financial analysts, Chris and _____, work
on last year's budget?   **N**   **O**

16. Roger, do you know whether it was _____ who
designed these brochures.   **N**   **O**

17. Our new sales representatives are Dave and _____.   **N**   **O**

18. I would recommend that _____ be appointed
treasurer.   **N**   **O**

19. As you asked, we made reservations for Cheryl and
_____.   **N**   **O**

20. Our financial advisor and _____ recommended
filing taxes electronically.   **N**   **O**

21. It was kind of you to invite _____ to the conference. **N**   **O**

22. Ask _____ to enter this data into the database.   **N**   **O**

23. As soon as Johanna and _____ arrive, we will
begin the presentation.   **N**   **O**

24. Carlos asked _____ to get bids from several
vendors.   **N**   **O**

25. When Roberta heard Bryce's voice on her message
service, she thought him to be _____.   **N**   **O**

26. The president congratulated _____ on their
successful sales campaign.   **N**   **O**

27. _____ would like to postpone the meeting until
the results of the research are presented.   **N**   **O**

28. Will _____ handle the presentation?   **N**   **O**

29. _____ is responsible for creating the production
schedule?   **N**   **O**

30. I would recommend Lydia rather than _____.   **N**   **O**

B. Supplying Pronouns

Directions: Complete the sentences below with the correct form of the following pronouns: *I, he, she, they, who,* or *whoever.*

1. Renee is a new employee _____ is going to have a successful career here.

2. If Brad had asked Jamie and _____, we would have driven him to the airport.

3. Both Peter and Diane work as computer technicians, and both _____ and _____ went to the same college.

4. Ask either of the research assistants, Naveen or _____ to help you find the needed information.

5. Bonnie and _____ are holding a videoconference with the Los Angeles office today.

6. _____ exceeds the sales quotas will receive a bonus.

7. You should give the completed forms to _____ is sitting at the front desk.

8. Two of the assistants, Becky and _____, are moving to new cubicles.

9. If _____ processes the invoice by Thursday, you will have your check on Monday.

10. _____ is the new head of Human Resources?

11. Invite _____ is interested in the topic of Web design.

12. Send _____ a copy of the latest user's manual.

13. Most of the designs were approved by Kate and _____.

14. Who is going to lead the workshop, Elias or _____?

15. Ms. Mendez will recommend only those employees _____ she knows are qualified.

16. Given the increase in sales during the past six months, _____ will have to hire additional staff.

17. Bruce Phan, _____ is our insurance agent, is joining another company.

18. Please give Phoebe and _____ your new Web address and cell phone number before you leave.

19. _____ will help organize donations for the food drive?

20. Who do you think is more likely to be successful, Bridget or _____?

21. She told our team, "I want _____ to beat the deadlines on this project."

22. Fax the information to Sylvi and _____ by 3 p.m.

23. If you were hiring the consultant, _____ would you choose?

24. At the videoconference, Stephen sat between Christina and _____.

25. We have no idea _____ replaced the toner in the photocopier.

26. Give _____ a signed copy of the contract.

27. Joel has been in this department longer than _____.

28. Perhaps it was _____ who misplaced the files.

29. Our new project should challenge _____ all equally.

30. Ask _____ for advice before you make your final decision.

C. Proofreading for Pronoun Errors

Directions: Underline any pronoun errors in the following sentences, and write your corrections on the lines provided. Write *OK* for any sentence that has no error.

1. The office assistant will contact we when the consultant arrives in the lobby.   _____

2. In your opinion, would Dana and her work well together?   _____

3. Mr. Rinaldo offered both of them some advice.   _____

4. Between you and I, all employees should have received health and retirement benefits.   _____

5. How could he blame either you or me for the error?   _____

6. Julia seems to enjoy working on the Web page as much as him.   _____

7. Ask Ms. Lewis if us office assistants may order copies of the reference manual.   _____

continued ●▸

8. No, I did not arrange a meeting with the marketing
    consultant who Ms. Delgado recommended.   _____

9. Finally, the issue was resolved by my supervisor, his
    assistant, and I.   _____

10. Leni, who you met at the conference, will be speaking to our
    staff this week.   _____

11. Between you and me, Bill should award the contract to the
    supplier whom is best equipped to handle the job.   _____

12. The two employees recognized for their outstanding service
    were Gwen and her.   _____

13. Ms. Pomery sent Jerry and I to the production meeting.   _____

14. Was it him who was responsible for negotiating the new
    contract?   _____

15. Ivan has more accounting experience than me.   _____

16. The new assistant will work with you and myself on setting
    up the network.   _____

17. When I first answered the telephone, I thought Robert
    to be him.   _____

18. The programmers who work best under pressure are José
    and me.   _____

19. I would much prefer to work with Max than with she.   _____

20. All invoices may be submitted electronically to Ms. Tate or me. _____

21. They might have avoided the problem if they had first
    checked with we technology people.   _____

22. Nina congratulated Karl and myself on winning the
    design award.   _____

23. Of course our company has a Web site; otherwise, our
competitors would have an advantage over us.   _____

24. To be honest, I wasn't sure that it was him.   _____

25. The most dedicated office assistant is her.   _____

26. Would you like to join Amy and I for lunch today?   _____

27. The new assistant has been helpful to both Hannah and I.   _____

28. The ability to evaluate applicants' skills is the key to the
success of we managers.   _____

29. Do you think both the president and her will attend the
dedication ceremony?   _____

30. I'd like to say thank you on behalf of my staff and myself. _____

D. Who Did What?

Directions: For each of the following sentences, select the pronoun in parentheses that
best completes the sentence. Write your choice on the lines provided.

1. (Who, whom) is the staff member responsible for updating
the information on our Internet site?   _____

2. Do you know (who, whom) we should contact for
information about the change in tax laws?   _____

3. (Whoever, Whomever) we hire for the teaching position
must have at least four years of teaching experience.   _____

4. Give this assignment to (whoever, whomever) has the
lightest workload.   _____

5. Jillian is the laboratory technician (who, whom) is
responsible for analyzing blood samples.   _____

E. Editing Practice

Directions: Underline any errors in the following sentences, and write your corrections on the lines provided. Write *OK* for any sentence that has no error.

1. Ms. Gazoorian said that she relies on we inventory analysts to find errors in the reports.

   _____

2. Pat and me had expected the freelancer to submit a bid for the entire project.

   _____

3. Would whomever left their cell phone in my office please retrieve it?

   _____

4. Mr. Destafano reminded Alicia and I to file all important documents before the end of the day.

   _____

5. Didn't you know that the city planner is Carrie Bullock, not her?

   _____

6. Jen's performance at the meeting was a surprise to all of us.

   _____

7. As you know, us tax preparers are always busy at this time of year.

   _____

8. According to Mike, the most useful networking software is one recommended by Lisa and he.

   _____

9. Just for a moment, I mistook James to be him.

   _____

10. I called for a vote and everyone approved the proposal, including me.

   _____

11. The office manager wants to know whom took the new phone list from her desk.

   _____

12. Please ask Michelle or he to demonstrate the presentation software.

   _____

13. According to the new medical plan, hourly employees receive the same benefits as us.

   _____

Copyright © Glencoe/McGraw-Hill

14. The assistant gave herself an hour to learn the new spreadsheet program.

_____

15. Us medical assistants would like to attend the workshop.

_____

16. Any job applicant should take a deep breath and relax him or her before an interview.

_____

17. Based on sales figures for last year, our new offices in Peru have allowed we to grow the market.

_____

18. Yesterday I worked later than him.

_____

19. Do you know whether Dr. Camillo and her have rescheduled the meeting?

_____

20. If you were me, would you apply for the job?

_____

F. Proofreading for Accuracy

Directions: Underline the six errors in the following memo. Write your corrections in the spaces provided.

To: Teresa Rivas
From: Gwen LaPlante
Date: February 12, 2002

As you know, some of we are in the process of selecting a _____

new presentation software package for the sales staff to use in _____

the field. Five other staff members and me have already reviewed _____

several software packages. It would be appreciated if you would _____

give ourselves your input, too. I think you are more familiar with _____

this software and its limitations than me. _____

Attached are copies of the software. If you can think of others _____

whom are qualified to look at them, please pass them along. Other- _____

wise, return the copies with your comments to I by Thursday. _____

Attachments.

CHAPTER 6 Expanding Language Skills

Section 6.1 Conjunctions

A. Classifying Conjunctions

Directions: Underline each conjunction in the following sentences. Then, on the line at the right, label each conjunction as *coordinating, correlative,* or *subordinating*.

1. Before Juanita processes the orders, ask her to double-check the account numbers. _____

2. We hired additional staff members for our Phoenix, Boston, and Detroit offices. _____

3. Spencer acts as if he were personally responsible for acquiring the Landau account. _____

4. Warren or Ramona will update our Web site. _____

5. Warren and Ramona are updating our Web site. _____

6. Not only Peggy but also Angelo will conduct the seminar. _____

7. Whenever you have time, please review the brochure. _____

8. The Morrises wanted to vacation in Canada, but their children wanted to vacation in Florida. _____

9. Although we have compared several models of computers, we have not yet decided which model to purchase. _____

10. Please proofread these invoices whenever you have time. _____

11. Both the customer service representatives and the programmers are responsible for our excellent service record. _____

12. As soon as you complete your analysis, contact the client in Spain. _____

continued ➡

13. The landscaping company planted trees, flowers, and shrubs outside the mall.

      _____

14. You may make flight reservations with a travel agency or with the airline.

      _____

15. Neither the attorney nor the paralegal had a copy of the contract.

      _____

B. Proofreading for Conjunction Errors

Directions: Underline any conjunction errors in the following sentences, and write your corrections on the lines provided. Write *OK* for any sentence that has no error.

1. The reason for inviting Ms. Perez is because she is considered an expert in estate planning.

  _____

2. Purchase orders for more than $500 must be approved by Allen or Martin.

  _____

3. This policy covers neither fire or flood damage.

  _____

4. During the meeting, the public relations firm not only agreed to produce the candidate's campaign advertisements but also to conduct the press conferences.

  _____

5. The team will have only two weeks to conduct training seminars, and they are certain that they will get the job done on time.

  _____

6. Book reviewers were selected because of their ability to be objective nor impartial.

  _____

7. We were instructed either to send the completed form to the Human Resources Department or calling Human Resources with the information.

  _____

8. Although the equipment installation was successful, the department manager was still apprehensive.

  _____

9. You may transfer the funds either by telephone and by Internet.

_____

10. Webster said that he will go to the presentation and that he might be late.

_____

11. The company was profitable before it became famous.

_____

12. Sydney answered the questions quickly, correctly, or authoritatively.

_____

13. Do not register for the conference except you are sure Mr. Burns will approve the travel
expenses.

_____

14. The reason the meeting has been postponed is that the flight has been delayed.

_____

15. When she returned from her trip, Ms. Torres looked like she was very tired.

_____

16. The new advertising campaign will stress our product's quality and our outstanding service.

_____

17. Being that our department has reduced its staff, we are all working overtime.

_____

18. Even though Ramon pretends like he is quiet, he is really quite outgoing.

_____

19. Kent has always enjoyed both creating advertisements and demonstrating new products to
customers.

_____

20. I especially enjoyed the lecturer's engaging manner but her interesting anecdotes.

_____

21. Like Ms. Leavis said, change is the only thing that's constant in business.

_____

continued ●➤

22. Patients may not have prescriptions renewed without a doctor's written permission.

_____

23. Both Reid and I enjoy taking photographs and jogging.

_____

24. Michael Bloomberg is the manager which is responsible.

_____

25. Each of the hospital technicians is experienced in analyzing blood samples and to identify blood types.

_____

C. Selecting the Correct Conjunction

Directions: On the line at the right, write the conjunction that would correctly complete each sentence.

1. Jason was surprised at the news, _____ he tried to remain calm. _____

2. Sometimes Rebekah acts _____ she were solely responsible for the office's management. _____

3. Yes, I'm certain _____ Allegra is responsible for getting the invoices approved in a timely manner. _____

4. Kendra and Damon work well as a team, _____ you said they would. _____

5. We will not reassign any operating room staff _____ Dr. Waite gives his approval. _____

6. _____ you specified, we have reinvested your stock dividend. _____

7. Do you know _____ Dr. Melrose has left? _____

8. As Heidi Simon explained, the reason we are advertising on the World Wide Web is _____ most of our customers are Internet users. _____

9. _____ I conducted the research, I investigated appropriate sites on the Internet. _____

10. The store was closed, _____ Leslie did not seem to mind. _____

D. Writing Skill

Directions: For each of the following conjunctions, write a sentence that uses each.

1. although

_____

_____

2. before

_____

_____

3. even if

_____

_____

4. since

_____

_____

5. that

_____

_____

6. unless

_____

_____

7. until

_____

_____

8. either ... or

_____

_____

9. whether

_____

_____

E. Proofreading Practice

Directions: Proofread the following memo and correct any errors. Write your corrections
on the lines provided. Assume that names of people are correct.

MEMO TO: All on-site staff

FROM: Francis Badillo, Presidant

DATE: September 1, <year>

SUBJECT: Overhead costs

We all know that this year have been very challenging for
hospital emergency centers. For the past few weeks, we have
been asking staff members for they're suggestions for effectively
streamlining common procedures. Of course, it goes without
saying that we can compromise neither our service or our
patients' care. Thanks to all of you that submitted your ideas
for consideration.

Department managers have begun reviewing all the submissions
presented by the staff. Beginning September 15, managers will
begin meeting to recommend appropriate actions and to
coordinate these changes between the many departments
throughout the hospital.

Being that these changes will affect all hospital staff, we
appreciate your patience and cooperation. Like always, you
have responded to a challenging situation in a most
professional manner.

_____

_____

_____

_____

_____

_____

_____

_____

_____

_____

_____

_____

_____

_____

_____

Section 6.2 Prepositions

A. The Correct Preposition

Directions: On the lines provided, write the correct prepositions to be used after the following words.

1. abide (a decision) _____

2. accompanied (item) _____

3. agree (a person) _____

4. agree (a thing) _____

5. attend (listen) _____

6. attend (wait on) _____

7. beneficial _____

8. buy _____

9. compare (likeness) _____

10. compliance _____

11. comply _____

12. confide (place confidence) _____

13. conform _____

14. consist (make up) _____

15. convenient (near) _____

16. correspond (match) _____

17. deal _____

18. depend _____

19. different _____

20. discrepancy (one thing) _____

21. enter (agreements) _____

22. identical _____

23. independent _____

24. inferior _____

25. plan _____

26. profit _____

27. retroactive _____

28. speak (tell something) _____

29. speak (discuss with) _____

30. wait (customer) _____

B. Proofreading for Preposition Errors

Directions: Underline any preposition errors in the following sentences, and write your corrections on the lines provided. Write *OK* for any sentence that has no error.

1. Melissa and I agree in the plan to expand the size of the computer memory. _____

2. Did you notice the discrepancy in Angela's estimate for the upgrade and Harris's bid for the job? _____

3. The two contractors agreed with the suggestion to revise their bids to accommodate our budget cuts. _____

4. In regard with our request, the estimates will be completed by next week. _____

5. Don't let yourself become angry with the new computer software. _____

6. Memorandums regarding the computer upgrades were distributed equally between the five department heads. _____

7. Make sure the department hiring policy is in compliance with the recent changes in state regulations. _____

8. As we anticipated, Taylor's invoice is almost identical to Leo's. _____

9. The staff's salary adjustment will be retroactive from March. _____

10. All of the stockholders should receive the company's annual report. _____

11. We expect to finish upgrading the computer server inside of the week. _____

12. See if you can get some extra schedules from Eri. _____

13. Our new corporate headquarters will be located opposite to the capitol building. _____

14. The proposals recommended in the second bid were quite different than the ones that were originally suggested. _____

15. The new department head will be selected from among these four candidates. _____

16. This computer server will be beneficial of both the clerical and the sales staff. _____

17. Our new in-house cafeteria is convenient to both fast meals and informal staff meetings. _____

18. We will enter in an exclusive contract with a major software distributor. _____

19. When you see the human relations director, ask her where the meeting's guest speaker went to. _____

20. The speed of this modem is different than the other. _____

21. We agree with the staff's recommendations. _____

22. Are you conversant to this new software interface? _____

23. Two data support technicians are planning on applying for the new supervisor's position. _____

24. The procedures for expanding the computer server can be adapted to the needs of each department. _____

25. We have adapted for the changes in our hiring policy. _____

C. Editing Practice

Directions: Underline any errors in the following sentences, and write your corrections on the lines provided. Write *OK* for any sentence that has no error.

1. We were pleased to hear about you accepting the new assignment. _____

2. As you know, these kind of personal digital assistants have just been approved for sale. _____

3. In the supply room is the toner and paper for the new printer. _____

4. As indicated earlier, the firm of Maris & Jaworski represent us in this lawsuit. _____

continued ●▶

5. Eli and I agree that the number of responses to the new job postings are very gratifying. _____

6. Are they the consultants whom Ms. Chin chose to complete the marketing research? _____

7. There's only two other companies that manufacture these kind of cellular telephones. _____

8. Either Nuygen or Steve are scheduled to give the presentation at the sales meeting. _____

9. Ms. Rodriguez was sure impressed when she saw the decrease in operating expenses. _____

10. All the nurses except Raymond and I attended the Emergency Treatment seminar. _____

11. I would of stayed later to finish the report if I knew the deadline had been changed. _____

12. Lee was some unprepared for the increased demand in Internet service. _____

13. Don't Carter know that the new E-mail system will not be in affect until June? _____

14. In our opinion, there new distribution center should be very effective. _____

15. The Marcus's leased a new car with a fuel-efficient engine. _____

16. Mr. Tan manages the Information Technology Department very good. _____

17. Every corporate manager at the branch office was asked to reduce his staff by 20 percent. _____

18. Only one of our contractors whom we consulted were able to meet our schedule. _____

19. Before you make the flight reservations for you and I, check the airline's Web site for their updated departure schedules. _____

20. Two of the consultants, Mr. Nourai and her, will answer questions about the software's new features. _____

21. Have you found the reason for the discrepancy in the two
sets of instructions?   _____

22. We plan on provide faster Internet service for all employees.   _____

D. Testing Your Writing Skills

Directions: Each of the following expressions contains a preposition. Use each of the
expressions correctly in a sentence. Write your answers on the lines provided.

1. adapted to

_____

_____

_____

2. consist of

_____

_____

_____

3. discrepancy between

_____

_____

_____

4. different from

_____

_____

_____

5. adapted to

_____

_____

_____

E. Proofreading Practice

Directions: Correct any errors in the following memo. Write your corrections on the lines provided.

Lupe Vega and I are planning on offering a seminar that is   _____

specifically designed to meet the needs of people training to be   _____

graphic designers. We would like for you to review the enclosed   _____

materials in regards to this proposed seminar.   _____

Lupe and myself estimate that about 200 people will attend the   _____

seminar. We are planning on charging each participant $150 for   _____

registration and materials. Our workshop will include several   _____

guest speakers. Beside some of the city's best-known graphic   _____

designers, we also will host the president's of two of Chicago's   _____

most prestigious design firms.   _____

Although Lupe and me have not yet decided where the seminar   _____

will be held at, we will be selecting a site inside of the next two _____

weeks. If you or your assistant need any additional copies of the _____

enclosed agenda, you may receive more off Jill De La Garza in   _____

the Continuing Education Department.   _____

Section 6.3 Adjectives

A. Comparing Adjectives

Directions: On the lines provided, write the comparative and superlative forms of the adjectives listed at the left.

Positive	Comparative	Superlative
1. good	_____	_____
2. reasonable	_____	_____
3. large	_____	_____
4. many	_____	_____
5. practical	_____	_____
6. angry	_____	_____
7. important	_____	_____
8. much	_____	_____
9. sharp	_____	_____
10. tactful	_____	_____
11. lively	_____	_____
12. important	_____	_____
13. bad	_____	_____
14. wide	_____	_____
15. profitable	_____	_____
16. thin	_____	_____
17. loud	_____	_____
18. beneficial	_____	_____

continued ➡

19. up-to-date   _____   _____

20. fine   _____   _____

21. strong   _____   _____

22. cautious   _____   _____

23. complete   _____   _____

24. little   _____   _____

B. Proofreading for Adjective Errors

Directions: Underline any errors in the following sentences, and write your corrections on the lines provided. Write *OK* for any sentence that has no error.

1. When Jon and I compared the two E-mail programs, we found that the first was good, but the second was definitely the best. _____

2. Writing this analysis should be more easy than completing the field work and research. _____

3. You should test a computer with these kind of options for Internet access. _____

4. Please request more bigger monitors for the graphic design department. _____

5. We would like to invest in mutual funds and tax free bonds for our retirement. _____

6. Ask Anne if them transcripts are the ones Mr. Ravitz wanted to send. _____

7. The supply of antibiotics must be shipped to the epidemic site by the most fastest method. _____

8. Our time to practice music seems short every year. _____

9. This laptop computer seems to be more smaller than the one we recently purchased. _____

10. Whom do you consider to be the most creative musician— Theresa or Michael? _____

11. Would Rudy prefer to have one of them low-radiation monitors for his computer?   _____

12. Neither of the three organic gardeners signed up for the composting workshop.   _____

13. We preferred the second DVD player because it produced clearer sound and a sharper picture than the first one.   _____

14. My new manager knows more about the company's history and development than any supervisor in the office.   _____

15. Juanita and I both like keyboards with infrared connections, but a good ergonomic keyboard often has the most features.   _____

16. In order to get the best rate, I signed a three year contract with an Internet service provider.   _____

17. Cheryl is definitely the most assertive of any of our marketing representatives.   _____

18. The new centralized distribution center is more fully automated than any facility in this part of Asia.   _____

19. Marty has more experience in intellectual property law than anyone else in our firm.   _____

20. Chu's troubleshooting techniques are certainly most unique.   _____

21. The department reviewed four of the bids for replacing the workstations and agreed that Capital Construction's was the better one.   _____

22. The batteries for these cellular telephones last more longer than the ones we bought recently.   _____

23. Joachin's report provides a comprehensive, up to date analysis of tourism in our market area.   _____

24. The award for volunteer service was the most biggest surprise I could have imagined.   _____

25. The judge granted the prosecutor a 15 minute recess to negotiate with the defense attorney.   _____

C. Editing Practice

Directions: Underline any errors in the following sentences, and write your corrections on
the lines provided. Write *OK* for any sentence that has no error.

1. Enrique files more billable hours than anyone in the firm. _____

2. The board of directors at the homeless shelter have voted to
   expand the charity's downtown facility. _____

3. The attorney generals of all fifty states met to discuss
   enforcement of the federal Voting Rights Act. _____

4. Natalie, is there any other instructions you would like to give
   us regarding the new spreadsheet program?. _____

5. The council members unanimously recommended that the
   new city manager should be her. _____

6. The schedule for the childrens' summer program will be
   posted shortly. _____

7. Who's the editor who changed the book's printing and
   production schedule? _____

8. Our clients were real excited when they learned that the
   plant in Malaysia had expanded its production capacity. _____

9. The revised edition of the user's manual is much more
   concise than the original. _____

10. Being that the school board has adopted new foreign
    language requirements, many students may choose to make
    up the extra classes during the summer session. _____

11. Janine has come to depend upon her mentor's advice. _____

12. Chang ordered external disk drives for Melissa and myself. _____

13. Who's proposal for the after-school program was adopted by
    the library committee? _____

14. Because Stuart did not feel good, he decided to work
    from home. _____

15. Are all the extra electrical cords around our desks in
    compliance with the city's new fire code? _____

16. Whomever needs additional instruction can request a sample CD-ROM that includes further practice. _____

17. The accountant which is in charge of the audit has requested additional information. _____

18. Mr. Taniguchi declared that neither he nor Ms. Spoleto are in favor of changing the company's telecommuting policy. _____

19. These kind of rush projects often require costly revisions and amendments. _____

20. California may have more expensive energy rates than any state in the continental United States. _____

D. Proofreading Application

> *Directions:* Correct any errors in the following letter, and write your answers on the lines provided.

Dear Ms. Richards, _____

Thank you for your recent inquiry regarding home equity loans _____

from Central Carolina bank. _____

Over the past year, as mortgage rates has fallen, the rates charged _____

by major credit cards have not. With more major credit cards, you _____

likely pay form 18 to 21 percent interest on your balance. With _____

our home-equity loan, you can borrow money for much lesser! _____

Doesn't our 8-percent loan sound more appealing than a credit _____

cards' high rate? Remember, too, that you're credit card interest is _____

not tax-deductible. _____

Stop being a homeowner whose paying too much in interest! To _____

learn more about a loan from Central Carolina Bank, call myself _____

at 910-555-6265. Schedule an appointment; you'll be real glad _____

you did!

Sincerely, _____

Section 6.4 Adverbs

A. Forming Adverbs

Directions: On the lines provided, write the adverb forms of the adjectives in
the left column.

ADJECTIVE	ADVERB
1. abrupt	_____
2. absolute	_____
3. actual	_____
4. apparent	_____
5. busy	_____
6. careful	_____
7. competent	_____
8. complete	_____
9. confident	_____
10. convenient	_____
11. direct	_____
12. entire	_____
13. equal	_____
14. happy	_____
15. honest	_____
16. immediate	_____
17. inefficient	_____
18. legal	_____
19. mutual	_____

20. obvious _____

21. persuasive _____

22. possible _____

23. practical _____

24. precise _____

25. professional _____

26. prompt _____

27. quiet _____

28. real _____

29. responsible _____

30. satisfactory _____

31. scarce _____

32. sole _____

33. specific _____

34. steady _____

35. true _____

36. trustworthy _____

37. universal _____

38. unnecessary _____

39. visible _____

40. whole _____

B. Proofreading for Adverb Errors

Directions: Underline any errors in the following sentences, and write your corrections on the lines provided. Write *OK* for any sentence that has no errors.

1. Mia and I only have researched the history of this industry. _____

2. If you don't feel good, Ashley, you should get some rest. _____

3. Ms. Marshall usually appears somewhat anxiously before the monthly status meeting begins. _____

4. The new air-filtration system is guaranteed to work satisfactory, so I'm confident that my allergy symptoms will improve. _____

5. The Harrises bid on the property, but we never received confirmation from the mortgage company. _____

6. Did you see on television where the two new Internet providers are merging? _____

7. When I heard Mr. Jackson speak at the business luncheon, his attitude about the firm's prospects sounded very differently. _____

8. You can use the program more quick when you install a larger processor. _____

9. We had both the interns prepare the presentation because they work good together. _____

10. The city wants to attract a new sports franchise in the worst way. _____

11. We will, naturally, reimburse you for the total price of the appliance; please send a copy of the invoice to the Customer Service Department. _____

12. I think that Robyn's plan for upgrading the wiring system is practically. _____

13. Please ensure that the server is disconnected complete before you begin the monthly maintenance. _____

14. Harry and Maria are upset only about vacation time awarded to veteran employees, not to recently hired workers.
_____

15. The judge must sure have intended to give the jury different instructions before the jurors were sequestered.
_____

16. Experienced investors advise strong against buying stocks at inflated prices.
_____

17. The information technology manager claimed that the program is exceptionally well designed and that it can easily expand to accommodate future demand.
_____

18. Members of the recycling committee feel badly about the delays in implementing the new plastics recycling program.
_____

19. Since the specifications have been changed so often, I can't hardly believe that the new product has been completed on time.
_____

20. Two people in the engineering department received some real exciting news about their patent application.
_____

C. Editing Practice

Directions: Underline any errors in the following sentences, and write your corrections on the lines provided. Write *OK* for any sentence that has no error.

1. Marketing analysts found that sales of DVDs increased some during the summer.
_____

2. Neither the defense attorney nor the prosecutor were aware of the new court date.
_____

3. Have you noticed that the HEPA filter makes the air smell freshly?
_____

4. The seminar is designed to help departments build more productive relationships with each other.
_____

5. This new voice-mail system is the best model of any that we have installed.
_____

6. Don't Suzanne or Jack usually request copies of the meeting agenda?
_____

continued ➡➡

7. Is Friday and Saturday the only two days that the workshop will be offered? _____

8. Only one witnesses testimony was needed to prove her innocence. _____

9. These kind of vacation packages are most popular among college students. _____

10. Be sure to review the manuscript very careful after it has been edited. _____

11. Our company needs to review its energy policy in the worst way. _____

12. The sales staff claims that this automobile rides smoother than any model. _____

13. Warren's staff agrees that he is a real loyal supervisor. _____

14. Mr. Chaney was satisfied with all them designs sent by the architecture firm. _____

15. Over the weekend, there was plenty of support specialists to answer customer queries. _____

D. Proofreading Practice

Directions: Some of the following sentences contain spelling errors, possessive errors, or vocabulary errors. Underline the error in each sentence, and write your correction on the space provided. Write *OK* for any sentence that has no error.

1. According to the official reports, the accident occured two miles north of the airport. _____

2. Alicia calculated the cost estamates carefully before submitting them to the manufacturing coordinator. _____

3. The Payne family recomended that we take a vacation to Hawaii. _____

4. Aparently, it was Mr. Rigney's decision to delay the shipment until the order was complete. _____

5. Although we expect 250 guests for the reception, the
accommodations at the West Side Hotel will easily meet
our needs. _____

6. In my opinion you are all ready overstaffed for this project
and may end up with little profit. _____

7. Send these copies to Ms. Richters; then ask each sister to sign
and return one of the copies. _____

8. The commercial showing families working together to
construct a neighborhood park is our's. _____

9. Since we purchased the jet ski, we have spent most every
weekend at the lake. _____

10. The companies plan is to discontinue its less profitable lines
and concentrate on its most successful products. _____

11. Lloyd maybe appointed to the design team that is working
on the construction plans for the arena. _____

12. Earl ordered a new devise that is supposed to sense even the
slightest amounts of smoke in the air. _____

13. Is it necessary to include payment with my order, or will the
company bill me later? _____

14. I am not certain weather Ms. Kagami plans to return to the
Tokyo office after next week. _____

15. We need to reserve the main conference room for an all-day
videoconferance with our manufacturing team in Indonesia. _____

E. Correcting Errors

Directions: Correct any errors in the following memo, and write your answers on the
lines provided.

MEMO TO: Customer Service Representatives   _____

FROM: Melissa Vascura   _____

DATE: May 15, <YEAR>   _____

SUBJECT: Customer Survey Results   _____

As you recall, we conducted a survey of our customer's at the   _____

beginning of April. Attached are the results of that survey, which   _____

thorough queried customers regarding our products and service.   _____

We asked participants to comment honest regarding their   _____

experience with repairs and replacements. We also inquired   _____

wether they found our Web site to be useful and easy to access.   _____

Calculating the results, we find that respondents noted us four   _____

our outstanding service in all the questionnaire's categorys.   _____

The customers have spoken! The survey says that customers have   _____

grateful noticed your efforts. Congratulations on you're hard   _____

work and dedicasion. By handling their questions and requests   _____

so prompt, you have earned their respect and admiration.   _____

CHAPTER **7** Applying the Mechanics of Style

Section 7.1 Sentence Enders

A. Punctuating Correctly

Directions: On the lines provided, indicate whether periods, question marks, or exclamation points are needed at the points marked by parentheses. If none of these marks is needed, write *None*.

1. Congratulations (_____) You certainly earned your promotion to senior analyst.

2. Mario wondered why the billing process was taking so long (_____)

3. Martin called all the regional sales representatives, didn't he (_____)

4. Will you please enter the figures into the spreadsheet program (_____)

5. That food was so greasy; I won't go to that restaurant until it updates its menu (_____)

6. Jorge, do you think Martin and Taylor will buy that house (_____)

7. At our next department meeting we will discuss the following:

    1. internet access policies (_____)
    2. travel procedures (_____)
    3. family leave policies (_____)

8. At our next department meeting we will discuss:

    1. internet access policies (_____)
    2. travel procedures (_____)
    3. family leave (_____)

9. Have you already mailed your application (_____) payment (_____) room deposit (_____)

10. May we have your reply by August 1 (_____)

11. Good luck (_____) We wish you success in your college career.

12. Mr. Ortiz made the recommendation, didn't he (_____)

13. Has the new manager met with the staff yet (_____)

continued ➡

14. That's a great idea (_____) Who suggested it?

15. Sergio asked who would be taking the high-speed train (_____) when it left for New York.

16. Are all of the child-care workers trained in CPR (_____)

17. After smelling smoke, Carson shouted, "Call 911 (_____)"

18. Answering all the questions (_____) honestly is the best strategy.

19. The base price of the computer is $900 (_____) Monitors are priced separately.

20. Can the PowerPoint slides be updated for the 10:30 presentation (_____)

21. Matt questioned the possibility of sending the report this morning (_____)

22. My expenses were $500 (_____) for the trip.

23. Her new business will move to South Harrison Blvd. (_____)

24. Has Simon finished the estimate for the mall construction (_____)

25. After graduation he plans to work for Office Systems, Inc (_____)

B. Punctuation Practice

Directions: Insert periods, question marks, and exclamation points as needed in the following sentences. Write *OK* beside correct sentences.

1. Ms. Dakis asked me to watch her children until 11 p.m.

2. Roberto Rossetti will be our guest speaker for the seminar

3. Karel asked if I could work next Saturday

4. The employees who were surveyed are interested in (1) health insurance, (2) flex time, and (3) dental insurance.

5. The employees who were surveyed are interested in:

    1. Health insurance
    2. Flex time
    3. Dental insurance

6. The employees who were surveyed are interested in the following insurance coverage:

    1. Health insurance

    2. Flex time

    3. Dental insurance

7. The employees who were surveyed are interested in the following insurance coverage:

    1. 95 percent want health insurance

    2. 98 percent want flex time

    3. 60 percent want dental insurance

8. The manager asked why the report did not include last month's production report

9. When is Madeline going to Jacksonville, Miami, and Tampa?

10. Congratulations, Ms. Washington, on landing the biggest contract in our company's history

C. Proofreading for Period Faults and Comma Splices

Directions: Check the following sentences for any period faults or comma splices. Write *OK* if the sentence is correct. Rewrite the sentence correctly if it contains errors.

1. Darleen and Patrice want to update the software. To increase the speed of their Internet connection.

    _____

    _____

2. Jerry had a question. About the dates for the conference.

    _____

    _____

3. Joleen hasn't confirmed her flight, Dana hasn't either.

    _____

    _____

4. When the supervisor leaves you in charge, you've got a big responsibility.

    _____

    _____

continued ➔

5. Gracie saw the paint samples. The carpet samples, too.

_____

_____

6. One of the applicants for the job had a degree, it was from the community college.

_____

_____

7. Leigh took Nelson to the warehouse. Ginger met them there.

_____

_____

8. Shipping costs are a major expense, every department is trying to reduce its shipping budget.

_____

_____

9. Mike proofread the report, and Emily approved it.

_____

_____

10. Jonas ran for class president, Carrie was his running mate.

_____

_____

11. The computer file with inventory figures was misplaced. The Data Processing Department found it.

_____

_____

12. Baxter is recruiting new nursing assistants. Doing an excellent job.

_____

_____

13. The development lies north of the city. A very desirable site.

_____

_____

14. The club members did an enormous number of volunteer hours this month; they set a new record.

_____

_____

15. The storm was merciless. Damaging much of the new construction.

_____

_____

16. Maeve reviewed the advertising copy. Since Moira wanted the brochure ready for next week.

_____

_____

17. The employee incentive plan was discussed, we received some useful input.

_____

_____

18. Jared began his research, then he was notified of his project's cancellation.

_____

_____

19. The children's program was a success. Because of the many generous volunteers.

_____

_____

20. When you have finished the report. Be sure to distribute copies to all the department managers.

_____

_____

D. Punctuation Application

Directions: In the following memo, strike through exclamation points, periods, and question marks that are incorrectly used. Write the correct punctuation beside the incorrect punctuation. Remember not to overuse the exclamation point.

MEMO TO: Rolf Starcke
FROM: Lauren Blevins
DATE: June 30, <year>
SUBJECT: Patrelli Account

Congratulations? Winning the Patrelli account from our competition is quite a coup? Ms. McDaniel, our new marketing VP, called just as soon as she saw the order! She asked me how you convinced Ms. Patrelli to buy from us?

Your outstanding multi-media presentation definitely made an impression on Ms. Patrelli? The video was entertaining and well paced! When you quickly and accurately answered her questions, she was favorably impressed and felt confident that you knew your product! Also, when you used our spreadsheet program to determine her potential profits, I saw her expression change from negative to positive?

You certainly did your homework for this presentation? Thanks for your hard work in landing this account.

Section 7.2 Commas

A. Correcting Comma Errors

Directions: Underline any errors in the use of commas in the following sentences, and write your corrections on the lines provided. Write *omit comma* for commas that are not needed, and write *OK* for any sentence that is correct.

1. Ashley Miller M.D. has developed new drugs for cancer treatment.

   _____

2. Concerned about our publicity campaign, we contacted a public relations firm.

   _____

3. Erin Andersen, who worked with us for five years, opened her own accounting firm.

   _____

4. Do you know, what our new digital subscriber line costs each month?

   _____

5. Only those residents, who live inside the city limits, should be able to vote in the bond election.

   _____

6. A copy of your birth certificate should be mailed directly to the immigration officials not to me.

   _____

7. The man, whom you met yesterday, donated part of his liver to his son.

   _____

8. July 4, 1826 marked the deaths of both Thomas Jefferson and John Adams.

   _____

9. Is the trade show in Seattle Washington?

   _____

10. By November 2005 we will know whether the city will need to issue bonds.

    _____

11. Construction on the bridge, which was to be completed this summer, was delayed by a labor dispute.

    _____

continued ➡

12. Sherman who is an architecture major is working on a job site this fall.

_____

13. Thank you Carter for helping with our volunteer effort.

_____

14. His ability to learn computer languages, in my opinion, will help him earn a promotion.

_____

15. Jessica approves all major expenditures and she approves all travel budgets.

_____

16. Alicia spoke, and Jared listened.

_____

17. Jocelyn, Lydia, and Susanna will attend the first session.

_____

18. You may buy the supplies in person, over the telephone or at the store's Web site.

_____

19. Cross-training shoes, kickboxing gear, workout clothes, etc. will be included in our fall sale.

_____

20. To prepare for a successful interview you must research the company's product and management philosophy.

_____

21. As soon as you complete the invoice return it to the Accounts Payable Department.

_____

22. For more information about repairs please call our Customer Service Department.

_____

23. The best strategy in my opinion would be a multi-media campaign.

_____

24. Our branch office will open on Monday August 15.

_____

25. Three of the candidates for the position, currently work at competing firms.

_____

B. More Comma Errors

Directions: Underline any errors in the use of commas in the following sentences, and write your corrections on the lines provided. Write *omit comma* for commas that are not needed, and write *OK* for any sentence that is correct.

1. Claire will take a course in technical writing, or a course in business communication.

_____

2. Mr. Blanton has forwarded for your approval, several prototypes for new office letterhead.

_____

3. Did you see that the company's public offering happens this week Jed?

_____

4. Change the company's address to 4,500 Congress Avenue.

_____

5. She set up a home office, and will begin telecommuting tomorrow.

_____

6. Errol agreed, but Katie disagreed.

_____

7. Employees use several types of Internet service providers: dial-up service, cable connections, direct subscriber lines etc.

_____

8. Mr. Xu flew from Hong Kong, boarded a high-speed train in New York, and attended a meeting in Boston.

_____

9. Francis, Devon, Bridger, and Ava, have shown their commitment to expanding our marketing.

_____

10. Enjoying the new digital video disk technology, will require buying new equipment.

_____

11. Toner, external drives, ergonomic keyboards, etc. are big sellers because we have very competitive prices.

_____

continued ➡

12. Knowing that the price of natural gas would probably increase Gilberto had our tanks filled this week.

_____

13. Before you interview the client, study her portfolio diversity and her recent purchases.

_____

14. No your flight has not been delayed.

_____

15. Matthew flew to Atlanta, where he met with several venture capitalists.

_____

16. Leah handles promotions for the trade show and Leslie is responsible for organizing the displays.

_____

17. Before we sign the contract we would like an engineer to inspect the building's foundation.

_____

18. Our house is located at 1,654 Delany Street.

_____

19. Have you told Mr. Wells, Ms Cortez, and Mr. Jackson, about the conference call?

_____

20. After the planning committee reviews the proposal it will make its recommendations to the city council.

_____

21. Because we were aware of the upcoming merger we were not surprised that several executives decided to retire.

_____

22. Our newest staff member Lamar Roberts graduated from Stonybrook in May.

_____

23. The most recent bond proposal which was on the November ballot was defeated.

_____

24. That brand's heaviest laptop weighs 2 pounds, 8 ounces.

_____

25. Lawrence Tyrell Ph.D. is the new engineering consultant.

_____

26. Our new employees will attend training sessions at Internet Solutions, Inc., in Phoenix Arizona.

_____

27. Will is an enthusiastic dynamic salesperson.

_____

28. You may have noticed Mr. Miller that next year's expenses have been reduced by 10%.

_____

29. The group's first record was released on April 5 1965.

_____

30. On March 16 200 schools will send students to the music contest.

_____

31. In July, 2002, the lease on our building will expire.

_____

32. James Barnett who is our legal counsel advised us to settle the complaint without going to court.

_____

33. For a free copy of our catalog simply E-mail your address to our Web site.

_____

34. Obviously we think that the voting procedures should be reviewed.

_____

35. We have at your suggestion installed more lighting in the parking lot.

_____

C. Punctuation Application

Directions: Assume that the following letter is correct except for comma usage. Underline any errors in the use of commas in the following letter, and write your corrections on the lines provided. Write *omit comma* for commas that are not needed.

Mr. Tucker Haden
Director
Austin Book Festival
400 Neches Street
Austin, TX, 78703

June 8, <YEAR>

Ms. Kara Blackstone
Web site Solutions
1,818 Academy Ave.
Austin, TX, 78712

Dear Ms. Blackstone:

Enclosed, please find the information you requested for the Austin Book Festival Web site. The packet includes author biographies, schedules for panels and speakers, lists of our supporters and contributors etc.

As I previously discussed with your assistant, Sarah Abboud, the book festival needs a Web site that can be easily updated and revised from our office. Previously we marked and proofread corrections for the Web site manager. That system was an awkward time-consuming process. Knowing how much Web site technology has improved we feel sure that you can help us streamline our procedures.

Access to an accurate schedule as you know is vital to people attending our speakers' lectures. We want the book festival to grow and our Web site an integral part of our expansion plan.

Please contact me, at 512-477-8701, after you have reviewed our materials. As we discussed previously, we hope to have our Web site operational, by August 1. We look forward, Ms. Blackstone, to reviewing your proposals.

Sincerely,

Tucker Haden

Section 7.3 Semicolons, Colons, and Dashes

A. Using Semicolons to Join Independent Clauses

Directions: Check the following sentences for any errors in the use of semicolons. Write *OK* if the sentence is correct.

1. Highway signs are clearly coded by their shape, indeed the octagon for STOP is instantly recognizable.

2. The enclosed brochure describes the transportation for the tour; the air-conditioned motor coach seems especially comfortable.

3. When you mark your ballot for class representatives, indicate the length of their appointment ap-pointments can be one semester, two semesters, or three semesters.

4. Partial payment is required when you make reservations for the class at the Student Union, you may, however, pay by credit card.

5. The British spelling of several words is different from the American spelling for example, British spellings include *labour, theatre,* and *criticise.*

6. Sean used the emergency telephone to call security; otherwise, he would have been trapped in the elevator for hours.

7. Fax machines are an essential office tool, the model combined with a scanner and copier is particularly popular.

8. Suzette bought her equipment at a Labor Day sale, she paid significantly less than she had budgeted for the items.

9. We are upgrading our advertising displays just in time; however, we still need to address our larger media campaign.

10. Our refund policy is generous, indeed, we want all our customers to be absolutely satisfied.

11. Plan your seminar paper that is, prepare a tentative outline before you begin your research.

12. Ruben Gonzales excelled in his studies, indeed, he graduated with honors.

13. Tanya is our patient advocate, and she values constructive criticism.

14. This shipment must be received tomorrow therefore, we need to rush delivery.

15. The office visited must be noted on the expense account moreover, you need to present receipts for each purchase of more than $20.

B. Using Semicolons, Colons, and Dashes

Directions: On the lines provided, indicate whether semicolons, colons, or dashes are needed at the points marked by parentheses. If none of these marks is needed, write *None*.

1. Let's draft the report before lunch (_____) we'll look at a typeset copy this afternoon.

2. Let's draft the report before lunch (_____) and look at a typeset copy this afternoon.

3. Remember (_____) Wear reflective clothing if you think you'll be out riding after dark.

4. Address the overnight package as follows (_____) Henry Abrahams, 24 Lyons Road, St. Louis, MO 63132.

5. Ms. Suzanne McCourt (_____) she's our office manager (_____) is extremely organized.

6. The computers' processing speeds were exactly the same; therefore, we looked at our next important consideration (_____) cost.

7. You will receive coupons worth $25 (_____) only repeat customers will receive them.

8. Charles met his deadline two weeks early (_____) quite a feat for someone with little previous editorial experience.

9. Your tour price covers the following (_____) all transportation, theater tickets, and dinner at The Green Room Restaurant.

10. Lee selected the tile and paint (_____) a nasty color combination.

C. Editing Practice

Directions: Underline any punctuation errors in the following sentences, and write your corrections on the lines provided. Write *OK* for any sentence that has no error.

1. The CD-ROM has been especially useful in answering customer queries—extremely useful!

   _____

2. Have the sales representatives—a crucial resource—been asked for their feedback?

   _____

3. Denise Beaufort hired a new lab technician, she seems competent and well-trained.

   _____

4. First brainstorm for new images—do you generally do that—then begin the design process.

_____

5. It is necessary: that we review our sales manual, revise as necessary, and distribute copies to all employees.

_____

6. Caprock Manufacturing will soon introduce a new portable storage device for data, it will be in retail stores next month.

_____

7. Our digital cameras have been sold; we should, however, receive a shipment before the holiday season.

_____

8. This product is unique—not only in design, but also in function.

_____

9. With your order, you will receive: a wireless computer mouse, a wireless keyboard, and information about acquiring a wireless Internet connection.

_____

10. Please send your completed loan application to: the Small Business Loan Department.

_____

11. Following this set of log-on procedures—have you tried it yet—will save you time.

_____

12. If you want more information about this mutual fund, Read Chapter III. of this book.

_____

13. Office managers must meet several criteria to be considered for the district level position, for instance, they must have at least five years' experience.

_____

14. The Board of Directors—which includes some very important business leaders—enthusiastically supports the new volunteer program.

_____

continued ➡

15. Jorge Gallatin is retiring this year, isn't he.

_____

16. You must preregister for the conference by October 5 to receive the discount; please include
your check for $150 with your registration form.

_____

17. Mr. de la Garza asked why the keyboards had not been tagged with inventory numbers?

_____

18. Mr. Villalobos called to say that he would not be in the office today, his flight from Chicago was
canceled because of the weather.

_____

19. Several people have registered for the training session, including: Steve Billings, Virginia Franks,
and Mercedes Geiger.

_____

20. Ms. Schlosser has reviewed your proposal, she will meet with you shortly.

_____

21. Will you please make the travel arrangements for the energy conference in Turkey?

_____

22. Based on our research Mr. Darcy we should revisit the security policies on all floors of the hospital.

_____

23. Should we ship this package for morning delivery or for afternoon delivery.

_____

24. The message from the conference was clear: we must ensure our children's safety.

_____

D. More Practice With Semicolons, Colons, and Dashes

Directions: Underline any punctuation or capitalization errors in the following sentences, and write your corrections on the lines provided. Write *OK* for any sentence that has no error.

1. We must hire a considerably larger support staff: our increased business demands it.

   _____

2. Charleston, South Carolina, is more famous than any other city in the state, actually, it is known throughout the South.

   _____

3. A midnight view of a cityscape can be impressive; that is, if you can view a city from the top of a skyscraper.

   _____

4. Jamal—you've met his brother, haven't you—was determined to excel in science.

   _____

5. Remember: Wallis needs to have a wake-up call at 6 a.m.

   _____

6. This city has several interesting golf courses, for example, the municipal course is very well designed.

   _____

7. The competition will begin in two days the participants are already nervous.

   _____

8. He is excited about making the sale, indeed the commission will double his salary.

   _____

9. Glynnis realizes now—what was she thinking—! that she should have finished her degree.

   _____

10. For our drive, we'll need the basics; food, water, a first-aid kit, and the daily newspaper.

    _____

E. Punctuation Application

Directions: Underline any punctuation errors and insert needed punctuation in the body of the following passage.

As you may have noticed posted on the Human Resources bulletin board, our company contributes to many charitable organizations. Our charitable activities include the following tutoring at East Woods Middle School delivering lunchtime meals for senior citizens, and hosting the local blood drive. All employees are encouraged to participate   employees may take up to four business hours per month for such activities.

In addition to tutoring, delivering meals and working at the blood drive, our company is now beginning a new volunteer project sponsoring a booth at the State Book Fair. The book fair's profits are used to support library projects throughout the state therefore you can think of volunteering at the company booth as a way to bring books to thousands of children in need.

A brief meeting about book fair will be held at noon on Wednesday October 5. The meeting will discuss volunteer opportunities and Stewart di Capo book fair director will give a short talk about the book fair's history. For more information about the book fair call Bev Roberts at extension 401 Lunch will be served and we look forward to seeing you there.

Section 7.4 Quotation Marks, Parentheses, and Apostrophes

A. Punctuating Correctly

Directions: Underline any errors in the use of quotation marks, parentheses, and apostrophes in the following sentences. Write your corrections on the lines provided. Write *OK* for any sentence that is correct.

1. You'll need to call for tickets as soon as they go on sale (the sales representatives expect the event to sell out by the end of the day.) _____

2. Miles wouldnt have attended if he had known the event was running so late. _____

3. "The report from the so-called consultant," James declared, "is incomplete and disappointing." _____

4. "The price of beef," according to the article, will rise sharply because of the shortage of European exports." _____

5. According to the article, "The price of beef will rise sharply because of the shortage of European exports." _____

6. The patients' representative said, "We demand that insurance companies cover these basic procedures"! _____

7. "Its an industry that is rebuilding after years of layoffs," the recruiter explained. _____

8. When the manuscript is delivered (did we pay for the more expensive morning delivery)? please ask the delivery person for a signed receipt. _____

9. The book's last chapter, "Surviving a Real Estate Boom-and-Bust Cycle", is the best part of the publication. _____

10. At the final meeting (April 4 or 5) we will discuss possible breaches of the computer's firewall. _____

11. When you complete the census form, mark with X's all the boxes that apply. _____

continued ➡

12. "At the beginning of the new fiscal year, all travel requests must be reviewed by the senior department head," the E-mail stated, "in addition, travel requests within the same 30-day period will be reviewed by the district supervisor." _____

13. Nellie announced that "an engineering degree also could lead to work in patent law." _____

14. Savitha specifically said, "Wire the money to First National Bank;" therefore, we followed her instructions. _____

15. All of the deductions will be taken by June 15 (our fiscal year ends June 10), therefore, we can claim all this year's equipment as a capital expense. _____

16. The following items will be on sale next week (look for our ad in Sundays newspaper): DVD players, personal digital assistants, and educational software. _____

17. Order extra copies (see our Web site) for a fraction of the original cost. _____

18. The sales representatives that have been out of the office dont know the results of the status meeting. _____

19. You can get additional computer space with a "zip drive," an external storage device. _____

20. Many managers cite the Latin phrase *carpe diem,* which means seize the day. _____

21. The headline for the advertisement will read, "Have you started planning for your retirement"? _____

22. The text for on-line ad will read as follows: "Buy computers on the Web and save 60%"! _____

23. Her so-called "model manager" missed her deadlines by two days. _____

24. Mr. Varadan asked, "Who's available to organize the monthly birthday party?" _____

25. "Does your company accept both debit and credit cards" asked Mrs. Chung? _____

26. Let's ask Levi "whether the deadline can be extended." _____

27. You should buy a digital camera (since you can E-mail digital photographs) to take to the reunion. _____

28. When you land in Newark, (a driver will meet you) you will have only a short drive into the city. _____

29. "All the news that's fit to print," is the historic slogan of The New York Times. _____

30. When Jack received the lottery prize, did he actually ask, "Are you sure I've got the winning numbers?" _____

B. Proofreading for Punctuation

Directions: Find the errors in the following sentences. Underline each error, and write the correction on the line provided. Write *OK* for any sentence that is correct.

1. The supervisor said, "Elizabeth Thomas is working in the Brooklyn branch, isn't she"? _____

2. Our technical support staff is adept (did you know that many have advanced degrees)? and they are expert problem-solvers. _____

3. Our new restaurant (the one in the warehouse district), is expected to earn the largest share of the profits. _____

4. Raquel was called "the number one candidate;" her Ph.D. would be an important asset to the department. _____

5. "If you need more time," said Ms. de la Rosa, We will extend your deadline by one week". _____

6. Because Ms. Nuygen is out of town (she's in Hackensack, New Jersey,) Mr. Rubin will answer your questions about the new accounts. _____

7. Look in the *Gourmet Magazine* article Sinless Summer Salads for an updated version of tomato aspic. _____

8. "Keep that manager on retainer as a consultant," the supervisor declared emphatically. "She's too smart to lose"! _____

9. Jonas said, "Call the emergency number immediately;" he didn't want to risk our safety. _____

continued ➡

10. Most people in the department wondered "whether Preston would coordinate holiday shipping." _____

11. We took the problem to our office's so-called "human calculator"; she solves these budget questions almost instantly. _____

12. Joseph he's our Human Resources director will give us media packets. _____

13. Our high school emphasizes "core curriculum:" science, math, and language skills. _____

14. I'll recite the poem The Chambered Nautilus at the city-wide fine arts festival. _____

15. It seems that many errors (too many to count!) were overlooked by the proofreaders. _____

16. Before Prince returns from his vacation—he's gone skiing again--! let's finish this product prospectus. _____

17. Most of the targeted market (nearly 90%) favored expanding business hours. _____

18. Full speed ahead seems to be the company's motto for selling more franchises. _____

19. The department had identified these tasks as our "number one priority": answering customer queries, reducing downtime, and increasing office efficiency. _____

20. The investment counselor emphasized, "Our strategy must be conservative." _____

21. Robert asked, "do you have any difficulty collecting overdue bills"? _____

22. Do you agree that the budget for office renovation is "bloated and excessive?" _____

23. "These one-day seminars," Henry exclaimed, "seem to last forever!" _____

24. To think that this office design was advertised as "affordable and up-to-the-minute!" _____

25. The receptionist said, "Mr. Colon will see you now;" she knew we had been anxiously waiting. _____

C. Punctuation Practice

Directions: Add quotation marks, parentheses, and apostrophes that are needed in the following memo. Underline any punctuation errors; then insert punctuation marks where needed.

MEMO TO: Catherine Ozimon
FROM: Andrew Simone
DATE: September 5, <YEAR>
SUBJECT: Construction Delays

As you know, construction on the new municipal buildings has affected traffic and parking around our building. (You may remember that the buildings were scheduled to be occupied in July) City officials havent always been able to notify us of street closings and the so-called "temporary traffic delays" have dragged on for months.

Our company could schedule employees' workdays around the traffic delays (if we only knew the city's schedule;) therefore, I contacted building supervisor James McDuff today. I told McDuff, "We can help you relieve some traffic congestion by adjusting our employees' hours when the streets are closed;" however, the city will need to give us some advance warning.

According to McDuff, "this is a workable solution". He couldnt imagine any difficulty in posting street closings on the city's Web site. I think this information could be a real "Gridlock Buster;" if we know streets will be blocked, we can stagger employees' arrivals. That way, workers wont waste precious time sitting in traffic.

I asked McDuff "whether he could give me a final completion date on the city's project." The answer was "no". Staggered arrival times wont eliminate our problem (or our employees' frustration;) however, this strategy may help keep aggravation to a minimum during the final months of city construction.

Student _____ Class _____ Instructor _____

Date Assigned _____ Date Completed _____

Section 7.5 Capitalization

A. Correcting Capitalization Errors

Directions: Underline any capitalization errors in the following sentences, and write your correction on the line provided. Write *OK* for any sentence that is correct.

1. We know that The Environmental Protection agency has jurisdiction in this case, but the EPA has not yet been informed of the pollution problem.   _____

2. Lou LaPorte has worked for IBM since graduating from the university.   _____

3. This is the bottom line: Work hard and have fun.   _____

4. Marguerite recommended that I read "Telecommuting And Loving It," which explains how more people can work from their own homes.   _____

5. We contracted with Office Temp Inc. to hire 10 temporary Writers and Editors.   _____

6. The Airport shuttle will shut down early during the holidays.   _____

7. We got the authorization from the Supervisor of our Baltimore office.   _____

8. The new High School auditorium is being built by Hill Country Construction Company.   _____

9. The mild climate in the south makes it popular with "snowbirds," retired people escaping cold winters in the northern states.   _____

10. Natan Weinstein is a Vice President of Silicon Hills Software in Austin, Texas.   _____

11. Today's schedule includes the following: A lecture on outpatient services, a meeting with the staff, and questions from hospital volunteers.   _____

12. Dr. McCully encouraged us to review the article "New Weapons In the War Against Cancer."   _____

13. Store managers report that fall sales were higher than anticipated in the following departments:

    a. luggage and accessories   _____

    b. women's sportswear   _____

    c. sporting goods   _____

14. Is Cathy a member of the American Bar Association? yes, she is a tax attorney.   _____

15. The head of our department announced, "all sales representatives who have met their quotas may attend the conference in Puerto Rico."   _____

16. This was the decision: The dispute will be resolved at the Federal Communications Commission hearing.   _____

17. Bost Bakery delivers the following products: breads, cakes, pies, and cookies.   _____

18. Be careful: the weather here can change in an instant.   _____

19. Kris's letter was critical, but he signed it with the salutation, "best regards."   _____

20. Janine won several prizes: a trip to the islands, a shopping trip at a department store, and a digital camera.   _____

21. He quit his work at the department to write a scathing analysis called *A Critical Look At Government Safety Standards*.   _____

22. Are the Canadian companies our major suppliers? Yes, our major suppliers are located in Montreal and Toronto.   _____

23. The hotel clerk gave us a hearty welcome: "Please be sure to visit our hospitality suite!"   _____

24. Some of the amenities in the conference facility are:

    a. an exercise room   _____

    b. a swimming pool   _____

    c. computer connections   _____

25. The market results were clear: our company had expanded its sales in every location.   _____

B. More Capitalization Practice

Directions: Underline any capitalization errors in the following sentences, and write your correction on the line provided. Write *OK* for any sentence that is correct.

1. Our Summer trip will take us to France and Germany. _____

2. The chapters are all numbered with Roman numerals. _____

3. We'll have two guests for dinner: Stan O'hern and Nora McCain. _____

4. The ranch seems far away, but it is located only five miles west of town. _____

5. I am enrolling in a History course at Taylor County College. _____

6. Their new offices occupy two floors in Hoover tower. _____

7. She recently transferred from accounting to the Business sales department. _____

8. Parts of the Rhine river are lined with medieval castles. _____

9. I'm fascinated by the development of armor in the Middle ages. _____

10. The department store has a wide variety of irish lace. _____

11. Our family will gather in Hoboken to celebrate the second day of hanukah. _____

12. The beaches of Bermuda are beautiful, but I think puerto rican beaches are more attractive. _____

13. Most recently, she had an internship at Merritt and Sisters company. _____

14. My interview will take place in the State of Washington. _____

15. We will head North to watch the fall foliage change color. _____

16. Our final destination will take us beyond the river to Ben White boulevard. _____

17. I am convinced that von Erich's analysis is sound. _____

18. She is a systems analyst at a major Information Technology firm. _____

19. The skull and bones club has always been surrounded by secrecy. _____

20. Either the Yankees or the Confederates could have won the battle of Bull run. _____

C. Capitalization Review

Directions: Underline any capitalization errors in the following sentences, and write your correction on the line provided. Write *OK* for any sentence that is correct.

1. The landscaping company bought John Deere Lawn Mowers to maintain the golf course. _____

2. The president of Oklahoma University, Former Senator Boren, will speak at the graduation ceremony. _____

3. We believe the Federal Government should intervene in this instance. _____

4. His Department has supported his application for tenure. _____

5. That botanist has been hired at the Ladybird Johnson wildflower center. _____

6. The Kiwanis club meets each month at Luby's Cafeteria. _____

7. By a wide margin, representative Lucas was re-elected to office. _____

8. Before we could close on the property, we picked up the abstracts at Stewart title company. _____

9. The menu consisted of peanut butter and jelly on Pepperidge Farm bread. _____

10. The company's contribution to the United Way campaign made an enormous difference. _____

D. Proofreading Application

Directions: Underline each capitalization error in the following letter. Write corrections in the spaces provided. If a line has no errors, write *OK*.

Dear Ms. Hinojosa,   _____

Thank you for alerting us to the unauthorized charges on   _____
your Credit Card.   _____

As you can see from the attached documents, we have   _____
adjusted your March Statement to make the following   _____
changes: _____
    a. removed the charge to Holiday rental car   _____
    b. adjusted the Charter House inn billing to eliminate   _____
       duplicate charges   _____
    c. changed your Account number to prevent further   _____
       security problems   _____

We appreciate your prompt attention in this matter: as you   _____
know, credit card abuse can be best contained by acting   _____
quickly. We have referred this matter to the attention of the   _____
fraud department of our Company. Mr. Spears, supervisor of   _____
that Department, will contact you soon.   _____

Sincerely,   _____

Maria O'sullivan, president   _____
American Fund credit, Inc.   _____
Dallas, Texas   _____

Section 7.6 Abbreviations

A. Identifying Abbreviations

Directions: In the space provided, write out the words that are abbreviated. Use a dictionary if needed.

1. M.D. _____

2. D.V.M. _____

3. ACLU _____

4. A.A. _____

5. ROTC _____

6. TDD _____

7. TOEFL _____

8. USDA _____

9. VDT _____

10. APB _____

11. AMA _____

12. ATM _____

13. COD _____

14. ET _____

15. EDT _____

16. SPF _____

17. UPC _____

18. WATS _____

19. PS _____

20. RDA _____

B. Abbreviations Errors

Directions: Underline any abbreviation errors in the following sentences, and write your corrections on the lines provided. Write *OK* for any sentence that is correct.

1. Ronald la Forge, Ph.D., has a private practice as well as a teaching appointment.

   _____

2. Because of the bad weather, Chicago flights are being routed through Saint Louis.

   _____

3. Both C.B.S. and N.B.C. provided special coverage during the Supreme Court hearing.

   _____

4. Please note my new address at 1922 Harrison Boulevard, N.W. _____

5. The courier should deliver the contracts to Mister Alex D. Rodriguez, 823 East 58 St., by noon.

   _____

6. Have you met Parker Adams, Jr., the owner of Coffee & More, Inc.?

   _____

7. We recently E-mailed our tax return to the I.R.S. _____

8. We opened a branch office in Pt. Washington this month. _____

9. Any changes in health benefits or payroll deductions must be made by Oct. 15.

   _____

10. Most of our facilities are located in the SW part of the country, but we plan to open franchises on the East Coast, as well.

    _____

11. Douglas Varadan, MD, has opened a practice in rural West Virginia.

    _____

12. Our primary supplier is S. Street Medical Supply Company on DeKalb St.

    _____

13. Because next Fri. is a holiday, classified ads for the Sunday paper must be received by Tues., July 1.

    _____

14. All carry-on luggage must fit in the overhead compartment and weigh no more than 45 lbs.

    _____

15. The invoice no. is printed on each form. _____

16. The fragile document, which measures 10 by 15 in, will be carefully preserved.

_____

17. The flight was scheduled to leave at 7:40 a.m., but engine repairs pushed the departure time back to 4 p.m.

_____

18. Two popular music festivals are in Austin and NYC.

_____

19. The water tank, with a capacity of 20,000 gal, has been repaired.

_____

20. Countries in Eastern Europe have welcomed investment from the U.S.

_____

21. The USDA booklets provide information about cooking beef safely.

_____

22. The company stocks its staff break room with 5 doz. bagels each morning.

_____

23. According to the AP reports, O.P.E.C. members have reached a new agreement.

_____

24. We have seen that Wall St. investors can be intimidated by interest rates.

_____

25. The Government National Mortgage Association bonds are popular now; the bonds are known as GNMAs (pronounced Ginnie Maes).

_____

C. More Abbreviation Practice

Directions: Underline any abbreviation errors in the following sentences, and write your corrections on the lines provided. Write *OK* for any sentence that is correct.

1. Doctors Williams and Lee have a joint practice.

_____

2. She continued her research after receiving her medical degree; therefore, she earned both an MD and a PhD.

_____

3. The new memorial to Franklin D Roosevelt has received critical praise.

_____

4. The Misses Haymaker have opened a new tearoom.

_____

continued ➡

5. The building was insured by Fox and Sterns, Ltd.   _____

6. Because the case is so complex, it has been referred to the
F.B.I.   _____

7. With the business changes at AT&T, our stock holdings may
be split.   _____

8. We attended the air show put on by members of the U.S.
Air Force.   _____

9. The program *Fresh Air* can be heard on many N.P.R. radio
stations.   _____

10. My mailing address is P.O. Box 4550.   _____

11. We plan to visit Nantucket on our trip to Mass.   _____

12. That entrée had only 2 grams of fat.   _____

13. How many km is it from Dresden to Bonn?   _____

14. His work was awarded Patent Number 600,454.   _____

15. No. 550, the Rainbow Suite, has both a sitting room and a
balcony.   _____

16. Consider this a rush job; it is due ASAP.   _____

17. The conference on interstate trade will feature a speech by
Gov. Gray.   _____

18. Rev. Liz Smith, D.D. has been appointed to our congregation.   _____

19. This laptop has a much larger R.A.M. than the earlier model.   _____

20. The new couple will live near the Air Force base at
San Diego, CA.   _____

D. Proofreading Application

Directions: There are five errors in the following memo. Underline the errors, and write the corrections in the spaces provided.

MEMO TO: Mister Jake Maloney, Human Resource Director   _____
FROM: Ms. Adrienne Cortez   _____
DATE: May 6, <YEAR>   _____
SUBJECT: Policy Coverage   _____

I would like to change my policy to add the vision and   _____

dental insurance programs that were made available in Feb. I   _____

understand that an additional $30 per month will be   _____

deducted from my paycheck, and that I can use any provider   _____

located in the state of Fla. In addition, I would like to note   _____

that the primary provider used by, Don Cortez, Jr. has   _____

changed. In the future, his primary physician will be   _____

Doctor Helene Velasquez.   _____

Thank you for your prompt attention in this matter   _____

Section 7.7 Numbers

A. Using Numbers Correctly

Directions: Underline any errors in the following sentences, and write your corrections on the lines provided. Write *OK* for any sentence that has no error.

1. The Internet connections will be installed in university dormitories by August 1st.   _____

2. The staff at Memorial Library is preparing for the institution's 125th anniversary.   _____

3. California will need to reduce its energy consumption by twelve to fifteen percent.   _____

4. Our new safety features will be installed in automobiles by 2,007.   _____

5. The cost for overnight mail is $35.00 per document.   _____

6. Our budget allows for us to spend only twenty-five percent of our income on housing.   _____

7. I will finish the report by the fifth of September or, at the latest, by the morning of the sixth.   _____

8. On June 10, 15 of our engineers will attend the conference on fuel cells.   _____

9. 89 percent of patients surveyed were pleased with the hospital's renovations.   _____

10. At the end of the season, you often can find swimwear at 2/3s off the retail price.   _____

11. The emergency dispatcher directed the firefighters to 1908 86 Street.   _____

12. About 1/3 of our lunch business is take-out orders.   _____

13. An annual subscription to the journal is $30.00; a two-year subscription is $50.   _____

14. The insurance adjuster claimed that it would cost more than six thousand dollars to repair the hail and wind damage.   _____

15. Make sure that the drive picks up the clients at ten a.m. tomorrow.   _____

B. Number Review

Directions: Underline any errors in the following sentences, and write your corrections on the lines provided. Write *OK* for any sentence that has no error.

1. The power plant will be operational April 5th, 2004. _____

2. Each commuter cup costs $.95 to produce. _____

3. This 19th century desk was built when Queen Victoria was a child. _____

4. When the Tour de France winner returned, several 1,000 people welcomed him home. _____

5. The brand-name soda costs $1.15; the store brand, however, is only $.50. _____

6. Our car insurance has a $500.00 deductible. _____

7. The lumberyard is located at 14,400 Capitol of Texas Highway. _____

8. The 6-page brochure will be less expensive if we can sub-contract some production work. _____

9. This container will not hold a gallon of liquid—its capacity is 3 quarts 3 pints. _____

10. 100 new recycling drop-offs will be installed this quarter. _____

11. Our operating income as $6,000,000 while income from other sources was $800,000. _____

12. The start-up company forecast annual revenues of $5 to $5.5 million. _____

13. The cleaning solution is two quarts of water to one and a half cups of detergent. _____

14. The first mortgage payment, $648.22, is due on the 1st of April. _____

15. Our company's first plant, built in the 1990's, was located near Houston Hobby Airport. _____

16. Paul ordered 6 55-gallon drums for mixing the chemicals. _____

17. On April 25 our second day-care center opened on 7th Street. _____

continued ➡

18. Each supplement contains one hundred percent of the folic
acid required by pregnant women.   _____

19. 500 copies of these coupons will be distributed in the mail.   _____

20. After some discussion, they arrived at a .6 percent portfolio
management fee.   _____

C. More Practice With Numbers

Directions: Underline any errors in the following sentences, and write your corrections
on the lines provided. Write *OK* for any sentence that has no error.

1. The hole in the ship's hull is approximately 9 inches by
24 inches.   _____

2. He injected each of the animals with three cubic centimeters
of vaccine.   _____

3. You can expect to receive a ten percent reduction on the
price of the floor samples.   _____

4. The bubble mixture is made from a 2:1 ratio of soap to water.   _____

5. The township passed an ordinance preventing lawn mowers
from being operated before eight a.m.   _____

6. We will observe the holiday on the 15 of November.   _____

7. Aunt Grace gave her nieces 10 $100 bonds.   _____

8. The practice room—only ten feet by 10 feet—is barely big
enough for the piano.   _____

9. The employees' stocks have risen by only .9 percent.   _____

10. The six percent return on the money market account is
higher than that of a regular saving account.   _____

11. On June 1 100 people will move their offices into the
new building.   _____

12. Nine o'clock is rather late to serve dinner.   _____

13. Of the nine three brothers and sisters are still living in the state.   _____

14. The meeting ended promptly at 3:30 p.m.   _____

D. Editing Practice

Directions: Underline any errors in the following sentences, and write your corrections on the lines provided. Write *OK* for any sentence that has no error.

1. The $.65 bialy is a bargain. _____

2. The professor's address is One Suydam Street. _____

3. The huge organ at the church cost more than two million dollars. _____

4. The reception room has nine tables, at least 40 chairs, and two television monitors. _____

5. The seventeenth-century construction is remarkably sturdy. _____

6. For their 10th anniversary, they took a weekend trip. _____

7. Paul, who is 13, will attend a new school in the fall. _____

8. We have gotten thousands of inquiries about our new product. _____

9. We increased our sales staff by hiring 7 new representatives. _____

10. 69 percent of our employees would like to see an on-site child care facility. _____

D. Proofreading for Accuracy

Directions: Proofread the inter-office message below. Underline each error and write your corrections in the space provided.

Ricardo, _____

Attached please find 7 samples of the prototype you _____
requested. 10 more will be ready by June 15th. _____

Our budget has remained close to our original estimate—our _____
costs are only five percent more than we originally predicted. _____
For your records, our expenses so far are $12,500.00. At this _____
rate, I would think that we could have a competitively priced _____
product in at least 3 more counties by the end of the quarter. _____

If you've got questions about the samples, just call me by four _____
o'clock. I'll be out of the office, returning on Friday, May 12. _____

CHAPTER 8 Sharpening Writing Skills

Section 8.1 Using Words Effectively

A. Using the Dictionary

Directions: Look up each of the following words in a dictionary. List the definitions, synonyms, and inflectional forms and derivatives for each word on the lines provided.

1. compensation
definition: _____
synonyms: _____
inflectional forms and derivatives: _____

2. disparate
definition: _____
synonyms: _____
inflectional forms and derivatives: _____

3. query (verb)
definition: _____
synonyms: _____
inflectional forms and derivatives: _____

4. reciprocate
definition: _____
synonyms: _____
inflectional forms and derivatives: _____

5. survey (verb)
definition: _____
synonyms: _____
inflectional forms and derivatives: _____

6. tangible
definition: _____
synonyms: _____
inflectional forms and derivatives: _____

B. Substituting Synonyms

Directions: Read the following memo. Look up the definition of each underlined word, and substitute an appropriate synonym for the word. Write your answers on the lines provided.

MEMO TO: Naomi Kaiser
FROM: George Han
DATE: September 30, <year>
SUBJECT: Revised Training Sessions

As you revisit the training session workshops, please consider
including scenarios such as the following: _____

• A wrathful customer asks for a full refund for an item that
has obviously been used repeatedly.   _____

• A customer arrives just before closing time with a byzantine
order to be filled.   _____

• A sales representative handles an impatient customer with
equanimity.   _____

• A sales clerk reports being bothered by a manager.   _____

Thank you for updating our workshops to keep the topics fresh
and lively. I appreciate your originality and hard work.

C. Using New Words

Directions: Look up the definition of each of the following words in a dictionary. Then use each word correctly in a sentence. Write the definitions and sentences on the lines provided.

1. ergonomics
definition: _____

_____

_____

2. nuisance
definition: _____

_____

_____

3. alternative (noun)
definition: _____
_____
_____

4. expenditure
definition: _____
_____
_____

5. zeal
definition: _____
_____
_____

6. asset
definition: _____
_____
_____

7. fiscal (adjective)
definition: _____
_____
_____

8. substantial
definition: _____
_____
_____

9. freelance (adjective)
definition: _____
_____
_____

10. criteria
definition: _____
_____
_____

D. Defining Words by Forming Sentences

Directions: Use each of the following words in a sentence that demonstrates your
understanding of the meaning of the word.

1. accommodate

_____

_____

2. equity

_____

_____

3. remittance

_____

_____

4. volume

_____

_____

5. consultant

_____

_____

6. synopsis

_____

_____

7. recommendation

_____

_____

8. negotiable

_____

_____

9. compensation

_____

_____

E. Systematic Vocabulary Building

Directions: For the next four weeks, add to your vocabulary five new words each week. Detach this page and place it in a notebook for ready reference.

Week 1   *new word* _____
           definition _____
           synonyms _____

           new word _____
           definition _____
           synonyms _____

           new word _____
           definition _____
           synonyms _____

           new word _____
           definition _____
           synonyms _____

           new word _____
           definition _____
           synonyms _____

Week 2   *new word* _____
           definition _____
           synonyms _____

           new word _____
           definition _____
           synonyms _____

           new word _____
           definition _____
           synonyms _____

           new word _____
           definition _____
           synonyms _____

           new word _____
           definition _____
           synonyms _____

continued ➡

Student _____ Class _____ Instructor _____

Date Assigned _____ Date Completed _____

Week 3   *new word* _____
　　　　　　definition _____
　　　　　　synonyms _____

　　　　　　new word _____
　　　　　　definition _____
　　　　　　synonyms _____

　　　　　　new word _____
　　　　　　definition _____
　　　　　　synonyms _____

　　　　　　new word _____
　　　　　　definition _____
　　　　　　synonyms _____

　　　　　　new word _____
　　　　　　definition _____
　　　　　　synonyms _____

Week 4   *new word* _____
　　　　　　definition _____
　　　　　　synonyms _____

　　　　　　new word _____
　　　　　　definition _____
　　　　　　synonyms _____

　　　　　　new word _____
　　　　　　definition _____
　　　　　　synonyms _____

　　　　　　new word _____
　　　　　　definition _____
　　　　　　synonyms _____

　　　　　　new word _____
　　　　　　definition _____
　　　　　　synonyms _____

F. English Translations

Directions: In the space provided, write the meanings of the following foreign terms that have become familiar in English speech and writing.

1. pro bono

_____

_____

2. per annum

_____

_____

3. de facto

_____

_____

4. vice versa

_____

_____

5. sine qua non

_____

_____

6. ad hoc (adjective)

_____

_____

7. faux pas

_____

_____

8. quid pro quo

_____

_____

9. a priori

_____

_____

G. Hyphenation Practice

Directions: Use diagonals (/) to indicate where each of the following words may be
divided into syllables. Example: in/di/ca/tion

1. assistance   _____

2. necessary   _____

3. recommend   _____

4. acknowledge   _____

5. immediate   _____

6. disinterested   _____

7. requirement   _____

8. certification   _____

9. substantial   _____

10. volume   _____

11. occasion   _____

12. quarterly   _____

13. permanent   _____

14. ingenuity   _____

15. electronic   _____

H. Using the Thesaurus

Directions: Next to each of the following sentences, list several words that may be
substituted for the word in italics.

1. One *clear* advantage to using this design is its flexibility.

_____

2. Marsha is a *hardworking* employee who gets the job done right every time.

_____

3. All the managers *backed* the proposal to allow workers to telecommute.

_____

4. We need to *change* our customer service procedures to ensure that customers' needs are being met.

_____

5. Joetta and Carl will *look over* the results of the survey.

_____

6. Stockbrokers are accustomed to making *fast* decisions about which stocks to purchase.

_____

7. Mr. Erikson said he would *concur* with our decision regarding the purchase of a videoconferencing system.

_____

8. Our development team has created a *top-notch* software product.

_____

9. Dwight Yeager suggested that we *implement* the change in hiring procedures immediately.

_____

10. Ms. Ruscilli's testimony on behalf of the defendant was very *effective*.

_____

I. Using the Right Word

Directions: Fill in each blank with an appropriate word from the following list. On the line at the right, write the letter that identifies the word selected.

a. appraise	**f.** definitive	**k.** precede
b. apprise	**g.** formally	**l.** proceed
c. comprise	**h.** formerly	**m.** statue
d. constitue	**i.** personal	**n.** stature
e. definite	**j.** personnel	**o.** statute

1. Each employee must complete a(n) _____ information form to be filed in the Human Resources Department.   _____

2. Before we _____ with the testing, you must get approval from your insurance company.   _____

continued ➡️

3. Mr. Gallagher was _____ sworn in as mayor on January 5. _____

4. He was _____ about the description of the suspect he gave to the police. _____

5. A lawyer must _____ clients of their rights. _____

6. Sheila's presentation will _____ the keynote speech. _____

7. Rosalie Pedrosa gave the _____ answer to the question. _____

8. Each subdivision in the housing development will _____ 30 lots. _____

9. The legislature approved a tougher _____ against industrial pollution. _____

10. Satish Patel was _____ with the accounting firm of Parkhurst and Owen. _____

J. Sound-Alikes

Directions: Choose the word in parentheses that correctly completes each sentence, and write the word in the space provided.

1. Michael's (principal, principle) reason for accepting the job offer was the opportunity for advancement. _____

2. To complete the warranty card, include the (cereal, serial) number of the item that you purchased. _____

3. I would appreciate your (assistance, assistants) with this lab procedure. _____

4. You must exercise (patience, patients) in dealing with customers who have a complaint. _____

5. One-third of the (residence, residents) in the apartment complex are eligible for a two-year lease. _____

6. We made a (miner, minor) adjustment to the blueprints for the Steele project. _____

7. If you are an employee of Meyer Memorial Hospital, we will (waive, wave) the membership fee for the health club. _____

8. The student advisory (council, counsel) will meet with
school officials next week to discuss the topic.   _____

9. Do you know (weather, whether) the new contract with the
technicians' union has been approved?   _____

10. We are working to (lessen, lesson) the number of backorders
we have for our products.   _____

K. Replacing Negative Words

Directions: In each of the following sentences, replace the negative word or words with
more positive wording. Write your answers in the space provided.

1. Because your company took too much time in processing the order, we missed our
shipping deadline.

_____

_____

2. You entered the data incorrectly, and the money was credited to someone else's account.

_____

_____

3. You are behind schedule, so we will have to delay the release date for the product.

_____

_____

4. What size processor do you want on your computer? We can't ship it until you give us all
the information.

_____

_____

5. The problem with your telephone service is not our telephone. Your wiring needs to
be repaired.

_____

_____

L. Antonyms

Directions: For each italicized word at the left, select the letter of the word that is most nearly opposite in meaning. Write your answers on the lines provided.

1. *coincide*   (a) correspond   (b) agree   (c) concur   (d) dissent   _____

2. *reinforce*   (a) strengthen   (b) abandon   (c) bolster   (d) support   _____

3. *impose*   (a) offer   (b) oblige   (c) demand   (d) intrude   _____

4. *expend*   (a) consume   (b) spend   (c) conserve   (d) waste   _____

5. *specify*   (a) designate   (b) suggest   (c) distinguish   (d) itemize   _____

M. Spelling and Vocabulary

Directions: Underline any spelling and vocabulary errors in the following sentences, and write your corrections on the lines provided. Write *OK* for any sentence that has no error.

1. We have updated many of our training videos by putting them in DVD format.   _____

2. The chapter on office systems proceeds the chapter on data storage.   _____

3. The merger between the two information technology companies is eminent.   _____

4. We are having better employee retention then we had last year.   _____

5. That supplier was charging exuberant prices for delivery and service.   _____

6. Our Internet advertising has had a positive effect on sales.   _____

7. The college recruiter gave us a detailed discription of the university's business and science classes.   _____

8. To be reimbursed, you will need to submit a receipt.   _____

9. Check all the colums of figures in all the appendices and addenda. _____

10. The simple computer modifikations will greatly increase your _____ processing speed.

N. Improving Sentences

Directions: In each of the following sentences, delete any unnecessary words or replace any overused words with more exact expressions. Write your answers in the spaces provided.

1. We'll continue on with the presentation after a short break.

_____

_____

2. I had a real bad experience with that vendor.

_____

_____

3. I'm sure this file will work fine after I've run the utilities program.

_____

_____

4. If you want to know how the novel ends, just turn ahead to the final chapter.

_____

_____

5. We never ever perform the maintenance procedures out of sequence.

_____

_____

6. If you would like to do some future planning, you might want to project the fall quarter sales.

_____

_____

7. We all had questions about the speaker's interesting analysis of the Supreme Court case.

_____

_____

continued ➤

8. The clerk had a pretty hard time pleasing such an exacting customer.

_____

_____

9. This courier service has always been good about delivering documents on time.

_____

_____

10. I think we found this product so great because we can use it in many applications.

_____

_____

O. Eliminating Clichés

Directions: For each cliché you find in the following sentences, substitute more effective wording. Write your answers on the lines provided.

1. Thank you for your recent communication regarding our business expansion.

_____

_____

2. Inasmuch as we wrote the program, we are the logical team to lead the training session.

_____

_____

3. Each and every sales representative needs to keep track of mileage.

_____

_____

4. I think the plans for the licensing arrangement with Giamatti Foods are on the right track.

_____

_____

5. After two weeks of intensive obedience training, our jumpy dog was as good as gold.

_____

_____

Section 8.2 Mastering Spelling Techniques

A. Proofreading for Spelling Errors

Directions: Underline any incorrectly spelled words in the following sentences, and write their correct spellings in the answer column. Write *OK* for any sentences that are correct.

1. Chris works as a computer technision in the Business Systems Department. _____

2. Were you able to pursuade Masaki to assist us in completing the telephone survays? _____

3. Two court-appointed attornies met with the defendant to discuss a possible plea bargain. _____

4. The banquet room can accommodate up to 300 people. _____

5. Financialy, we are in an ideal position to expand our business. _____

6. Our sales representatives are commited to providing excellent service to all customers. _____

7. Do you know if this pen contains permanant ink? _____

8. We will need to overcome several obstacals in order to achieve our sales goal. _____

9. You will be eligible for a promotion in one year. _____

10. A good administrator is energetic, recourcefull, and decisive. _____

11. Over one-half of our internal documents are transmited by E-mail. _____

12. Order the miscellaneus computer supplies from Office Clearinghouse. _____

13. When interest rates are high, few people can get morgages. _____

14. Customer demand for our new keyboarding software has exceded our expectations. _____

continued ●▸

15. We will basicaly start from scratch in designing our new line of active wear.   _____

16. Did you percieve anything unusual about Joel's request?   _____

17. Our company offers extended warrantys on every washer and dryer we manufacture.   _____

18. The weather service issued a travel advisery due to the heavy snowfall.   _____

19. An independant auditor was brought in by the stockholders to review the company's pension plan.   _____

20. Check with your insurance agent about the deductable on your automobile insurance.   _____

B. Spelling Practice

Directions: On the lines provided, spell the phonetically written words that are enclosed in parentheses in the following sentences.

1. The refinery was refitted in order to better (dispoz) of hazardous waste.   _____

2. The waiter knew we were in a hurry, so he was very (prampt) in bringing our entrée.   _____

3. The Senate (konkurd) with the House of Representatives' decision.   _____

4. We are looking for a new (vender) to provide lunch in the breakroom.   _____

5. The presentation had just enough (repetishun) to remind listeners of important points.   _____

6. We find it most economical to (advertize) on local radio stations.   _____

7. Staff writers produce most of our documents, but we must (okazunully) contract with freelance editors.   _____

8. Newspaper prices went up due to an (inkres) in
   newsprint costs.   _____

9. Our aquifer was stringently tested to see whether it was in
   (komplyuns) with drinking water regulations.   _____

10. My (skejul) is so full, I won't be able to meet with you
    until Friday.   _____

11. This contractor's price is within the budget of our (klient).   _____

12. Because billing costs are high, the veterinarian asked us to
    pay the full (amaunt) of the office visit.   _____

13. He was (konshus) that his message was being poorly
    received.   _____

14. Eileen clearly stated the (perpus) of the emergency
    staff meeting.   _____

15. The insulated windows are expensive, but that will save a
    (substanshul) amount in energy costs.   _____

16. The team listened to numerous proposals before making
    its (disizhen).   _____

17. Despite the change in the economy, the board voted to
    (proseed) with the company's building project.   _____

18. The (inishel) blueprint was for a much larger building.   _____

19. We completed our first (faz) of the project only slightly over
    our budget.   _____

20. The editorial staff does not handle (teknikul) issues such as
    computer upgrades.   _____

C. Spelling Checkup

Directions: On the line provided, write the letter that represents the correctly spelled word in each group. If none of the words is spelled correctly, select *d*.

1. (a) responsibilety   (b) responsibilaty   (c) responsibility   (d) none   _____
2. (a) consciensious   (b) conscientious   (c) consietious   (d) none   _____
3. (a) liability   (b) lieability   (c) lyabilaty   (d) none   _____
4. (a) preceed   (b) presede   (c) preseed   (d) none   _____
5. (a) committment   (b) commitment   (c) comittment   (d) none   _____
6. (a) judgement   (b) judgment   (c) judgmente   (d) none   _____
7. (a) forgetable   (b) forgetible   (c) forgettable   (d) none   _____
8. (a) technitian   (b) technician   (c) tecknition   (d) none   _____
9. (a) ocasional   (b) occassional   (c) occasional   (d) none   _____
10. (a) equivalint   (b) equivalant   (c) equivalent   (d) none   _____

D. Selecting the Right Word

Directions: From the words in parentheses, select the one that correctly completes the meaning of the sentence, and write it on the line provided.

1. The director and I had met one another, but we had not been (formerly, formally) introduced.   _____

2. The new managing editor (least, leased) a duplex while she looked for a house to buy.   _____

3. The best (advise, advice) I could have received would have been to proofread my work carefully.   _____

4. Harold has always worked (quiet, quite) hard, but he still was surprised to receive a promotion.   _____

5. You must be well prepared for your interview, but (assertive, asertive) about your qualifications.   _____

6. Anna was (intense, intent) on her violin lesson and practiced for hours without a (break, brake). _____

7. Harold is (casual, causal) about procedures, but he is serious about his product. _____

8. The most recently hired employees are (illegible, ineligible) for the company's stock offerings. _____

9. Next week, the (defendants, defendents) will tell the prosecutor their side of the story. _____

10. The staff tries to keep (patients, patience) from waiting too long to see a doctor. _____

E. The Correct Form of Words

Directions: In the space provided, write out the correct form of the words in parentheses. Use a dictionary if needed.

1. We called the airline for (confirm) of our flight's arrival time. _____

2. Lauren's rigorous exercise program ensures that she is the (healthy) member of our family. _____

3. Technicians (modify) the program to meet individuals' needs. _____

4. That community has an (abnormal) high percentage of leukemia patients. _____

5. Your question can only be answered by a person familiar with (administrate) policy. _____

6. The city ballet's (perform) of Swan Lake was breathtaking. _____

7. The architects (submit) both a blueprint and a model of the plan they proposed. _____

8. The electrician's (recommend) could improve our building's air conditioning system. _____

9. The primary (enhance) to the building was the addition of landscaping. _____

continued ➡

10. We did not know of this competitor's (exist) until we saw
their advertisements on the Internet.   _____

11. The (account) conducted an independent audit of
our finances.   _____

12. There is no (possible) that the change in operating systems
will affect the computers' performance.   _____

13. Federal law requires that this building be (access) to people
using wheelchairs.   _____

14. Do you have all the tools you need for the DSL (install)?   _____

15. Davis is still adjusting to his new (supervise) position.   _____

16. James' (participate) in the volunteer effort made the lunch
delivery proceed smoothly.   _____

17. Although the station (temporary) raised the price of gas, we
soon saw the price fall by 10 cents per gallon.   _____

18. Her military experience makes her (knowledge) about many
of the helicopter's features.   _____

19. Since we have made a down payment, we are (commit) to
buying the downtown loft.   _____

20. In an (evacuate) of the building, we will use stairs rather
than elevators.   _____

F. Troublesome Words

Directions: In the sentences below, underline the incorrectly spelled words, and write their correct spellings in the answer column. Indicate correct sentences by writing *OK*.

1. My parents' class is preparing to celebrate their fourtieth reunion.   _____

2. If you compliment Suzanna in public, it will only embarrass her.   _____

3. Working with such well-known authors was a great privelege.   _____

4. The golfer's swing at the nineth hole was absolutely perfect.   _____

5. Repitition is to be expected in a refresher class such as this one.   _____

6. We have had precious little time to develope an alternative proposal.   _____

7. I read in the newspaper that the final verdic was in the plaintiff's favor.   _____

8. The difficult procedure was conducted in the doctor's primary office.   _____

Section 8.3 Structuring Phrases and Clauses

A. Sentences With Unclear Thought Units

Directions: The following sentences contain misplaced words, phrases, clauses, or confusing thought units. Rewrite each sentence so that its meaning is clear and reasonable.

1. I was only willing to buy the computer with the extended warranty.

   _____
   _____

2. Maurice and Martin agreed that his suggestion deserved further discussion.

   _____
   _____

3. Last week I saw the Picasso exhibit while in Los Angeles.

   _____
   _____

4. Refer to my memorandum to all senior staff about the new security measures dated August 14.

   _____
   _____

5. Students who have reviewed their notes can easily pass the exam for two hours.

   _____
   _____

6. The shoes are most appropriate for small children with the Velcro closure

   _____
   _____

7. Make sure that all the bills have return address labels mailed today on the envelopes.

   _____
   _____

8. These contracts should be filed near the door in the lateral file.

   _____
   _____

9. Before you mail the invoice for the Craig's air conditioner repair, please make a copy of it.

_____

_____

10. The consultant's evaluation included suggestions for improving communication, which will be discussed at the staff meeting.

_____

_____

11. Sales representatives do not have access to the inventory system. This has caused delays in filling orders.

_____

_____

12. Replying to the E-mail, the customer's query was handled by Madison.

_____

_____

13. Here are some guidelines for rebooting your system from the support staff.

_____

_____

14. Jack Davis successfully presented our case to the Senate, thus proving that he is a capable lobbyist.

_____

_____

15. In the status report from you, it says the highway project is behind schedule.

_____

_____

16. Francis Gallagher returned an E-mail to his supervisor sitting at the airport.

_____

_____

17. Being an organic gardener, the natural fertilizer was the only choice.

_____

_____

continued ➡

18. The information about the author's lecture is posted beside the elevator on
the bulletin board.

_____

_____

19. We offer a wide variety of software for all employees, which you can purchase at a special
discount.

_____

_____

20. Do you know where they repair printers quickly and reliably?

_____

_____

B. *Because* **Clauses**

> ***Directions:*** Thought-unit errors with *because* often misstate people's reasons for acting.
> Correct any such errors in the following sentences.

1. Andrea barely listened to the speech the mayor made because she was distracted by a deadline
at work.

_____

_____

2. Maureen completed the research you requested ahead of schedule because she will be leaving
for a conference tomorrow.

_____

_____

3. Lori did not process the contract you submitted because the paperwork was incomplete.

_____

_____

4. Mr. Fujimoro will not attend the session because he is preparing his keynote address.

_____

_____

5. Professor Levine did not review the book proposal Mike submitted because he was in a faculty
meeting.

_____

_____

C. *Which* Clauses

Directions: Misplaced *which* clauses can cause confusion. Correct any misplaced *which* clauses in the following sentences.

1. I researched the manuscript at the British Museum, which contained an important piece of evidence.

_____

_____

2. Continued miscommunication with the client could result in us losing the contract, which neither of us prefers.

_____

_____

3. The board of directors recently appointed Ms. Briix to head the library, which meets once a month.

_____

_____

4. The new position would attract highly qualified candidates, which was posted on the Internet.

_____

_____

5. The column appeared in Monday's paper, which was highly critical of the corporation.

_____

_____

D. *Who Did What*

Directions: The following sentences contain misplaced or confusing phrases and clauses.
Rewrite each sentence so that its meaning is clear and reasonable.

1. I found the file searching my hard drive.

   _____

   _____

2. The utilities program recovered all the corrupted information, thus justifying the expense.

   _____

   _____

3. After saying goodbye to our guests, the kitchen was a mess.

   _____

   _____

4. If not on time, the train fare will be free.

   _____

   _____

5. Accepting the customer's praise, the compliment was very much appreciated by Stewart.

   _____

   _____

6. If eligible, we will join the credit union.

   _____

   _____

7. The child asked a question of the museum docent entering the exhibit for the first time.

   _____

   _____

8. The book fair was a success, thus confirming our suspicion that young people enjoy
   such activities.

   _____

   _____

9. Before finally deciding on the movie, the entertainment choices seemed limitless.

_____

_____

10. Climbing down from the ladder, the hammer was still at the top of the stairs.

_____

_____

E. Confusing Pronoun References

Directions: The following sentences contain unclear pronoun references. Rewrite each
sentence so that its meaning is clear and reasonable.

1. They say the new artificial heart has vastly improved on the earlier model.

_____

_____

2. I looked in the shoe store all morning, but I could find only three of them that fit.

_____

_____

3. The fireworks were moved to a smaller park. This created massive parking problems.

_____

_____

4. Will and LeRoi were late because he missed his train connection.

_____

_____

5. Lydia asked Sandra to return the book to the library as soon as she finished reading it.

_____

_____

6. After the clerk put the soda in the bag, I checked it to make sure the lid was secure.

_____

_____

continued ➡

7. Lorraine has problems going to sleep at night. This means she's terribly tired all afternoon.

_____

_____

8. They say the city's convention center may still be completed on schedule.

_____

_____

9. She put the bucket beside the ladder, then asked me to hand it to her.

_____

_____

10. When Angie took Barbara to the airport, she drove her car.

_____

_____

Section 8.4 Writing Effective Sentences

A. Improving Sentences

Directions: In the space provided, rewrite each sentence to improve it.

1. Mary Margaret did not fail to make all her deadlines last year.

_____

_____

2. He is experienced, if not more experienced, than the other accountant.

_____

_____

3. I was preparing the office budget when the new CEO toured the office.

_____

_____

4. The project is demanding, challenges are exciting.

_____

_____

5. The corporation wanted to increase its involvement in the community, and so I suggested we participate in the Big Brothers/Big Sisters program.

_____

_____

6. Matthew wanted to learn more about creating Web sites, so he signed up for a seminar at the community college.

_____

_____

7. Only reports dealing with the reported global warming phenomenon will be reported on at the international trade conference on Saturday.

_____

_____

continued ❯

8. Attached are the E-mail addresses you requested in your June 16 message.

_____

_____

9. He is, considering his work and academic experience, a very strong job candidate.

_____

_____

10. Germaine is, given the delicate nature of the negotiations, the best mediator for the situation.

_____

_____

11. Colleen likes the new Web browser more than Dwayne.

_____

_____

12. To increase efficiency, cubicles were replaced with open work areas and the desks moved closer together.

_____

_____

13. Rafael convinced the product engineers to test his design, and they had rejected it originally.

_____

_____

14. To avoid confusion about how to complete this type of transaction, you should revise the instruction manual.

_____

_____

15. Three of the seven responses were incorrect.

_____

_____

16. Mr. Nouri stated that the product testing had been successful and manufacturing would begin in January.

_____

_____

17. It wasn't hard to understand why Natalie Ramos was promoted to Chief of Staff.

_____

_____

18. Christian is logical, detailed, and likes to troubleshoot problems.

_____

_____

19. The report was tedious to read, not because it was long but it was poorly written.

_____

_____

20. Jackson is interested, as you mentioned yesterday, in working on the production staff.

_____

_____

B. Coordination and Subordination

Directions: Choose the proper subordinate or coordinate conjunction for each of the sentences below.

1. The price of the coat is reduced (and, because) the lining has been damaged. _____

2. The Human Resources Department will hire the caterer (since, and) the Editorial Department will write the brochures. _____

3. The other offices were acceptable (but, although) this office has the best location. _____

4. We will walk the dog (or, because) we will work in the garden. _____

5. The waiters will bring coffee (when, and) the table has been cleared. _____

C. Joining Sentences

Directions: In the space provided, rewrite each pair of sentences as one sentence. Use a subordinating conjunction to join the sentences.

1. Ms. Wong was in India on business. Her department was reorganized.

_____

_____

2. Irene will distribute the flyers. Marlon will make the telephone calls.

_____

_____

3. We preregistered for the conference. We could not confirm hotel accommodations.

_____

_____

4. The customer service representatives were able to attend the seminar. The marketing manager had rescheduled the staff meeting.

_____

_____

5. We start our carpool at 6 a.m. The downtown traffic becomes congested.

_____

_____

6. Bruce was given the option of telecommuting. He lives more than an hour's drive from work.

_____

_____

7. Other sites were reviewed for the new offices. This site was closest to the airport.

_____

_____

8. The stock of copier paper was getting low. Ryan ordered a new supply to be sent from the warehouse.

_____

_____

9. Ms. Khin delayed the status meeting. Mr. Stansberry, the managing editor, had arrived.

_____

_____

10. All the teams practiced hard. They had never practiced harder before.

_____

_____

D. The You-Attitude

Directions: Rewrite each of the following sentences to use the you-attitude and positive wording.

1. Reagan is anxious to hear your critique of her proposal.

_____

_____

2. We have received your complaints regarding our personal digital assistant.

_____

_____

3. Do you know who is to blame for ordering the shipment incorrectly?

_____

_____

4. We regret that we will have to delay shipment of your order until all the items have arrived from the manufacturer.

_____

_____

5. You have to give me the complete report by Thursday, November 18.

_____

_____

E. Active and Passive Voice

Directions: Make the following sentences more positive by changing them from passive voice to active voice. Write your answers in the space provided.

1. New procedures for tracking shipments and deliveries have been adopted by the sales department.

   _____

   _____

2. The Web site was reviewed by a number of consultants.

   _____

   _____

3. Emma has received helpful mentoring from her supervisor.

   _____

   _____

4. Suzanne was named for a promotion by the division manager.

   _____

   _____

5. A copy of the personnel policy was received by all supervisors.

   _____

   _____

6. Additions to the HMO coverage were discussed by Marguerite Duran.

   _____

   _____

7. Instructions for recycling household waste were included on the flyers.

   _____

   _____

8. The staff at the start-up company was surprised by the news of the upcoming layoffs.

   _____

   _____

9. Norbert was congratulated by Ms. Garrison for posting the company's highest sales.

_____

_____

10. Sharilyn was often discouraged by setbacks in her recovery, but her goals were never lost sight of.

_____

_____

F. Balancing Sentences

Directions: Rewrite each of the following sentences to balance the elements. Write your answers in the space provided.

1. Grace was the logical choice for the Web Master position because she is knowledgeable, detail-oriented, and has much creativity.

_____

_____

2. The senior staff reviewed preliminary budget figures this morning and copies distributed to department managers for review.

_____

_____

3. We will need to staff our new office, and we will need to hire a claims specialist and an insurance adjuster.

_____

_____

4. Roxanne can proofread the pamphlet just as well, if not better, than Kris.

_____

_____

5. A competent trial lawyer must speak to and confer clients regularly during a case.

_____

_____

continued ➡

6. Harris spends more time on the road than home.

_____

_____

7. Has Katie finished the design for the Web site or has her assistant?

_____

_____

8. My DSL Internet browser provides as much flexibility as, if not more flexibility, than the cable service's browser.

_____

_____

9. Our survey indicates that high school students know as much about computers as college students.

_____

_____

10. The seminar on Internet research was practical and gave much information.

_____

_____

11. For the agreement to be binding, both parties must agree to and abide the terms described in the letter of intent.

_____

_____

12. Our law firm has offices both in Austin and San Jose.

_____

_____

13. Our software specialists are skilled in problem-solving and have the ability to answer questions.

_____

_____

14. Business class passengers can be as demanding as passengers traveling in first class.

_____

_____

15. This laptop computer is lightweight and small in size.

_____

_____

16. Any incidents of harassment should be reported to the supervisor, and notify the personnel director.

_____

_____

17. Ask the electrical engineer whether she is aware of and agreeable the changes in the blueprints.

_____

_____

18. Mr. Shimanek discussed the trip he met with the minister of trade.

_____

_____

19. The defendant would neither plead guilty nor would he accept a plea bargain.

_____

_____

20. Do you know if Ashley visited Bangkok or her brother?

_____

_____

G. Writing More Effective Sentences

Directions: Read the following sentences from a memo. Rewrite any sentences that need
to be improved or combined.

1. Our annual Red Cross Blood Drive has been rescheduled. It conflicted with the yearly
   sales meeting.

   _____

   _____

2. Coordinator James Simon can answer any questions you may have about the project. Assistant
   Coordinator Suzanne Thompson also can help you with questions.

   _____

   _____

3. We had complaints about the backlog at last year's blood drive, and we have improved our
   scheduling system.

   _____

   _____

4. You are encouraged to help with a worthwhile cause.

   _____

   _____

5. More lives can be saved if we donate more blood.

   _____

   _____

Section 8.5 Building Effective Paragraphs

A. Sentences, Paragraphs, and Messages

Directions: From the following list, select the word or words that *best* complete the sentences. Write your answers in the blanks.

bury	main idea
choppy	one
connections	readability
eight	sentence length
first	sentence structure
five	six
length	structure
even	topic sentence
odd	twenty
ten	unity
transitional	vary
two	

1. A written message should have _____ purpose, and each paragraph in that message should have a single _____.   _____

2. A business writer's goal should be to _____ sentences by changing their _____ and _____.   _____

3. The main idea of a paragraph is often stated in a(n) _____, which is often the first sentence in the paragraph.   _____

4. You can create _____ between sentences and between paragraphs with _____ words and phrases.   _____

5. Combining several short paragraphs into one paragraph keeps a text from looking _____.   _____

6. The ease with which something can be read is called its _____.   _____

7. Most sentences in a message should be between _____ to _____words in length.   _____

8. The first and last paragraphs of a message should be short, usually between ___ and _____ lines long.   _____

continued ➡

9. If sentences are too long, they can seem to _____ the main idea. _____

10. A paragraph generally should have no more than _____ to _____ lines. _____

11. When all of a paragraph's sentences support its main idea, the paragraph can be said to have _____. _____

12. In general, an _____ number of paragraphs in a message creates a more pleasing appearance. _____

B. One Main Idea

Directions: Read each of the following paragraphs. Underline any sentences that do not develop the main idea of each paragraph.

1. The Akron Public Library is pleased to announce that it is now part of a statewide library exchange system. If you have a valid library card with the Akron Public Library, you can become a member of BookShare just by filling out a form. BookShare allows you to check out books in hundreds of municipal and university libraries throughout Ohio. There's no charge for the service. There are 25 branch libraries in the Akron Public Library system. Stop by any branch of the Akron Public Library, and, within minutes, you can have a card that will help you read your way across the state.

2. The Meals on Wheels program is looking for noontime drivers to deliver lunch to elderly city residents. If you can spend lunch with us once a week, we can offer you a rewarding experience that's worth more than a tank of gas. All the meals we deliver are designed to meet individual's particular dietary needs. We can tailor your delivery area to a route close to your home or work; we'll get you back to where you started in less than an hour. We promise. Call our office at 340-2000 to get more information about how you can take us to lunch!

C. Making Smooth Transitions

Directions: From the following list, select the transitional word or phrase that best links each of the following pairs of sentences, and write your answer in the blank. Do not use the same word or phrase more than once.

at present	consequently
especially	finally
for example	in addition
in fact	moreover
nevertheless	on the other hand
second	specifically
such as	that is
then	therefore

1. Security in our office has been upgraded. _____ , key cards have been issued to all employees and are required for access at all entries. _____

2. We are, _____ , planning to expand our product line to include more wireless computer equipment. _____

3. Terrance has proven to be adept at legal research. _____, he is skillful at preparing legal briefs. _____

4. Employees are encouraged to take continuing education classes at the university. _____, the company will reimburse employees' tuition for work-related classes. _____

5. Several members of the nursing staff want to attend the in-house training sessions. They are _____ interested in learning new infection-control techniques. _____

6. All our divisions have become more productive. _____, our profit margin has increased. _____

7. Our travel agency is now booking winter holidays. _____, we are accepting reservations for spring tours. _____

8. First, Carter will outline the sales history. Second, Evan will present the multi-media show. _____, John and Emma will answer any questions. _____

continued ➡

9. On the one hand, our sales have increased. _____, our expenses have escalated.

    _____

10. Ed Cohen has been with the firm for only a short time. _____, he has been named a full partner.

    _____

11. The company has expanded its health care offerings this year. _____, the company is offering coverage with Blue Cross/Blue Shield and Central Western HMO.

    _____

12. We find that most of the residents in our facility spend the holidays with their families. _____, we will close one wing of the building during that time.

    _____

13. Any schedule changes, _____ lengthy layovers at airports, should be allowed for in your travel itinerary.

    _____

14. Meet with your insurance agent to increase your automobile coverage. _____, you should plan to update your life insurance.

    _____

15. Most automobile accidents are avoidable; _____, careful drivers can prevent such accidents from happening.

    _____

D. Varying Sentence Length

Directions: Rewrite the following long sentences, making each one into two or more sentences. Insert transitional words or phrases as needed.

1. In an effort to minimize our operating expenses for the remainder of the fiscal year, our vice president of operations, Melissa Strauss, has requested that all managers review their budgets for the period of July to December and cut the personnel and training segment from $50,000 to at least $35,000 and to accomplish this savings, we would like each manager to suggest expenses that can be canceled or postponed.

   _____

   _____

   _____

2. As part of the Women's Leadership Council meeting on November 5 at the Stauffer Inn, a panel of managers will discuss their career tracks.

_____

_____

_____

3. The company's tuition-reimbursement plan is designed to support employees who wish to continue their education, and it does so by paying for the complete cost of tuition for approved courses, and naturally we encourage all interested employees to take advantage of this opportunity.

_____

_____

_____

Directions: Rewrite the following short sentences to combine them into one longer sentence.

4. Effective March 1, all employees are required to use the new Travel and Expenses form. This form is to be used to report all company-related travel expenses.

_____

_____

_____

5. Olivia and I are coordinating the production team. Matthew will obtain the bids. Joshua will make the schedule. Yolanda will oversee quality control.

_____

_____

_____

E. Smooth Communication

Directions: Rewrite the following paragraph from a company newsletter so that the
message is communicated more smoothly.

    Laredo Communications took part in National Health Awareness Week.
National Health Awareness Week was April 21–25. Heath information
sessions were held in the company cafeteria. They were held Monday
through Friday. Regina Velasquez was on hand to answer questions. She
is a registered nurse. She answered questions about health-related issues.
Ms. Vernon shared information and literature about preventive health care.
She also shared information and literature about health maintenance.

_____

_____

_____

_____

_____

_____

_____

_____

F. Making Paragraph Decisions

Directions: Break the following excerpt from a message into four effective paragraphs. At
the points marked (T), insert an appropriate transitional word or phrase.

    In August, one of our supervisors, Tony Garza, suggested that we
investigate ways to reduce the paperwork in our division. (T) we asked
Tony and his two assistants to analyze the procedures in their department
and to submit some recommendations for reducing unnecessary paperwork. Not surprisingly, they found that we now make and distribute far
too many copies of routing forms. (T) we now distribute 23 copies of
purchase orders throughout the company. (T) they found that 16 of the
employees who received these purchase orders simply file the copies for
future use. (T) Tony and his co-workers found that other routine forms are
copies that are distributed unnecessarily. (T) copies of budget estimates
for each project are sent to every manager in the division. (T) copies
should be sent only to members on the project team, their supervisors,
and the division vice president. When Tony and his two assistants
complete their report, we will share their findings with you. (T) if you
have suggestions for reducing paperwork, please let us know.

_____
_____
_____
_____
_____
_____
_____
_____
_____
_____
_____
_____
_____
_____
_____
_____
_____
_____
_____
_____

G. Editing for Accuracy

Directions: Underline any errors in the following sentences, and write your corrections on the lines provided. Write *OK* for any sentence that has no error.

1. Kim Fox said, "I hope that Harry working so hard will pay off for him in the long run." _____

2. Are you sure that the flight has been delayed until tomorrow? _____

3. Our CEO thinks that the best proposal is your's. _____

4. Has you ordered the latest version of the tax software for all our accountants? _____

5. Obviously, its in our best interest to offer exceptional customer service. _____

6. For every item you recycle, you save the city money and landfill space. _____

continued ➡

7. Of all our competitors, Buena Suerte Industries is most highly regarded for their fair prices and excellent service. _____

8. In my opinion, Mick's sales record is superior to Suzanne. _____

9. At our vice presidents' suggestion, we purchased the cellular telephone system. _____

10. Did you find out if Leo's and Max's class meet tonight? _____

H. Proofreading Practice

Directions: Underline errors in the following memo, and write your corrections in the spaces provided.

MEMO TO: Lorenzo Murphy _____
FROM: Katherine Leffler _____
DATE: July 5, <YEAR> _____
SUBJECT: independence Day festival _____

Your staff did a great job yesterday of handling the holiday _____
crowds at Independence park. _____

All your preparations for directing the crowds to the pedestrian _____
bridge paid off. The view of the fireworks was great from the _____
bridge, and moving people their eased congestion in other areas _____
of the park. _____

In addition, city employees did a terriffic job of directing traffic _____
out of the park. We have as you know had bad accidents there in _____
the past; the extra staff in the parking areas was a very good idea. _____

Thank you for your departments' hard work. I hope your team's _____
holiday was a safe and pleasant one. _____

Section 8.6 Revising, Editing, and Proofreading

A. Using Proofreader's Marks

Directions: Using the proofreaders' marks introduced in section 8.6 of your text, make corrections in the following sentences.

1. Many of our Company representatives attended the global warming conference in Seattle Washington.

_____

_____

2. Our store ofers a three year warranty on every electronic appliance we sell.

_____

_____

3. You may place orders four our latest computer upgrades with our regional sales person.

_____

_____

4. In August we will send stockholders copyes of the anual report.

_____

_____

5. When may we expect to recieve your decision.

_____

_____

6. You may at any time withdraw money from your certificate of deposit account.

_____

_____

7. Our Web site provides up to date weather reports and stock options.

_____

_____

8. Please send the contracts to the New york office.

_____

_____

continued ➡

9. Be sure that you sign the authorization form, to.

_____

_____

10. Unless we obtain a written release from form the patient we cannot release information to the insurer.

_____

_____

11. Has the Doctor received the results of my tests?

_____

_____

12. Febuary 20 will mark our 15 year in busniess.

_____

_____

13. Will you be able to complete the report by 4:00 P.M.?

_____

_____

14. The contract for the Mishibishi acount has been aproved.

_____

_____

15. Which para legal is researching the Kramer vs. Hawley case?

_____

_____

16. Most of the files for our salespresentation have been completed.

_____

_____

17. Will you be able to respond to the E-mail message by 5p.m.?

_____

_____

18. Ms. Mendez wil travel to our offices in Albuquerque New Mexico and San Antonio Texas.

_____

_____

19. Occassionally our computer network is shut down to instal program upgrades.

_____

_____

20. Our new offices will be in the Easton business complex on Morse Rd.

_____

_____

B. Improving Tone and Organization

Directions: Rewrite the following memo to improve tone and organization.

MEMO TO: All Employees
FROM: Security Department
DATE: May 16, <YEAR>
SUBJECT: Facility Security

Employees who fail to observe this new procedure will be subject to company discipline.

Employees are hereby warned not to remove company property from the site unless it is vital to their work and is approved by the appropriate supervisor. Employees must obtain a property pass from the security guard, and they must have the guard sign the pass. But first they must receive approval from their supervisor to take company property from the site. This property must be fully described on the pass.

_____

_____

_____

_____

_____

_____

_____

_____

_____

_____

_____

_____

C. Revising Tone

Directions: Revise the following sentences so that they reflect a positive tone.

1. Unfortunately, a backlog of orders for our high-resolution computer screens makes it impossible for us to ship your order for two weeks.

   _____
   _____

2. We have already told you that we cannot pay you for 30 days.

   _____
   _____

3. You carelessly omitted your social security number on your application.

   _____
   _____

4. We have received your October 8 letter in which you complain about our service.

   _____
   _____

5. Do you really think that we will refund your money?

   _____
   _____

D. More Effective Sentences

Directions: Revise each sentence according to the directions in italics. Write the revised sentence in the space provided.

1. The editing presentation for the senior staff was organized by the copyediting department, primarily by Michael.
   Change to active voice.

   _____
   _____

2. The support makes our office routines go smoothly.
   Substitute more colorful verbs, adjectives, and adverbs.

   _____
   _____

3. The cultural exchange program has been so successful over the past two years that our
European affiliates have adopted it.

   Begin the sentence with a prepositional phrase.

   _____

   _____

4. Georgia Pine Company greatly regrets that it must close its manufacturing plant in Savannah.

   Begin the sentence with an adverb.

   _____

   _____

5. The reason that we are flying to Seattle on Saturday instead of Monday is so that we can take
advantage of reduced weekend airfares offered by the airline.

   Eliminate unnecessary words.

   _____

   _____

6. Deanna is illegible to enter the competition because of the new rules that went into affect
on Monday.

   Use the correct word.

   _____

   _____

7. To apply for a staff position with Cardinal Credit Services, prospective employees must fully
complete an application that outlines their background and qualification for employment at
Cardinal Credit Services.

   Eliminate unnecessary words and repetition.

   _____

   _____

8. Come to our sale on computer equipment.

   Use more specific, colorful words.

   _____

   _____

9. Materials regarding your child's performance have been sent by our office for your review.

   Change to active voice.

   _____

   _____

E. More Effective Language

Directions: In the space provided, revise the following paragraph from a memo to improve the language and the sentence structure.

Our company employs a relocation specialist. This specialist, Sydney Roberts, works in the Human Resources Department. Her job is to help employees in relocating to another city. She helps with the details involved in selling a home, moving to another location, and finding an affordable home in that location. She has prepared a booklet titled "Tips for Moving" that answers questions that are frequently asked about relocating. She also can tell you about the company's policy on the company buying your existing home so that you can purchase a new home in the city to which you are moving.

_____

_____

_____

_____

_____

_____

_____

_____

_____

_____

_____

_____

F. Being More Specific

Directions: In the spaces provided, rewrite the following sentences using more specific and colorful nouns, verbs, adjectives, and adverbs.

1. I'm sorry I can't go to the important meeting.

_____

_____

2. She parked her new car in the garage.

_____

_____

3. The office manager said that we should change the policy.

_____

_____

4. Eleanor did the report on the new office machines.

_____

_____

5. Geraldo went to Detroit for the conference.

_____

_____

G. Identifying Questionable Content

Directions: Block and query questionable content in the following sentences. Use a different letter of the alphabet to label each block. Write the reason for your query in the space provided.

1. You are booked on Flight 6257, which leaves Dallas at 2:15 a.m.

_____

_____

2. The bank statement listed all our checks except the three written yesterday: 3198, 3199, and 3300.

_____

_____

3. The conference will be held from February 29 to March 1, 2003.

_____

_____

4. For only $1995, you will receive 12 issues of our magazine—one each month for the entire year.

_____

_____

5. Our department store's after-Christmas sale will begin December 25, promptly at 8 a.m.

_____

_____

H. Editing for Conciseness

Directions: Without changing the meaning, rewrite the following items, omitting any overused words. Underline any words that are overused and should be omitted.

1. The media room contains some extremely sensitive equipment that is easily damaged by extreme temperature or humidity fluctuations. You must be very careful not to damage the equipment when you use these machines. Monitor the temperature and humidity controls very carefully.

_____

_____

_____

2. Marin County Realty has four company cars and three company vans. The corporate vans are two years old, and the company vans are four years old. As your company accountant, I recommend selling your current corporate vehicles and leasing new ones.

_____

_____

_____

I. Editing for Consistent Sequence

Directions: In the space provided, rewrite each item to make it consistent in sequence.

1. We will conduct field surveys on July 16, September 4, and August 8.

_____

_____

2. Esperanza Enterprises plans to open plants in Durango, Coahuila, and Sonora.

_____

_____

3. The nurse will conduct health screenings at 9:30 a.m., 2:30 p.m., 11:45 a.m., and 1:15 p.m.

_____

_____

4. The gift certificates are available in the following denominations: $25, $50, $100, and $75.

_____

_____

5. By your criteria, should Megan, Karen, or Stephan get the assignment?

_____

_____

6. Breyer, Marshall, Connor, and Ruth were recently appointed to the board of directors.

_____

_____

7. The job candidate interviews are scheduled for 8:30 a.m., 9:45 a.m., 1:30 p.m., and 11 a.m.

_____

_____

8. The convention facilities are available in April, June, and May.

_____

_____

9. The following purchase orders have not been filled: M1639, M1643, and M1640.

_____

_____

10. Kim Millbrook, Dolores Cantu, and Sharyl Ramos should receive copies of the contract.

_____

_____

J. More Proofreaders' Marks

Directions: Make the changes indicated by the proofreaders' marks. Write the corrected sentences in the spaces provided.

1. Deborah Fosse, Mr. Chin's assistant advised me to schedule an appointment to discuss the programing changes.

_____

_____

2. Our 3 computer programmers are extremely knowledgable; indeed they are among the best in the industry.

_____

_____

continued ◆▶

3.] CONSUMER TRENDS [

Many computer users subscribe to a cable service for INTERNET access. Such services provide access to E-mail, bulletin boards, and news groups.

_____

_____

_____

4. Ms. Phylis Parson
5305 N. Main St.
Columbus, OK 43235

_____

_____

_____

K. Editing for Courtesy

Directions: In the space provided, rewrite the following message to improve the tone. Add transitions as needed, and break the message into paragraphs. Also, include any details necessary to make the message complete.

TO: Barry Hines

FROM: Tri-State Import Motor Repairs

Hi, Barry!

Tri-State Import Motor Repairs, your neighborhood auto repair shop, wants to remind you that you're due for an oil change. Be smart, Barry, and bring your car in for service now. Otherwise, you'll have expensive problems later. At Tri-State, we use only quality parts and have excellent, factory-trained mechanics. But you have to do the legwork. If you don't keep up your maintenance schedule, we can't be responsible for the results. So come on in. For a short time, we are giving a special service to customers. We'll give you a ride to and from work on the day of your service appointment as long as it isn't too far. We're proud of this extra service. Call our Service Department for an appointment.

_____

_____

_____

_____

_____

_____

_____

_____

_____

_____

_____

_____

_____

_____

L. Detecting Embarrassing Mistakes

Directions: Spelling checkers would not find the correctly spelled, but incorrectly used, words in the following sentences. Underline each incorrectly used word, and write the correct word in the space provided.

1. Angelika requested a wireless mouse fore her computer. _____

2. The community college offers an intensive coarse in building Web sites. _____

3. Please direct your questions about employee benefits to the personal director. _____

4. Dr. Patel has a great deal of patients when working with children. _____

5. The board of directors has finally agreed upon the new sight for the company headquarters. _____

6. The Human Resources director covered all the policy changes accept access to the parking garage. _____

7. The attorney hoped that the case would be settled without coming to trail. _____

8. My sister is pursuing a perspective client. _____

9. The detective uncovered evidence to support there claims. _____

10. Our principle concern has been the cost of health benefits. _____

M. Proofreading for Content Errors

Directions: Use proofreaders' marks to insert omitted words and letters, and to delete repeated words in the following sentences.

1. Ms. Rabin will direct the overseas operations, including those Korea.

2. Do you prefer a morning or an training class?

3. The back-ordered items arrived on Thursday, and and the invoice arrived.

4. Your on-line order requires the following information: your name, telephone number, telephone number, and credit card account number.

5. Colleen returned her answered machine; in addition, she ordered two sets bookends and tree mouse pads.

N. Proofreading for Punctuation Errors

Directions: Use proofreaders' marks to insert, delete, or change punctuation as needed in the following sentences. Then, write the corrected sentences on the lines provided.

1. Those attending the convention will need to register by Monday October 6 to confirm hotel reservations.

2. Jay Martin has worked for the Tennessee based company for five years.

3. Corinne's exact words were "Deliver the order immediately!

4. Oliver wrote the memo then he proofread it.

5. Cheryl Ianelli M.D. will deliver the keynote speech at the American Medical Association conference.

O. Proofreading for Number Usage Errors

Directions: Use proofreaders' marks to make corrections in number usage in the
following sentences.

1. The two-day seminar on desktop publishing costs $199.00 and covers 6 different applications.

2. 300 customers were surveyed, and only eight percent were dissatisfied with the company's service.

3. The restaurant on the interstate highway will open at 6:00 a.m. each day, 7 days a week.

4. Your rebate form must be received by June first.

5. The new addition measures fourteen feet by sixteen feet.

P. Proofreading on the Computer

Directions: Yesterday you began the following message and saved it on your computer
before proofreading it. Proofread the paragraphs now, correcting any errors
you find. Write your corrections on the lines provided.

Increasingly, businesses are contracting with independant firms _____

that provide alternative dispute resolution services. Such firms _____

provides mediation and arbitration services to clients as _____

constructive ways too resolve employment-related disputes. _____

Most alternative dispute resolution firms employ former judges _____

and experienced attornies, these professionals serve as mediators _____

and arbitrators. These neural parties has diverse background and _____

include people of different ages, races, and religions. _____

continued ➡

CHAPTER 9 Writing E-mails, Memos, and Letters

Section 9.1 Planning Good News, Bad News, and Persuasive Messages

A. Direct Approach

Directions: Based on the information given, compose a message that uses the direct approach. Begin with the most important point, continue with supporting information, and close with an upbeat ending.

SITUATION

As a reservations manager at Hilton Lodge and Convention Center, you are writing to Ms. Camille Barrett regarding arrangements for the Plains States Literary Council Convention next month. You want to inform Ms. Barrett that your facility can accommodate her request for special displays at the convention. Write the body paragraphs for a letter to Ms. Barrett.

_____

_____

_____

_____

_____

_____

_____

_____

_____

_____

_____

_____

_____

_____

_____

_____

_____

_____

B. Indirect Approach

Directions: Using the information given, compose a message that uses the indirect approach. Begin the message with a buffer that presents background information. Continue with reasons and explanations, then present the bad news, and end with a buffer.

SITUATION

You are a graduate of City College and have been invited to speak at the school's upcoming alumni weekend on September 16–17. You would like to attend, but you have other commitments. However, you are willing to participate in a later event. Write the paragraphs for a letter that turns down the invitation.

_____

_____

_____

_____

_____

_____

_____

_____

_____

_____

_____

_____

_____

_____

_____

_____

_____

_____

_____

_____

C. Persuasive Approach

Directions: Using the information given, compose a message that uses the persuasive approach. Begin the message with an attention-getting opening. Follow the opening with information that generates the reader's interest. Continue with additional information to create a desire on the reader's part, and close by asking the reader to take the desired action.

SITUATION

As a sales representative for Coyote Cable, you are writing to potential customers. Your goal is to encourage recipients to add Internet Cable Access (ICA) to their existing cable service. ICA will provide customers Internet access through their televisions. You describe your company's introductory package: For a subscription fee of $22 per month, customers will receive unlimited Internet access using their television. Your company is the only cable service in the city offering this service, and the price is very reasonable. The $22/month subscription fee is an introductory offer in effect until December 1. After that time, the price of adding Internet service will go up to $50/month.

_____

_____

_____

_____

_____

_____

_____

_____

_____

_____

_____

_____

_____

_____

_____

_____

_____

_____

Student _____ Class _____ Instructor _____

Date Assigned _____ Date Completed _____

D. Improving Message Content and Presentation

Directions: Revise the following paragraphs from a memo so that the message is clear, concise, correct, and courteous. Write your corrections in the space provided.

This year, once again, as we did last year, we have the opportunity to give something back to our community. Your participation in the United Way Campaign provides essential funding for teen counseling, summer camp for children from low-income familys, job training for unemployed adults, and much more. If you would like to, please review the attached brochure that lists the more than 30 community agencies and programs that benefit from your gifts to United Way.

Last year, United Way agencies assisted more then 5,000 people in our community, and the need for community support continues to grow. Cutbacks in goverment programs mean that groups that have 501c(3) status or United Way can be the only source of aide for many people.

United Way hopes to raise $50,000 this year—an ambitious but attainable goal. We need your help to make this goal a reality. Look at the attached flier regarding contribution options. All contributions are tax deductible and your company will match every dollar of each employee's contributions.

_____
_____
_____
_____
_____
_____
_____
_____
_____
_____
_____
_____
_____
_____

E. Special Formatting Techniques

Directions: Using some of the special formatting techniques discussed in Section 9.1, organize the following information to make reading and understanding easier.

The Antique Restorer's Catalog is pleased to offer these new products.

A roll-top desk for children, item #AH 02331133; $33'' \times 26'' \times 19^{1}/_{2}''$; $269.

Insinglass sheet replacements for stove doors, item #AH-02250107; $6'' \times 9''$; $52.99

Revolving bookcase kit, item #AH-02003175; $31''$ H $\times$ $17''$ square; $99.

We also offer a new line of Arts and Crafts style furniture and hardware. See our new catalog for a complete selection. Order any time by calling 1-800-946-2232.

_____

_____

_____

_____

_____

_____

_____

_____

_____

_____

_____

_____

_____

_____

_____

_____

_____

_____

_____

_____

Section 9.2 Formatting Business Documents

A. Block Style Letter

Directions: Format the following letter using the block style. Include all necessary letter parts, such as a salutation and a complimentary closing. Use your name in the closing.

Current date/ Ms. Jane Burdett/ Contractor/ 472 Rockway Drive/ Portland, ME 34595

As we discussed in our telephone conversation yesterday, I have chosen the ceramic tile rather than the linoleum option for the upstairs bathroom floor. Also, I would like to replace the sink with a two-sink vanity.

Enclosed are the ceramic tile samples and a diagram showing the pattern for the floor tiles. When you have reviewed these plans, please let me know your time frame for finishing the project. You may leave a message on my cell phone (595-3342) or my answering machine (709-0992).

_____

_____

_____

_____

_____

_____

_____

_____

_____

_____

_____

_____

_____

_____

_____

_____

_____

_____

_____

_____

_____

_____

B. Modified-Block Style Letter with Indented Paragraphs

Directions: Format the following letter using the modified-block style with indented paragraphs. Supply all the necessary letter parts.

Current date/ Ms. Aidan Coulson/ Great Lakes Consulting / 132 Chambon Avenue / Toronto, Ontario M4T 2Z8/ CANADA/ Subject: Task Force Candidates

Aidan, it was a pleasure to meet with you in Toronto last week to discuss our partnership on the North Plains project.

Based on our discussion, the next step is to establish a task force to review the existing advertising campaign. At your suggestion, enclosed is a list of the names of Lake Sinclair account managers who have the experience to handle such a high-profile account. Also enclosed are samples of their work. I think you will agree that any of these candidates would be an asset to the project.

When you have a chance to review the enclosed materials, please call me at 313-555-9263 to discuss your recommendations for the task force.

LAKE SINCLAIR ADVERTISING, INC. / Nathan V. Powers, Vice President / c: Roman Durban

_____
_____
_____
_____
_____
_____
_____
_____
_____
_____
_____
_____
_____
_____
_____
_____
_____
_____
_____
_____

continued ➡

Student _____ Class _____ Instructor _____

Date Assigned _____ Date Completed _____

_____

_____

_____

_____

_____

_____

_____

_____

_____

_____

_____

_____

_____

_____

_____

_____

_____

_____

_____

_____

C. Proofreading Practice

Directions: Underline any errors in the following sentences, and write your corrections in the space provided.

1. Three-fourths of the completed surveys has been processed.   _____

2. Brittany said that the engineers who have the expertise in that area are Leroi and her.   _____

3. The production manager assigned the inventory analysis to Nick and myself.   _____

4. The new computer system, which includes digital imaging and recording technology, has not been used to their full potential.   _____

5. The informal survey shows that a number of employees is requesting a change in performance review policy.   _____

6. All of the CD-ROM labels should be forwarded to Chan and Associates, which are the assembler of those packages.   _____

7. Keith Williamson and Sarah Chaney have doubled the sales in their district; obviously, they work well with one another.   _____

8. You will view the results different, Ryan, when you review the survey procedures.   _____

9. Will the new courthouse be located opposite to police headquarters?   _____

10. With only one week remaining before the deadline, it looks like we will be able to complete the report in time.   _____

D. Personal-Business Letter

Directions: Write a short personal-business letter in the space provided. To make your letter realistic, write to an actual person or a company. For example, you might write to a company requesting a catalog.

_____

_____

_____

_____

_____

_____

_____

_____

_____

_____

_____

_____

_____

_____

_____

_____

_____

_____

_____

_____

_____

_____

_____

_____

_____

E. Letters and Memos

Directions: From the following list, select the word or words that *best* complete the sentences.

message memos	letterhead
routing slip	country
guide words	initials
street address	salutation
subject line	modified-block format
watermark	

1. Callers' telephone numbers and messages may be recorded on _____.   _____

2. Carriers such as Federal Express and United Parcel Service need a _____ in order to complete a delivery.   _____

3. When writing an international address, one should NOT abbreviate the name of a _____.   _____

4. A _____ refers to the address and other information printed at the top of business stationary.   _____

5. To channel messages to specific people, you might attach a _____ to the document.   _____

6. The person who writes a memo should put his or her _____ after the name on the FROM line.   _____

7. A letter using _____ places many parts of the text—such as the dateline, the closing, and the writer's identification—in the center of the page.   _____

8. Memo headings such as SUBJECT and DATE are called _____.   _____

9. A _____ is the greeting that precedes the body of a letter.   _____

10. You can see a stationery's _____ by holding the paper up to the light.   _____

11. A _____ identifies the topic of a letter.   _____

Section 9.3 Writing E-mails, Memos, and Letters

A. Differences Among Types of Business Writing

Directions: From the choices listed with each item, identify the type of message that is described.

1. _____ can be delivered 24 hours a day.
   a. E-mails   b. Memos   c. Letters   _____

2. _____ are delivered by an interoffice mail delivery system.
   a. E-mails   b. Memos   c. Letters   _____

3. _____ are delivered by mail or courier services.
   a. E-mails   b. Memos   c. Letters   _____

4. _____ are sent instantly through the Internet.
   a. E-mails   b. Memos   c. Letters   _____

5. _____ are not private or confidential; in addition, they may be easily forwarded to others.
   a. E-mails   b. Memos   c. Letters   _____

6. _____ are printed on letterhead.
   a. E-mails   b. Memos   c. Letters   _____

B. Transmitting Messages by Various Modes

Directions: For each of the following tasks, decide which form of message is most appropriate for the situation.

E-mail

Memo

Letter

1. A customer has not paid an invoice from last month. The payment is 10 days past due, and you want to inform the customer that payment is needed.   _____

2. You are in charge of the company blood drive to be held two days from today. You need to send a reminder to all those who have volunteered to donate blood.   _____

3. You need to provide the people in your department with the routine updates of a product's production schedule.   _____

4. You have confidential information to share with your company attorney.   _____

5. You want to share data with other company supervisors about the costs of upgrading a laptop computer.   _____

C. Recognizing Homonyms

Directions: Some of the following sentences contain homonym errors that would not be corrected by a computer spell-checking program. Underline the incorrect word and write the correct word in the space provided. Write *OK* for any sentence that has no error.

1. The journalist sited several authoritative sources.   _____

2. Because the evidence was so complex, the district attorney herself persecuted the case.   _____

3. She made a conscience effort to compete the analysis on time.   _____

4. We least another office when our contract expired.   _____

5. I would advice you to get a second opinion from another doctor.   _____

6. You will need to be discrete in handling this personnel information.   _____

7. The company health plan covers employees' minor dependents.   _____

8. You may be libel for damages if someone has an accident on your property.   _____

9. We will device another plan to replace the old one.   _____

10. Brian and Elaine had their house apprised before they put it on the market.   _____

D. Planning a Memo

Directions: You are writing a memo to your supervisor, Angelika Weber, providing her with information about a proposed budget change in a project. Using the information below, write a memo that clearly states your proposal. Your memo should contain guide words and a copy notation.

- You and the project coordinator, Jim Wade, have reviewed the budget for the Jimenez project and have determined that more money is needed for travel.

- You and Jim Wade will need to travel to Memphis at least once each month for five months for status meetings with the client. The current travel budget is $1,900; you propose increasing the travel budget to $4,800.

- Attached are copies of the current budget and the revised budget.

_____

_____

_____

_____

E. Subject Lines for Memos

Directions: The following subject lines for memos are wordy. Rewrite each subject line to be more concise.

1. The Policy of Amundsen Industries Regarding Employee Use of Company Computers

_____

_____

2. New Procedure Instituted by Human Resources for Enrolling in Health Coverage

_____

_____

3. Orientation Meeting for New Employees in All Departments Hired in September

_____

_____

4. Recent Promotion of Andrea Callas to Head of the Pathology Lab

_____

_____

5. Code of Ethics for the Classroom That Applies to All Students

_____

_____

F. Using E-Mail

Directions: Read the description of the E-mails below. In the space provided, describe how each E-mail should be edited or modified.

1. The subject line of an E-mail reminding the department of the monthly birthday party reads as follows: Subject: URGENT: Monthly Birthday Party.

_____

_____

2. The Human Resources director sends an E-mail to all department heads that contains confidential personnel information.

_____

_____

continued ➡

3. The project director sends all staff members a four-page E-mail outlining changes in travel reimbursement procedures.

   _____

   _____

4. The office manager sends the following E-mail message: REMEMBER THAT THE STAFF MEETING HAS BEEN CHANGED FROM 3 P.M. TO 2 P.M. THANKS.

   _____

   _____

5. To make sure that your E-mail to an important client is error-free, you use a spell- and grammar-check program before sending it.

   _____

   _____

G. Standard Memo Format

Directions: Revise the following memo, correcting any errors in format and style.

Memo To: Jenna Stafford
FROM: Mrs. Gretta Langfur
Date: 7/12/<YEAR>
SUBJECT: Payroll Change Effective August 1

Dear Jenna,

Beginning Friday, August 1, payroll checks will be distributed twice each month instead of only once. The checks will be available on the first and the fifteenth of each month.

Beginning immediately, employees may have their checks deposited to their bank accounts automatically. If employees choose direct deposit, they should complete the necessary forms in the Human Resources office.

Employees have requested these changes. Please let me know about any feedback you receive regarding payroll distribution and direct deposit.

Enclosure

rg

Student _____ Class _____ Instructor _____

Date Assigned _____ Date Completed _____

_____

_____

_____

_____

_____

_____

_____

_____

_____

_____

_____

_____

_____

_____

_____

_____

_____

_____

_____

_____

_____

_____

_____

_____

_____

_____

_____

_____

_____

_____

_____

_____

H. Memo Parts

Directions: Your supervisor, Paul Hilgedick, has asked you to type a memo with the following information and to include a distribution list with the following names: Liza Jones, Dena Livingston, LeVon Bardo, Jack McCarty, and Will McDaniel. Include reference initials and an enclosure notation.

The employee insurance policy needs to be revised this month for the upcoming contract ratification. Since you served as a member of this committee for the last contract, the union would like your assistance again.

Several issues about the current insurance policy have been brought to my attention. Attached is a copy of the concerns I have received from other employees. Please review this information and schedule a meeting with the other members of your committee to discuss alternatives.

If you are unable to serve on this committee, please let me know by the end of this week so I can identify a replacement.

_____
_____
_____
_____
_____
_____
_____
_____
_____
_____
_____
_____
_____
_____
_____
_____
_____
_____
_____
_____
_____
_____
_____
_____

I. Writing a Memo

Directions: Following the guidelines on pages 394–399 of your textbook, write a memo based on the following situation. Use the standard memo format for plain paper.

SITUATION

As the manager for the men's clothing department at Old Khaki, you need to inform employees of a new fall clothing line. You will attach a brochure about Safari!, the new clothing line, to the memo. To promote the line, the store is holding a one-month sale on Safari! items. In addition, the store is offering employee incentive bonuses to the two top salespersons for this month. If employees have questions, they should contact you by the end of the week. Include the file name of the memo (Safari.doc) in your memo.

_____
_____
_____
_____
_____
_____
_____
_____
_____
_____
_____
_____
_____
_____
_____
_____
_____
_____
_____
_____
_____
_____
_____
_____
_____
_____

J. Outdated Expressions and Redundancies

Directions: Underline any outdated expressions or redundancies in the following
  sentences, and write your revisions on the lines provided.

1. Geoff wants to build a team that can cooperate together to
   complete the project.   _____

2. In the event that the test results are inconclusive, the doctors
   will schedule more tests.   _____

3. Please advise us as to the date on when you plan to occupy
   the building.   _____

4. At the present time, all customer service representatives
   are busy.   _____

5. Ray advised us as to the date when we could expect to
   receive our first paychecks.   _____

6. Will you kindly stop by my office when you return from
   lunch.   _____

7. Due to the fact that Mr. Sharpe is in Tokyo, Ms. Nagimoto
   will conduct the meeting.   _____

8. From past experience, we know that a successful
   international trade show takes months of preparation.   _____

9. At next week's meeting, we will continue on with our
   discussion of the warehouse commission.   _____

10. The consultant submitted the same identical studies to
    both companies.   _____

11. Implementing the consolidation plan is our chief main goal
    for the next year.   _____

12. Jesse needs to face up to the fact that sales are declining.   _____

13. I trust that you will agree with my recommendations
    regarding the new computer system.   _____

14. Your comments on the allegations are duly noted.   _____

15. It has been our customary practice at the clinic to have patients sign in at the reception desk.   _____

16. Would you kindly notify the team of a change in our next meeting date.   _____

17. We plan to meet up with our colleagues at the national convention.   _____

18. If you need clarification, refer back to the notes from last month's board meeting.   _____

19. Most of the surveys will be sent via U.S. mail.   _____

20. Herewith is the contract request form you mentioned.   _____

Section 9.4 Informing and Requesting

A. Making an Announcement

Directions: Prepare an announcement about the relocation grand opening of a favorite downtown café in your city. Include all necessary details.

_____

_____

_____

_____

_____

_____

_____

_____

_____

_____

_____

_____

_____

_____

_____

_____

_____

_____

_____

_____

_____

_____

_____

_____

_____

B. Creating a Flier

Directions: Create a flier appropriate for posting on a bulletin board about a meeting of a student organization. In the spaces provided, identify the *who, what, where, when, why, how,* or *how much* to include on the flier.

1. *who*

    _____

    _____

2. *what*

    _____

    _____

3. *where*

    _____

    _____

4. *when*

    _____

    _____

5. *why*

    _____

    _____

6. *how*

    _____

    _____

7. *how much*

    _____

    _____

C. Clear Sentences

Directions: Rewrite the following sentences to make sure they communicate clearly.

1. Hanging in the closet, I saw that the uniform had become wrinkled.

   _____

   _____

2. Jacqui sent me the name of the consultant where we could identify our company's problems.

   _____

   _____

3. To show sales growth, charts were used by the regional manager.

   _____

   _____

4. The new utility rates became effective August 1 that were approved by the regulatory board.

   _____

   _____

5. To succeed in your courses at school, a number of hours each day will be required for study.

   _____

   _____

6. Leaving the office, my car seemed to be acting up.

   _____

   _____

7. Before putting tax forms in the mail, signatures will be added.

   _____

   _____

8. Opening the window, the sky looked overcast.

   _____

   _____

9. Under the stack of books, I found the article that I had been looking for.

   _____

   _____

D. Complete Requests

Directions: You work in the Reservations Department of a major New York hotel. Today you received the following request:

Dear Reservations Manager:

   Next month I will be in New York on business and would like to book a room. Please let me know the cost and availability of rooms.

Sincerely,

Directions: List some of the important details omitted from this letter. Then write the letter, supplying all the details needed to make the request complete.

_____

_____

_____

_____

_____

_____

_____

_____

_____

_____

_____

_____

_____

_____

_____

_____

_____

_____

_____

_____

E. Precise Sentences

Directions: The following sentences are imprecise. Rewrite them, supplying any details needed to make them specific.

1. Please send me information about your company.

   _____

   _____

   _____

   _____

2. Do you have a vacancy at your spa during spring break?

   _____

   _____

   _____

   _____

3. Please send me the DVD dealing with effective people skills.

   _____

   _____

   _____

   _____

4. I wish to order a copy of the book and video on how to build children's toys.

   _____

   _____

   _____

   _____

5. As I am investing in the stock market, I need annual reports and other information.

   _____

   _____

   _____

   _____

6. May I use your company library in the near future?

_____

_____

_____

_____

7. We are interested in having our class reunion in your hotel banquet hall. Would you be able to accommodate us?

_____

_____

_____

_____

8. Will you be able to complete the work on schedule?

_____

_____

_____

_____

9. I want to start a garden. Please send me information you think would be helpful.

_____

_____

_____

_____

10. What online services do you recommend that I subscribe to?

_____

_____

_____

_____

F. Writing to Inform

Directions: Read the following scenarios and write a short message communicating the information. Decide whether you would use a direct or indirect approach to convey the information. Supply any details needed to make the message specific.

1. The company health fair will be held on Friday.

_____
_____
_____
_____

2. Beginning next week, the building management company will begin towing cars illegally parked in the parking lot.

_____
_____
_____
_____

3. Jack LaMascus has been promoted.

_____
_____
_____
_____

4. We can no longer allow employees to bring children and pets to the office on weekends.

_____
_____
_____
_____

5. Benefits counselors will be in the office next week. They will discuss the company's new health insurance package.

_____
_____
_____
_____

G. Writing Claim Letters

Directions: The *Sun-Times*, 800 West Third Avenue, Toledo, Ohio 46059, has billed you for a month's delivery of both daily and Sunday newspapers. You ordered only the daily newspaper, however, and you have not received copies of the Sunday edition. Your bill is for $12 for 24 issues of the daily paper, and $8 for 4 Sunday issues. Write a letter to Mr. Sinclair Jackson, Circulation Manager, and request that your account be adjusted.

_____
_____
_____
_____
_____
_____
_____
_____
_____
_____
_____
_____
_____
_____
_____
_____
_____
_____
_____
_____
_____
_____
_____
_____
_____
_____
_____
_____
_____
_____

Section 9.5 Responding to Requests

A. Thinking Positively

Directions: Using positive words can lighten the burden of answering a problem request. In the left column is a list of negative words. In the right column, replace the negative word with a positive word or phrase.

Negative Words	Positive Words
1. cheap	_____
2. complaint	_____
3. careless	_____
4. liable	_____
5. lazy	_____
6. shoddy	_____
7. failure	_____
8. problem	_____
9. mediocre	_____
10. overpriced	_____

B. Saying No Tactfully

Directions: Analyze the following sentences. Then, on the lines provided, rewrite the sentences so that they say *no* more tactfully.

1. You may not have free multiple copies of our report.

_____

_____

_____

2. Our office will not contribute this year.

_____

_____

_____

3. You neglected to tell us what finish you want on your bookcase.

_____

_____

_____

4. You are not qualified for this position because you do not have the necessary skills.

_____

_____

_____

5. I do not have time to speak to your organization on February 23.

_____

_____

_____

6. We do not have enough brochures to fill your request.

_____

_____

_____

7. The fact that you did not follow maintenance instructions for your hair dryer means that we will not replace it.

_____

_____

_____

8. When our leasing agreement expires, we will take our equipment to a company that keeps its promises.

_____

_____

_____

9. You did not tell us your arrival time; therefore, we cannot book your hotel room.

_____

_____

_____

C. Improving Replies

Directions: Correct and improve the following replies to customer correspondence. Write revisions on the lines provided.

1. We do not have the luggage you requested for your upcoming vacation.

_____
_____
_____
_____

2. Here is the coffee maker you ordered. As you can see, it takes a special filter.

_____
_____
_____
_____

3. We received your check.

_____
_____
_____
_____

4. I did not have time to answer your query last week.

_____
_____
_____
_____

5. Write again next month and we may have the item in stock.

_____
_____
_____
_____

D. Be Sales-Minded

Directions: The Association of Office Managers has asked you to speak at its monthly meeting on February 15. The topic is efficiency in office systems. You have a project due February 10, and you did not receive the invitation until January 26; therefore, you do not have enough time to prepare a good speech. Write a letter of refusal to chairperson Marjorie Pinnell, 928 West Magnolia Street, Smithville, VA 24070. Suggest another topic that you have prepared, or give her information about Harriet Evans, a colleague who spoke on office systems at a similar meeting.

_____

_____

_____

_____

_____

_____

_____

_____

_____

_____

_____

_____

_____

_____

_____

_____

_____

_____

_____

_____

_____

_____

_____

_____

_____

E. Error Hunt

Directions: Underline all the errors in the following adjustment letter, and write your corrections in the spaces provided.

Ms. Marietta Johnston   _____

7190 Colorado Blvd   _____

Lincoln, Nebraska 68505   _____

Dear Ms. Johnston,   _____

Thank you for your letter of August 29 in which you mention the   _____

performance features of your new Regal Vaccum Cleaner that   _____

you resently bought from Sloan's Appliances.   _____

As you will recall, our service represnative examined your   _____

machine and located several kmechanical defects. The sucsion   _____

was malfunctioning and causing dust to escape from the tank.   _____

We discovered a split in the hose where it fit into the tank. Its   _____

now operating properly; there should be no dust escaping   _____

unneccesarily from the machine.   _____

If you experience any farther problems, Mrs. Johnston, please   _____

bring your machine in immediatly and we will repair it as soon as   _____

possible. Please except this coupon for a 10 percent discount off   _____

any merchandise in our store. Just remember—Sloan's is hear to   _____

serve you.   _____

Sincerly yours,   _____

F. Reviewing Requests

Directions: From the following list, select the word or words that *best* complete the sentences.

preprinted reply cards	you
problem requests	we
guide words	them
tickler file	prompt

1. A company's response to correspondence should be _____.   _____

2. Letters requiring negative responses from a company are called _____.   _____

3. Negative statements often stress _____, while positive comments stress _____.   _____

4. A _____ reminds a user to check on a particular action.   _____

5. _____, which often have printed messages, allow companies to respond to large numbers of requests promptly.   _____

CHAPTER 10 Writing Specific Communications

Section 10.1 Persuasive Communications

A. Targeting Audiences

Directions: For each product or service listed, determine the audience(s) you would target. Select your audience on the basis of such factors as age, geographical location, income, occupation, or lifestyle.

1. Copyshop, a multipurpose printer, scanner, copier, and fax machine

_____

_____

2. Don't Bug Me!, a natural insect repellent lotion for sensitive skin

_____

_____

3. *Ski Land and Sea*, a new monthly magazine

_____

_____

4. The Supply Closet, an office supplies store

_____

_____

5. Isabel Sent Me, a line of classic women's clothing sold through professional consultants

_____

_____

B. Planning a Sales Letter

Directions: BizShare, a new business networking group, is being organized in the community to help small businesses form useful relationships. It is designed specifically for business owners who would like to promote and expand their business. You have been appointed the marketing chairperson of the group. Your assignment is to write a letter mailed to small business listed in the local Yellow Pages and belonging to the local chamber of commerce. Your letter should persuade business owners to attend the organizational meeting, become charter members, and pay the group's dues. Plan the letter by writing two sentences for each category indicated below. The two sentences should work together to form a paragraph.

1. Attracting Attention

_____

_____

_____

_____

2. Establishing a Relationship

_____

_____

_____

_____

3. Appealing to Buying Motives

_____

_____

4. Persuading Someone to Act

_____

_____

_____

5. Providing the Opportunity to Act

_____

_____

_____

_____

C. Identifying Sales Appeals

Directions: Read the following sales appeals to identify the specific want or need to be satisfied in each case. Write that want or need in the space provided.

1. If you could not read this letter, imagine how different your life would be. Help someone learn to read by sending a contribution to the Literacy Guild.

   _____

   _____

2. Late getting home to fix dinner for your family? A healthy five-course meal is at your fingertips. Just call Healthy Gourmet when you leave the office, and dinner will be delivered when you arrive home.

   _____

   _____

3. Let us help you look the part—we'll put you in the driver's seat of a new luxury executive sedan.

   _____

   _____

4. Look great while you're feeling comfortable. With Jean Hinson sportswear, you don't have to choose between being active and looking terrific.

   _____

   _____

5. The SecureInc. security system protects your loved ones and your hard-earned property from vandalism and break-ins.

   _____

   _____

6. The BeautySleep mattress ensures that when you wake up, you're ready to face the day.

   _____

   _____

7. You work hard, and your money will, too, at Martson Investments, Inc.

   _____

   _____

8. Shopping at Jo-Mart gets you more for your dollar.

   _____

   _____

continued ➡

9. The Energy Glider's aerobic workout and muscle toning adds up to a firmer, fitter you.

_____

_____

10. The Enviro-Cean air purifier will make your home virtually dust free. In addition to clear air, our purifier gives you extra time, since it all but eliminates the need to vacuum.

_____

_____

11. No more rushing from the restaurant to the movie: Flicks and Feast combines two terrific ideas—a great meal and a great film.

_____

_____

12. Treat yourself to a revitalizing all-day spa at our new facility on Westmoor Boulevard—you'll be glad you did!

_____

_____

D. Revising for Improvement

Directions: Rewrite the following paragraph from a sales letter to give it more of a you-attitude and to correct mechanical errors.

Midwestern Mutual Life Insurance has developed an Early Retirement Policy designed to help people save enough money to retire at age fifty-five. To accumulate enough money, savings can mount up quickly. Please find the information card that is enclosed and fill it out. A representative will call to set up an appointment to discuss how you can begin accumulating savings for after you quit work.

_____

_____

_____

_____

_____

_____

_____

_____

E. Writing Collection Letters

Directions: Each of the following statements appears in a separate letter in a series of five follow up-collection letters. Based on how firmly the letter is worded, identify the order in which the following statements would be sent in the series of five follow-up letters.

a. To avoid a letter from our attorney, please send $528, the balance owed on the living room set you purchased from our Nottingham store. We must receive the balance by March 1. _____

b. The busy holiday season has come and gone. Please remember that you have an outstanding balance for the living room set you purchased from our Nottingham store. Please be sure to remit your payment of $528 by January 15. _____

c. Did you receive a statement from us a few weeks ago? We anticipated receiving your $528 payment by now. If you have a problem paying the total, please call 1-800-555-2340 to arrange for installment payments. _____

d. To avoid damaging your credit rating, you must pay the $528 balance on your account by February 1. _____

e. Please send your $528 payment today. I know the fact that we haven't received it must be an oversight on your part. _____

F. Editing Practice

Directions: Underline any errors in the following sentences, and write your corrections in the space provided. Write *OK* for any sentence that is correct.

1. Chris Whitley, former state senator from Cincinnati, is a Senior Partner with the law firm of Duncan, Dodge, and Dilbert. _____

2. My supervisor, Donell Lawton, knows more about those remediation systems than any engineer in the company. _____

3. If two-thirds of our stockholders agrees with the proposed changes, the board of directors will move forward with the plan. _____

4. More than likely it was she who ordered the energy saver program that is used on our network computers. _____

continued ➡

5. Both Corey and Marshall have extra copies of the new requisition forms; ask any of them if you should need more forms. _____

6. Although changing systems will be challenging, I'm looking forward with using an integrated software package. _____

7. Company policy states that no employee can engage in consulting work without he or she first gets permission from management. _____

8. Read the first chapter, "Marketing for Results", for an overview of our new campaign. _____

9. Most of our L.A. customers have signed up for the conference on Tuesday, February 10. _____

10. The Manufacturing Department will hire 6 additional employees to handle the increase in production. _____

G. Improving Letter Writing

Directions: The following letter is a draft of a first follow-up collection letter. Improve the writing in the letter based on your knowledge of the collection process.

Dear Mr. Rohmer:

Why haven't you responded to the two statements we have sent you? This letter is our reminder that a balance of $121.50 is due on your account.

If you believe our statement to be in error, please let us know at once. If you would like to discuss installment payments, please call me at 1-800-555-2781 to arrange a payment plan. A preaddressed envelope is enclosed for your convenience.

Sincerely yours,

_____

_____

_____

_____

_____

_____

_____

_____

_____

Section 10.2 Claim and Adjustment Communications

A. Recalling Terms

Directions: Add the words that *best* complete the sentences below.

adjustments

claim letter

claimant

equitable adjustment

penalty

1. Only by evaluating business experience, examining company policy, and using common sense can a business make a(n) _____.

   _____

2. A(n) _____ is a person who makes a claim against a company.

   _____

3. Consumer protection laws allow customers to cancel certain contracts without _____.

   _____

4. Examples of _____ include partial credit, refunds, and exchange of merchandise.

   _____

5. A letter written to address a problem with a product or service is called a(n) _____.

   _____

B. Improving a Claim Letter

Directions: Rewrite the following claim letter to make it more effective. Add any information needed to make the letter specific.

Dear Toy Joy Sales Manager:

I just spent $500 on your "Welcome Back" playhouse for my daughter. After lugging back this huge box from the store, I found that I could not assemble "Welcome Back" because two important parts—the roof and the door—are missing!

Needless to say, the surprise for our daughter's birthday was less than complete. Please send me the parts I need!

Sincerely,

_____

_____

_____

_____

_____

_____

_____

_____

_____

_____

_____

_____

_____

_____

_____

_____

_____

_____

_____

_____

_____

C. Writing an Adjustment Letter

Directions: Assume you work at Everett and Company, a popular hardware and garden store that caters to upscale customers. More than a year ago, a customer purchased an expensive pair of garden clippers; recently, he returned them in a very damaged condition. Write an adjustment letter that addresses the customer's request to have the garden clippers replaced. Add any information needed to make the adjustment letter specific.

_____

_____

_____

_____

_____

_____

_____

_____

_____

_____

_____

_____

_____

_____

_____

_____

_____

_____

_____

_____

_____

_____

_____

_____

_____

Section 10.3 Public Relations Letters

A. Creating Goodwill

Directions: You work for Crafty Types, a popular store that sells craft supplies. Your store
is relocating to a larger site, and you must draft a letter informing customers of
your move. Write a lively, interesting message to Crafty Types customers,
sharing the news. Include any details that will add realism. Write your message
in the space provided.

_____

_____

_____

_____

_____

_____

_____

_____

_____

_____

_____

_____

_____

_____

_____

_____

_____

_____

_____

_____

_____

_____

B. Promoting a New Business

Directions: Think of a business enterprise that interests you—one that you might like to start someday. In the space below, write a PR letter in which you introduce yourself and announce the nature of your business. Your aim, of course, is to establish a positive public opinion and to attract customers.

_____

_____

_____

_____

_____

_____

_____

_____

_____

_____

_____

_____

_____

_____

_____

_____

_____

_____

_____

_____

_____

_____

_____

_____

_____

_____

_____

_____

C. Attracting New Customers

Directions: Assume that five years have passed since you established the business you announced in Exercise B. An industrial park, new housing communities, and a retirement village have opened in your area, increasing the entire business community's potential for new customers. In the space below, write a PR letter designed to attract new customers to your business and to persuade them to join your other satisfied customers.

_____
_____
_____
_____
_____
_____
_____
_____
_____
_____
_____
_____
_____
_____
_____
_____
_____
_____
_____
_____
_____
_____
_____

D. Polishing the Public Image

Directions: Assume that you work for Western Gas and Electric Company. Read the following sentences from letters to be sent to WG&E customers, and revise them to build a more favorable image of WG&E.

1. Your electric bills are high because your outdated home appliances are energy hogs.

   _____

   _____

2. You are hereby informed that Western Gas & Electric will sponsor the Oceanside Symphony Orchestra to celebrate our donation to the Symphony Fund on Wednesday evening, April 8, at 8 p.m.

   _____

   _____

3. By scheduling more of your power usage during off-peak hours, money can be saved as well as avoiding "brownouts."

   _____

   _____

4. As part of our mission to educate the public about the need for energy conservation, we have enclosed a most informative pamphlet.

   _____

   _____

5. To make sure our stockholders get a good return on their investment, we have applied to the State Utilities Commission for a rate increase.

   _____

   _____

6. Now, for the first time in our history, you will be given the opportunity to spread your utility payments over a 12-month period.

   _____

   _____

7. We in the Customer Service Department would like to offer our congratulations on your upcoming marriage to Lorenzo Adams

   _____

   _____

Section 10.4 Social-Business Communications

A. Writing Thank-You Letters

Directions: You have worked for Magna Industries for three years. Recently, when your department manager retired, you were promoted to her job. As a result, many of your friends and colleagues sent congratulatory notes, two of which are shown below. In the space provided, write a thank-you letter for each.

1. From Joanie A. Bennett, Magna Industries President:

Congratulations on your promotion to manager of Direct Mail—and welcome to the Magna management team!

Since you joined Magna three years ago, you have certainly developed a reputation for problem solving and maintaining customer satisfaction. We are sure that you will continue developing your record of service in your new position.

All of us at Magna are confident that you will be a superior manager and will have a most successful career with our firm. We look forward to working with you and your department. Please let me know whenever I may be of service to you.

_____
_____
_____
_____
_____
_____
_____
_____
_____
_____
_____
_____
_____
_____
_____
_____
_____

2. The second letter is from James Richenberry, Magna's national sales manager. Richenberry has been a friend and valued business associate during your tenure at Magna. You work closely with him and his staff, and your mutual cooperation has been very effective.

Congratulations! I'm really happy—but of course not surprised—to hear the news about your promotion to Direct Mail manager.

As a sales manager, I value strong customer relations, so I especially appreciate all your efforts to communicate effectively with top customers and provide all customers with exemplary service. It's been a pleasure working with you!

My best wishes to you in your new position. I know that you will do a superb job, and I look forward to working more closely with you.

Sincerely,

_____

_____

_____

_____

_____

_____

_____

_____

_____

_____

_____

_____

_____

_____

_____

_____

_____

_____

_____

_____

_____

_____

_____

_____

B. Recognizing Types of Social-Business Communication

Directions: Read the descriptions of special business situations and occasions below. Then write the type of social-business communication you would need to write in response.

1. A co-worker has announced his engagement.   _____

2. The manager of your team has been promoted to the district office.   _____

3. You have received a present marking your 10th anniversary with the company.   _____

4. Your supervisor has just returned from the funeral of a family member.   _____

5. A client has recommended your business to other colleagues and associates.   _____

C. Handling Invitations

Directions: Practice your skill at handling invitations by completing the following assignments.

1. As chair of the entertainment committee for Fonda San Pedro Industries, you must write the formal invitation to the company's annual dinner dance. In the space below, write the invitation as you want it to be printed. The reception begins at 7 p.m., followed by dinner at 8 p.m. The event will take place on Saturday, May 20, in the Springfield Manor Hotel's Lincoln Room.

_____

_____

_____

_____

_____

_____

_____

_____

_____

_____

_____

_____

2. You have received a formal invitation from Richard and Elena Nunez to attend their dinner party on Friday, November 10. In the space below, write to *accept* their invitation.

_____

_____

_____

_____

_____

_____

_____

_____

_____

_____

_____

_____

_____

_____

3. In the space below, write to *decline* the formal invitation to Richard and Elena Nunez's dinner party.

_____

_____

_____

_____

_____

_____

_____

_____

_____

_____

_____

_____

_____

_____

Section 10.5 Form Paragraphs, Form Letters, and Templates

A. Advantages and Disadvantages of Using Form Letters

Directions: You work for a travel agency that is planning to use form letters to promote vacation and weekend getaway packages. Your supervisor has asked you to identify the advantages and disadvantages of form letters and to present the findings at a staff meeting.

List five advantages of using form letters.

_____

_____

_____

_____

_____

_____

_____

_____

_____

_____

_____

_____

_____

List three disadvantages of using form letters.

_____

_____

_____

_____

_____

_____

_____

_____

_____

_____

_____

B. Types of Form Letters

Directions: Based on the advantages listed previously in Exercise A, the travel agency decides to use form letters for different situations. Select the type of form letter that would be most appropriate for each situation.

a. Form letter

b. Form letter with variables

c. Letters with form paragraphs

1. Providing information about upcoming cruises to potential customers. _____

2. Responding to a job applicant. _____

3. Forwarding tickets for a client's upcoming cruise. _____

4. Proposing a travel itinerary for a client. _____

5. Requesting information to update a client's travel profile. _____

C. Preparing a Letter With Form Paragraphs

Directions: In your position in the Human Resources Department of Palm City Plastics, you handle all correspondence with job applicants. You use form paragraphs to streamline the process. Joaquin Lavelle, a job applicant, has sent a résumé and application letter to the Human Resources Department. The personnel manager has asked you to write Mr. Lavelle requesting that he complete an application form and provide three references. Your office will schedule an interview when the information is received.

From the list below, select four form paragraphs that you would include in the body of a letter to Mr. Lavelle. In the spaces provided, write the numbers of the form paragraphs you would use in the order that they would appear in the letter.

1. Thank you for your interest in our company. We would be delighted to discuss career opportunities with you.

2. We are not able to increase our staff at this time. However, we anticipate positions opening in several specialized areas in the next six months.

3. Your qualifications impressed us. Please stop by our office to complete an application. On your application, please include names and addresses of three references.

continued ⟶

4. The qualifications you listed on your application form impressed us. Please submit a résumé to us that includes the names and addresses of three references.

5. When we receive the information requested, we will call to schedule an interview.

6. Thank you for your interest in Palm City Plastics. We look forward to hearing from you.

7. We will keep your application on file and notify you when a suitable position becomes available.

8. You're qualifications are impressive. However, we have hired a candidate whose qualifications best match the position for which you interviewed. If you would like, we will keep your application on file and contact you when any opening becomes available in your area of interest.

9. If you would like to keep your application on file, please contact the Human Resources Department at the number above.

_____

_____

_____

_____

D. Writing Form Letters

Directions: As the administrative assistant to the president of Tradewinds Basket Company, one of your responsibilities is to respond to the routine correspondence of Brian Dresden. You compose letters and Mr. Dresden, company president, signs them. Because of the volume of routine correspondence, you decide to use form letters. Write form letters, form letters with variables, or letters with form paragraphs for each of the following situations.

1. Write body paragraphs of a form letter used for catalog requests. Enclose a 10-page catalog with the letter.

_____

_____

_____

_____

_____

_____

_____

2. Write body paragraphs of a form letter with variables that responds positively to requests from local charitable organizations. Variables will be the receiver of the contribution (for example, the Central Iowa Literacy Council) and the amount of the contribution.

_____

_____

_____

_____

_____

_____

_____

_____

3. Write form paragraphs that respond to requests for plant tours. Write a paragraph to cover each of the following items:

a. A goodwill opening paragraph.

_____

_____

_____

_____

_____

_____

_____

_____

b. Daily tours are conducted Monday through Friday from 9 a.m. to 4 p.m. from April through November. Groups are limited to 25 participants.

_____

_____

_____

_____

_____

_____

_____

_____

continued ●→

c. Tours can be arranged by Jeni Briand at 1-800-555-4252.

_____

_____

_____

_____

_____

_____

_____

d. Tradewinds Basket Company Factory Store, across the street from the plant, is open from 9 a.m. to 4 p.m., Monday through Saturday. Basket and gift items are available.

_____

_____

_____

_____

_____

_____

e. A goodwill closing paragraph.

_____

_____

_____

_____

_____

_____

_____

CHAPTER 11 Preparing and Writing Reports

Section 11.1 Technology and Reports

A. Types and Purposes of Reports

Directions: Identify the type of report that would be written for each of the following situations. On the line to the right of each description, write the choice that best identifies the type of report.

1. You are asked to report on your progress toward completing an assignment.   _____

2. Your company wants to identify a computer consultant to perform monthly sales analyses. You ask three companies to submit proposals and bids.   _____

3. A sales representative has just demonstrated a new copier; you report to your supervisor why purchasing the copier is a good idea.   _____

4. A product is a month behind its release schedule. Should the marketing department continue to promote it? Explain to the vice president of marketing why the department should continue its scheduled promotional campaign.   _____

5. You have been given surveys completed by business communications students. You are asked to report on the results of the questionnaires.   _____

6. You are helping with the fund-raising project for a school organization. At monthly meetings, you present reports on the work completed for the fund-raiser.   _____

7. The travel agents in your office compile monthly reports on the customer service requests they have received.   _____

continued ➟

8. A metropolitan hospital is exploring the need for opening outpatient surgery centers in neighboring suburbs. As a member of the oversight committee, you prepare a report explaining the plan's benefits and drawbacks. _____

9. The manager of patient services is asked to prepare a report explaining to the hospital board why the hospital should develop a new children's wing. _____

10. The facilities manager of the hospital is asked to report each month on the construction of an outpatient surgery center. _____

B. Gathering Information

Directions: Select a topic of your choice related to a hobby, your current job, or a possible future career. State your topic clearly. Then, using one or more of the following indexes—*Reader's Guide to Periodical Literature, the Business Periodicals Index*, or *The New York Times Index*—develop a list of a minimum of 10 secondary sources about your topic. These sources should be from publications that are no more than three years old. Include sources from Internet databases and Web sites. Be sure to include the following information for each source:

- Author
- Title of article
- Title of periodical
- Date of publication
- Page numbers

1. _____

   _____

2. _____

   _____

3. _____

   _____

4. _____

   _____

5. _____

   _____

6. _____
_____

7. _____
_____

8. _____
_____

9. _____
_____

10. _____
_____

C. Reliability of Sources

Directions: Select one article from the sources identified in Exercise B. Prepare a one-page
report about the reliability of the information in the article based upon the
following criteria:

1. Does the source provide current information on the topic?

2. Is the source reliable? Why or why not?

3. Is the information pertinent to your topic?

4. Is the author an authority on the subject? What evidence do you have?

5. Does the author identify his or her opinions?

_____
_____
_____
_____
_____
_____
_____
_____
_____
_____
_____

continued ➡

_____

_____

_____

_____

_____

_____

_____

_____

_____

_____

_____

_____

_____

D. Survey Questions

Directions: Critique the following questions based upon their value for use in a questionnaire intended for students who eat in the campus cafeteria. Write your answers on the lines provided. This questionnaire will help determine which foods students would like in the cafeteria.

1. Which foods would you most like to see in the cafeteria? Rank the following with 1 being the most liked and 5 being the least liked:
   _____ burgers
   _____ salads
   _____ pizza
   _____ casseroles
   _____ deli sandwiches

_____

_____

_____

_____

_____

_____

2. What foods do you think should no longer be served in the campus cafeteria?

_____
_____
_____
_____
_____
_____

3. Do you like desserts? _____Yes _____ No

_____
_____
_____
_____
_____
_____

4. Which foods do you suggest that the cafeteria serve in the future?

_____
_____
_____
_____
_____

5. How often do you eat in the cafeteria?
_____ most days
_____ 2–3 times a week
_____ once a week
_____ never; please explain: _____
_____ other; please specify: _____

_____
_____
_____
_____
_____
_____

E. Primary Sources

Directions: Write 10 questions for a questionnaire to survey students on your campus
regarding one of the following topics:

1. Using Internet browsers

2. Online shopping

3. Required departmental courses

4. On-campus housing

5. Campus tutoring services

1. _____

   _____

2. _____

   _____

3. _____

   _____

4. _____

   _____

5. _____

   _____

6. _____

   _____

7. _____

   _____

8. _____

   _____

9. _____

   _____

10. _____

    _____

F. Conducting and Analyzing the Survey

Directions: Using the questionnaire developed in Exercise E, survey students in one of your classes. Tabulate their responses and prepare a two- to four-page analytical report on the results. In the space provided, indicate the findings you will analyze in your report.

_____

_____

_____

_____

_____

_____

_____

_____

_____

_____

_____

_____

_____

_____

_____

_____

_____

_____

_____

_____

_____

_____

_____

_____

_____

_____

_____

_____

_____

_____

_____

G. Using Keywords to Search for Information

Directions: List two keywords to use for an Internet search of the topics.

1. business ethics _____ _____

2. stock market investing _____ _____

3. computer programming _____ _____

4. job search _____ _____

5. home mortgages _____ _____

6. day-care services _____ _____

H. Searching the Internet for Information

Directions: Conduct a search on one of the following topics using the tips for searching the Internet found on pages 464 and 465 of your textbook. If you do not have Internet access, conduct a search of print materials.

- Interviewing
- Cultural diversity
- Public speaking
- Telecommuting
- Office design
- Negotiation

1. Write the topic you selected.

_____

_____

_____

2. Write at least four keywords used in your search.

_____ _____

_____ _____

_____ _____

Student _____ Class _____ Instructor _____

Date Assigned _____ Date Completed _____

3. Locate four sources of information on your topic. Provide the following information for each source you locate:

- **Name of the Internet source or the title of the publication**
- **Date the Internet site was accessed or publication was printed**
- **Brief description of the information provided by each source**

Internet Source Name	Access Date	Description
1.		
2.		
3.		
4.		

I. Working Bibliography

Directions: **1.** Using 3″ × 5″ cards or 4″ × 6″ cards, prepare bibliography cards for sources on one of the topics from the list in workbook Exercise 11.1H.

2. Prepare at least one bibliography card for each of the following types of sources:

- Book
- Magazine article
- Internet publication or Web site
- Reference book or online database
- Dictionary
- Newspaper

J. Note Taking From Sources

Directions: Select one article on the topic you selected for Exercise 11.1H, and prepare two note cards using the guidelines on page 466 of your textbook.

K. Documentation Formats

Directions: Prepare three separate 3″ × 5″ cards (or 4″ × 6″ cards) in each of the three formats described on pages 469–470 in your textbook: Chicago Style, APA Style, and MLA Style. Use a different card for each of the three documentation formats.

L. Documenting Electronic Sources

Directions: Review the information given on page 470 of your textbook on preparing citations from electronic sources. If you have access to the Internet, look up a source dealing with one of the topics given in workbook Exercise 11.1H. Locate at least three types of secondary information sources listed on page 460 of your textbook. Create a bibliography card for each source using 3″ × 5″ or 4″ × 6″ cards.

M. Key Terms for Technology and Report Writing

Directions: Choose the word from the list below that *best* completes the following sentences.

Web browser	bibliography
pilot test	justification report
analytical report	plagiarism
paraphrasing	CD-ROM
periodic report	informative report

1. The type of report explaining why a new staff member was hired would be called a(n) _____.   _____

2. A report prepared at regular intervals is called a(n) _____.   _____

3. A(n) _____ gives facts without making recommendations.   _____

4. A report that draws conclusions and makes recommendations is called a(n)_____.   _____

5. To navigate the World Wide Web, you would use a(n) _____.   _____

6. Using another person's words without giving the original author credit is called _____.   _____

7. The list of sources used in a report is called the _____.   _____

8. To check the quality of your survey, you might conduct a(n) _____.   _____

9. Rephrasing someone else's ideas in your own words is called _____.   _____

10. Many library sources are now available in _____ format.   _____

Section 11.2 Writing Informal Reports

A. Specific Subjects

Directions: Below are general subject lines used in informal reports. Revise each subject line into one that tells the reader more specifically about the contents of the report. Add details if necessary.

1. SUBJECT: Products

SUBJECT:_____

_____

_____

2. SUBJECT: Positions

SUBJECT:_____

_____

_____

3. SUBJECT: Profits

SUBJECT:_____

_____

_____

4. SUBJECT: Technology

SUBJECT:_____

_____

_____

5. SUBJECT: Books

SUBJECT:_____

_____

_____

B. Writing an Unsolicited Informal Report

Directions: Your townhome complex wants motorists to drive through the housing facility more slowly. The posted speed is 15 miles per hour, but some residents and guests drive much faster. This potentially dangerous situation worries joggers, walkers, and parents of small children. You would like to add speed bumps to the streets to slow traffic. Write an informal report to Jeff Bankston, president of the homeowners' association, expressing residents' concern. Mention other housing complexes that have added speed bumps, and include any other information you would like the president to share with the association board.

_____
_____
_____
_____
_____
_____
_____
_____
_____
_____
_____
_____
_____
_____
_____
_____
_____
_____
_____
_____
_____
_____
_____
_____
_____
_____

C. Tone and Organization

Directions: You are the manager of the local softball team, which is supported by PeopleFirst Bank and Consumers' Best Foods. The team includes men and women. Using an appropriately informal tone, rewrite the following report, which will be sent to the head of the bank and the food store. Organize the information into paragraphs.

We have finished a 10-game season in the Hyde Park League, with 6 wins and 4 losses, coming in third in the League. Twenty players reported for the season opening: fourteen starters and six substitutes. Last year, we had 21 people on the roster. Janie Woo, an accountant, assisted me as manager. Our home games were held every Tuesday at 7 p.m. at Macrae Field. We appreciated the fans' support, but we hope even more will attend next year. Next year, would it be possible to post the game schedule at both PeopleFirst Bank and Consumers' Best Foods and run the schedule in local papers? Having copies for players to distribute would be helpful, too. These might be ways to improve attendance. This year, new equipment purchased from supporters' funds included eight new uniforms, a dozen softballs, six bats, one bench, two fielders' gloves, and a new catcher's mitt. We estimate that we will need $1,200 for next year. May we count on you for this support?

_____

_____

_____

_____

_____

_____

_____

_____

_____

_____

_____

_____

_____

_____

_____

D. Unsolicited Report

Directions: Think of an idea that would improve the operation or facilities of your school. For example, you may have an idea for increasing student attendance at school events, or for improving Internet access for students. In the space provided, write a one-page unsolicited report describing your idea. Explain why a specific improvement is needed and how you think the change should be implemented. Address your report to a staff person who has the authority to put your idea into effect. Route the report through your instructor.

_____

_____

_____

_____

_____

_____

_____

_____

_____

_____

_____

_____

_____

_____

_____

_____

_____

_____

_____

_____

_____

_____

_____

_____

_____

_____

_____

E. Revising Sentences From Reports

Directions: The following sentences were selected from reports. If a sentence is correct, write *Correct* in the space below it. If a sentence has errors, rewrite the sentence correcting each error.

1. Everyone accept Ms. Shin has approved the reccommendation.

   _____

   _____

2. Mr. Weinstein, whom I met at the sales conference, is someone whose opinions I have come to trust.

   _____

   _____

3. Mr. Cannon will screen perspective employees for the position.

   _____

   _____

4. The principle rules are posted on the bulletin board.

   _____

   _____

5. We discovered that their interested in expanding the service.

   _____

   _____

Section 11.3 Writing Formal Reports

A. Preparing to Write Formal Reports

Directions: Complete each sentence by writing the name of the correct report part in the space provided.

1. The _____ tells what the report is about, who prepared it, and when it was prepared.

2. The _____ shows where the principal elements of a report are located within the text.

3. The _____ provides background information such as who requested the report, why the report was needed, and how the report was developed.

4. The _____ gives the reader an overview of the report's contents.

5. The _____ gives all the details of a report—all the factual material and the sources of these facts.

6. The _____ lists the findings and makes recommendations based on these findings.

7. The _____ indicates the books and periodicals that were used in preparing the report and provides other information such as tables, charts, questionnaires, and letters that may be referred to as exhibits.

8. The problem that the report addresses is called its _____.

9. The section of the report that describes how research was conducted is called _____ .

B. Defining the Purpose and Scope

Directions: The scope of many reports is too general or too vague. Revise the following report titles to make each one more specific and meaningful, as in the example shown. Add details as necessary.

Sample: Advertising   <u>Changes in Online Advertising</u>

1. Job Performance _____

2. Early Retirement _____

3. Holidays _____

4. Jogging _____

5. Study Aids _____

C. Organizing the Report

Directions: Prepare an appropriate outline for a report on one of the topics listed in
workbook Exercise 11.3B.

_____

_____

_____

_____

_____

_____

_____

_____

_____

_____

_____

_____

_____

_____

_____

_____

_____

_____

_____

_____

_____

_____

_____

_____

_____

_____

D. Objective Reporting

Directions: A business report should be objective, without personal opinions and attitudes. Revise the following sentences to eliminate personal and subjective references.

1. I think that all staff members should receive further computer training.

_____

_____

2. I think the members of the senior class will agree that the placement office needs to expand its services.

_____

_____

3. In our opinion, the bank should be open until 7 p.m. on weekday evenings and on Saturday mornings for customer convenience.

_____

_____

4. Most of us think the outdated computers need to be replaced.

_____

_____

5. It seems that the reorganized workspace is proving effective.

_____

_____

6. In my opinion, using spreadsheets will make compiling monthly sales reports easier.

_____

_____

_____

E. Proofreading for Grammar Errors

Directions: Underline any grammar errors in the following paragraphs. Write your corrections in the space provided.

Mr. Justine Simone, our management consultant has completed   _____

an analysis of the employer morale survey conducted March 14.   _____

He reports that 95% or our employees responded.   _____

On Tuesday, April 20, at 10:00 a.m. in the main conference room,   _____

Mr. Simone will present the results of the survey. He will   _____

distribute copys of teh full report and a summary of the findings   _____

to each attendee. In addition, Mr. Simone will interpet his   _____

findings and present reccommendations for improvement.   _____

Section 11.4 Keeping Meeting Records

A. Meeting Vocabulary

Directions: In the space provided, write a definition of each term as it applies to a business meeting of an organization. Use a dictionary as needed.

1. Quorum

_____

_____

2. Agenda

_____

_____

3. Motion

_____

_____

4. Carry

_____

_____

5. Chairperson

_____

_____

6. Preside

_____

_____

7. Record

_____

_____

8. Call to Order

_____

_____

continued ➡➡

9. Table

_____

_____

10. Minutes

_____

_____

11. Adjourn

_____

_____

12. Second

_____

_____

B. Recording the Minutes

Directions: As the recorder for the Student Volunteers Association, you must prepare the minutes of yesterday's meeting from the notes that follow. Prepare formal minutes of the meeting.

1. Date, Time, Place: September 28, <YEAR>, 5 p.m., Regal Conference Room

2. Chairperson: Sam DePew, President

3. Call to order & quorum: Call to order at 5:10 p.m.; quorum established (30 percent required)

4. Present: R. Ball, L. Crenshaw, J. Toombs, M. Robbins, K. Fischer, P. Lucas, J. Shaw, V. Christie

5. Absent: V. Owen, O. Williamson, J. Riffle

6. Approvals: Minutes of the May 25 meeting; treasurer's report; audit report

7. Committee reports: Bylaws, Membership, Program

8. Unfinished businesses: Fund-raiser: Motion by Shaw, chairperson of Ways and Means Committee, to raffle a summer weekend stay in Cincinnati and tickets to Kings Island; sale of $5 tickets to begin Nov. 1. Profits to go to Ronald MacDonald House. Carried.

9. New business: Motion to accept the invitation of the Monroe Community Leaders' Association to have a Student Volunteers representative speak at their

November 15 meeting with Robbins. Seconded and carried. Motion by Lucas to contribute $500 to the United Way. Motion seconded and failed.

10. Tabled: Discussion of Spring Garage Sale until January meeting.

11. Adjournment: 6:25 p.m. Next meeting scheduled for October 8 at Pizza King at 6 p.m. for member recruitment.

_____

_____

_____

_____

_____

_____

_____

_____

_____

_____

_____

_____

_____

_____

_____

_____

_____

_____

_____

_____

_____

_____

_____

_____

_____

_____

_____

C. Proofreading Minutes

Directions: Underline any spelling errors in the following sentences from the minutes of meetings. Write your corrections on the lines provided. Write *OK* for any sentence that has no spelling error.

1. Hernandez anounced that the fund-raising campaign will be held in May.

   _____

2. Their were no additions or corrections to the minutes of the April 13 meeting.

   _____

3. The board reccommended increasing the health insurance deductible.

   _____

4. Olsen thanked Mobuktu for serving on the Personnal Committee.

   _____

5. Izaks complemented the employee council for it's work on the flextime survey.

   _____

6. Sese reported that salary adjustments should appear on the October 30 payroll check.

   _____

7. Felix moved that the seperate statement of principle on loan payments should be calculated.

   _____

8. Husted pointed out that the miscelaneous expenses included the purchase of a desktop copier.

   _____

9. The next meeting is scheduled for Feburary 10 at 4 p.m.

   _____

10. Hong presented a calender of activities for the winter months.

    _____

11. The motion was seconded and carried that the audit report be excepted.

    _____

12. The group agreed to lobby legislators at the Capitol.

    _____

13. The group agreed that members' relatives should not be illegible to receive the scholarship.

    _____

14. The company selected for the printing job was Denzel Graphics.

    _____

15. There being no further business, the meeting was ajourned.

    _____

Section 11.5 Preparing News Releases

A. Analyzing a News Release

Directions: You are the head of a large civic organization that supports a home for at-risk children. Your group sponsors a benefit dinner to raise money for the children's home. Your public relations chair has resigned, and you have asked the organization's secretary to draft a news release for your approval. The news release is shown below:

The El Paso Civic Club is planning its annual dinner dance. Tickets, which cost $50, are available from Jennifer Polaski, 448 West Madison, Nomesville, OH 48999. Please call 614-555-8000 for questions or reservations.

The El Paso Civic Club has hosted this event for 15 years. Ticket sales support the at-risk youth at the Children's Village on State Route 31. To support this important community service, be sure to order tickets before the August 26 deadline.

1. Compose four alternative titles for this news release.

   a. _____

   b. _____

   c. _____

   d. _____

2. Write three different opening sentences for the news release.

   a. _____

   _____

   b. _____

   _____

   c. _____

   _____

B. Function of the News Release

Directions: In the space provided, write *Yes* for each situation that is an appropriate subject for a news release. Write *No* if the situation is inappropriate.

1. A major corporation in a mid-sized city has decided to expand its industrial complex north of the city. _____

2. Candidates are being interviewed for the human resources manager position at XYZ Corporation. _____

3. Marshall Douglas is observing 25 years with Hong Kong Imports. _____

4. Employees of Educational Publishers spend four weekends in May painting and repairing houses in flooded areas in the southern part of the state. _____

5. Jefferson McHenry, CEO of a multinational corporation, will retire at the end of the year after 17 years in the position. _____

C. Writing News Releases

Directions: In the space provided, identify the who, what, when, where, and why in the opening paragraphs of the following news releases.

1. The El Paso Civic Club is planning its annual dinner dance. Order tickets, which cost $50, from Jennifer Polaski, 448 West Madison, Nomesvillle, OH 48999. The dinner will be held September 15 from 7 to 11 p.m. at the Regency Inn.

   Who: _____

   What: _____

   When: _____

   Where: _____

   Why: _____

2. Lara Croftson, president of Croftson & Associates, has been named chair of the Omaha Downtown Council's Board of Directors for the coming year. She will succeed H. Ron Wils III, executive vice president of State Insurance.

   Who: _____

   What: _____

When: _____

Where: _____

Why: _____

3. Ribs of Texas plans to expand into Eastern Europe by opening ten restaurants there over the next seven years.

Who: _____

What: _____

When: _____

Where: _____

Why: _____

4. Los Angeles-based 21st Century Fitness disclosed Thursday that it will open a chain of exercise centers across the United States next year. Spokesperson Maggie Sak says the centers will be for men and women age fifty or older who want a health center based on the needs of older people.

Who: _____

What: _____

When: _____

Where: _____

Why: _____

5. As part of a cost-saving program, Little Fitters, Inc., the nation's leading snack maker, will announce layoffs Monday. The layoffs, which will hit the Nashville area hardest, will take place immediately.

Who: _____

What: _____

When: _____

Where: _____

Why: _____

continued ➡

Chapter 11 **Preparing and Writing Reports** **309**

6. Corporate Computer Training in Oklahoma City is opening a new center on Classen Boulevard on August 15. The training center will have a staff of 10 full-time and 6 part-time instructors who will conduct courses for business and industry computer technicians.

   Who: _____

   What: _____

   When: _____

   Where: _____

   Why: _____

7. Central Oregon Power and Light is beginning an energy reduction program for all Piedmont-region customers, beginning April 1. The program, which hopes to encourage customers to conserve electricity, is open to all COP&L residential and business customers.

   Who: _____

   What: _____

   When: _____

   Where: _____

   Why: _____

8. Donna Marcelli, former city attorney for Columbia, Missouri, has been appointed the new state attorney general. She was appointed by the governor to fill the term of Thomas Daimler, who was recently elected to the state supreme court. The appointment is effective immediately.

   Who: _____

   What: _____

   When: _____

   Where: _____

   Why: _____

D. The Form of the News Release

Directions: Revise the draft of the news release shown in Exercise 11.5 A in the workbook.

_____

_____

_____

_____

_____

_____

_____

_____

_____

_____

_____

_____

_____

_____

_____

_____

_____

_____

_____

_____

_____

_____

_____

_____

_____

_____

_____

_____

_____

_____

_____

_____

_____

_____

CHAPTER 12 Working With Technology

Section 12.1 Ways Technology Affects Communication

A. Telephone Communication

Directions: You work as an administrative assistant at a firm that employs 22 people. You and one other administrative assistant handle all incoming telephone calls. To better handle telephone calls, you investigate the advantages and disadvantages of using a voice mail system in the office. Based on your findings, you decide to recommend to the office manager that a voice mail system be used. List the advantages and disadvantages of voice mail that you would mention in a memo to the office manager.

ADVANTAGES OF VOICE MAIL

1. _____
   _____

2. _____
   _____

3. _____
   _____

4. _____
   _____

5. _____
   _____

6. _____
   _____

continued ➛

DISADVANTAGES OF VOICE MAIL

1. _____

   _____

2. _____

   _____

3. _____

   _____

B. Using Voice Mail

Directions: As a Web-design coordinator for Planet X Travel, your job responsibilities include meeting with co-workers and attending professional conferences on a regular basis. You rely on voice mail to track calls you have received and to respond to callers in a timely manner. In the space provided, compose an appropriate voice mail message for each of the following situations.

1. A greeting for internal calls from co-workers in your company.

   _____

   _____

   _____

2. A response to a voice mail message from Christina Kwan, a graphic designer at Planet X. Christina left a message asking you to attend a meeting on Thursday, June 10. You will be out of the office at a conference from June 8 through June 11. You will return to the office on June 12.

   _____

   _____

   _____

3. A greeting for external calls from outside the company. This greeting will be used for calls received while you are attending the conference from June 8 through June 11.

   _____

   _____

   _____

   _____

C. Using Business Communication Technology

Directions: In the space provided, describe how each form of technology assists communication in the workplace.

1. Voice mail

_____

_____

_____

_____

2. Electronic mail (E-mail)

_____

_____

_____

_____

3. Fax machines

_____

_____

_____

_____

4. Pagers

_____

_____

_____

_____

5. Personal computers

_____

_____

_____

_____

D. Expanding Your Knowledge

Directions: Read the classified advertisement section of your local newspaper. Cut out one advertisement for each of the following jobs: administrative assistant, programmer, and retail salesperson. What technical skills are required for each position?

1. administrative assistant

_____

_____

2. programmer

_____

_____

3. retail salesperson

_____

_____

E. Correcting Errors

Directions: Underline any errors in the following sentences. Then on the lines provided, rewrite each sentence to eliminate any errors.

1. Technology has influenced teh way busynesses communicate, especially with regard to productivity.

_____

_____

_____

2. Voice mail enables co-workers to send and retrieve telephone messages at there convenience.

_____

_____

_____

3. Word processing software reduces the need from traditional currection materials and retyping.

_____

_____

_____

4. The internet is a system of computer networks that link computers form around the world.

_____

_____

_____

5. Pagers may include short text displays that allow peoples to send breif messages.

_____

_____

_____

6. Both voice mail and E-mail enabel you to communicate with many person at once.

_____

_____

_____

7. Cellular phones and pagers are particularlly useful for people who are frequently away from her offices.

_____

_____

_____

8. Many people dapend on E-mail to communicate quickily in the workplace.

_____

_____

_____

Section 12.2 Using Technology to Communicate

A. Recalling Key Terms

Directions: Each of the following acronyms is a Key Term covered in Section 12.2 from your textbook. Define each term and describe how the technology is used in today's workplace.

1. 2G cell phone

_____

_____

_____

_____

_____

2. PCS

_____

_____

_____

_____

_____

3. GPS

_____

_____

_____

_____

_____

4. PC

_____

_____

_____

_____

_____

5. DSL

_____

_____

_____

_____

_____

B. Selecting Technologies

Directions: For each task described, select the appropriate technology or technologies from the list. Write the correct letter in the space provided.

A. Smart phone

B. Personal computer

C. Scanner

D. Laser printer

E. Digital video camera

1. Create a document that incorporates a spreadsheet of a company's projected earnings. _____

2. Produce a company brochure in color. _____

3. Send a written message from one location to another using the telephone only. _____

4. Incorporate a photo of a new product into the company's Web site. _____

5. Conduct a meeting in different locations using audio, graphics, and video. _____

C. Selecting Appropriate Software for the Job

Directions: For each of the following situations, identify the type of software from the list that would be most appropriate for completing the job.

A. Database software

B. Desktop publishing software

C. Integrated software

D. Spreadsheet software

E. Word processing software

1. Drafting a letter about upcoming events to be sent to several clients. _____

2. Preparing a newsletter for various companies statewide. _____

3. Merging a spreadsheet into a report. _____

4. Creating a mailing list with customers' names, addresses, and telephone numbers. _____

5. Preparing a table for a company's annual fiscal review. _____

D. Proofreading Practice

Directions: Proofread the following E-mail message, correcting the spelling, punctuation, and grammar errors. You may want to reword sentences that are unclear or abrasive. Write your edited version on the lines provided.

To All Employees:

Our senior vice president, Ana Hensley, and myself is confident that the current acquisition will strengthen our reputation as the premier publisher of educational Software programs. Your probably aware that on August 21 Hanson Publishing Company acquired Cyber Software Design, making Hanson the nations largest publisher of educational software programs. As a result of the acquisition, a number of staff members form Cyber will be joining our present staff.

If you would like more details of this acquisition visit the company's Intranet home page on the World Wide web.

Student _____ Class _____ Instructor _____

Date Assigned _____ Date Completed _____

_____
_____
_____
_____
_____
_____
_____
_____
_____
_____
_____
_____
_____
_____
_____
_____
_____
_____
_____
_____
_____
_____
_____

Section 12.3 Communicating With the World

A. Reviewing Key Points

Directions: After reviewing Section 12.3 in your textbook, answer the following questions.

1. What is the difference between the Internet and an intranet? What is an extranet?

   _____

   _____

   _____

   _____

2. What are hypertext links? Provide an example of how a hypertext link can help a customer visiting the Keds homepage, for example.

   _____

   _____

   _____

   _____

3. How are smart cards used presently? What features may appear on smart cards in the future?

   _____

   _____

   _____

   _____

4. How can laptop computers, tablet PCs, and handheld devices assist workers such as sales representatives, real estate agents, and reporters?

   _____

   _____

   _____

   _____

5. How do embedded computer devices simplify tasks?

   _____

   _____

   _____

   _____

B. Retail on the Internet

Directions: The production team at Williams Electronics beat all their deadlines and came in under budget. Your supervisor has just asked that you send a gift to all four-teen members of the production team, leaving the details to your discretion. However, the total amount should not exceed $800.00. Using the Internet, search for a company, such as Red Envelope, that can meet your needs, pro-viding gifts for both men and women. On the lines provided, write the URL addresses that you visited, a description of the products the sites offer, and the average price of the gifts. Then state which company you chose and why.

_____

_____

_____

_____

_____

_____

_____

_____

_____

_____

_____

_____

_____

_____

_____

_____

_____

_____

_____

_____

_____

_____

Directions: Your company, located in Kansas City, wants you to attend a training conference in San Diego, and you must schedule the plane trip for yourself. Your training is scheduled to begin at 2:00 p.m. on Monday and ends Wednesday at lunch. However, you must be back in your office for an important closing Thursday at 10:00 a.m. Using the Internet, visit sites such as Travelocity and Priceline, as well as the homepage for specific carriers, such as American, Delta, and Southwest. Use the chart below to rank your flight choices from most preferred to least preferred.

URL of Web site	Departure Date and Time	Arrival Date and Time	Cost

C. Electronic Communication

Directions: Describe how each of the following technologies can enhance communication in the business world.

1. Bluetooth

_____

_____

_____

_____

_____

2. Voice Browsers

_____

_____

_____

_____

_____

3. Peer to Peer

_____
_____
_____
_____
_____

4. XML

_____
_____
_____
_____
_____

D. Communicating With Others

Directions: Communicating with other staff members is essential in any business, yet it can often be time-consuming. Write a short description for each of the following tools that allow people to communicate without face-to-face contact. In your descriptions, explain how the user can incorporate the six Cs of business communication.

1. E-mail

_____
_____
_____
_____
_____

2. Instant Messaging

_____
_____
_____
_____
_____

continued ➡

3. Virtual Reality Training

_____
_____
_____
_____
_____

4. Groupware

_____
_____
_____
_____
_____

5. Teleconference

_____
_____
_____
_____
_____

Section 12.4 Teleworking as a Way to Communicate

A. Reviewing Key Terms

Directions: After reviewing Section 12.4 in your textbook, define the following Key Terms.

1. Telework

_____

_____

_____

_____

2. Hot desking

_____

_____

_____

_____

3. Hotelling

_____

_____

_____

_____

4. Ergonomics

_____

_____

_____

_____

Student _____ Class _____ Instructor _____

Date Assigned _____ Date Completed _____

B. Finding Telework Employment

Directions: Read the classified advertisement section of your local newspaper or that of a large city nearby. In addition, do a search on the Internet to find at least three telework jobs that interest you. Write down what the job requirements are, what skills are required, and list any special considerations that you, the employee, must meet (such as access to E-mail, the Internet, and fax machines).

_____

_____

_____

_____

_____

_____

_____

_____

_____

_____

_____

_____

_____

_____

_____

_____

_____

_____

_____

_____

_____

_____

_____

_____

C. Productivity in the Home Office

Directions: For each item in the chart, describe at least two ways teleworkers can increase their productivity in the home office.

	Productivity in the Home Office
Time	
Convenience	
Quality of Work	

D. Advantages and Disadvantages of Telework for the Employer

Directions: As more employers turn to incorporating teleworkers in their organization, they must consider how it affects their bottom line. Based on the information covered in Section 12.4, list the advantages and disadvantages of teleworking that an employer must consider.

Advantages of Telework for the Employer

_____

_____

_____

_____

_____

_____

_____

continued ➡

Disadvantages of Telework for the Employer

_____

_____

_____

_____

_____

_____

E. Increasing Vocabulary

Directions: For each italicized word at the left, select the letter of the word that is closest in meaning.

1. *excise*	a) avoid	b) tax	c) stimulate	d) hide	_____
2. *merger*	a) division	b) occupation	c) franchise	d) joining	_____
3. *accrual*	a) skilled	b) deficit	c) growth	d) installment	_____
4. *equitable*	a) fair	b) excessive	c) overdue	d) exact	_____
5. *fiscal*	a) intricate	b) minor	c) balance	d) financial	_____
6. *proprietor*	a) assistant	b) client	c) owner	d) partner	_____
7. *consecutive*	a) alternate	b) sequential	c) supervisor	d) substitute	_____
8. *advocate*	a) oppose	b) facilitate	c) doubt	d) recommend	_____
9. *comprehensive*	a) thorough	b) incomplete	c) reasonable	d) inexpensive	_____
10. *initiative*	a) cautious	b) duplicate	c) first move	d) observe	_____

CHAPTER 13 Communicating With Customers

Section 13.1 The Importance of Good Customer Service

A. Remembering Key Terms

Directions: Using the Key Terms in Section 13.1 in your textbook, define the terms that follow.

1. customer service

_____

_____

2. external customer

_____

_____

3. internal customer

_____

_____

4. referrals

_____

B. Customer Service Statements

Directions: Circle *T* if the statement is true and circle *F* if the statement is false.

1. If you represent a company in any capacity, the customer will believe that you can help him or her with a need or a concern.   **T**   **F**

2. You should treat customers, with the guidelines of company policy, the way you would want to be treated.   **T**   **F**

continued ➡

3. Customer service is a function that should be practiced only in some business organizations.   **T**   **F**

4. Customer satisfaction occurs when the customer's wants and needs are met and when the customer feels valued by the company.   **T**   **F**

5. Most chief executive officers report that it is easier to attract new customers than to keep existing ones.   **T**   **F**

6. Top management should provide support and specific directives to key employees to ensure that customer service is carried out adequately.   **T**   **F**

7. Many businesses derive much of their new business through referrals or recommendations from satisfied customers.   **T**   **F**

8. Internal customers are self-sufficient and rarely serve as team players.   **T**   **F**

9. A company may deal with external customers through its Web site, face-to-face contact, the telephone, or other modes of communication.   **T**   **F**

10. The following is an example of a situation involving an external customer: A marketing executive asks an accountant in the Accounting Department for the credit rating of a customer.   **T**   **F**

C. Turning Ill Will Into Goodwill

Directions: The following items contain negative statements or questions. In the space provided, rewrite each item making it more positive and, thus, more customer oriented.

1. I can't help you until you do a better job of explaining your complaint.

_____

_____

2. Sorry, that route is booked. Try us again another time.

_____

_____

3. What's your problem?

_____

_____

4. Don't blame me; management just changed its mind.

_____

_____

5. Don't you understand what I'm trying to tell you? Pay attention, and I'll say it again.

_____

_____

6. Unless you have the warranty information, I can't help you get your laptop repaired.

_____

_____

7. Hold on a minute while I search for your account information. It should be somewhere in our records.

_____

_____

8. All lines are busy. No one can take your call now. Stay on hold or hang up and dial us again.

_____

_____

9. Before we can give you a refund, I need the order number and reason for return.

_____

_____

10. You should have realized that the rebate offer expired a few weeks before you submitted it.

_____

_____

Section 13.2 Maintaining Good Customer Service

A. Recalling Key Points

Directions: Circle *T* if the statement is true and circle *F* is the statement is false.

1. Customer service is a problem-solving function that applies only when there has been a customer complaint.   **T**   **F**

2. Employees at all levels should be trained to communicate with customers.   **T**   **F**

3. An organization that is customer-focused considers customers its top priority.   **T**   **F**

4. Customer service involves maintaining a positive attitude and remembering that customers are important to any business.   **T**   **F**

5. Customers depend more on us than we do on them.   **T**   **F**

6. Any employee who comes into contact with a customer directly or indirectly can influence that customer's perception of your company's products and services.   **T**   **F**

7. First impressions are important in establishing a good relationship between customers and your organization's representatives.   **T**   **F**

8. You should avoid addressing a customer by his or her name.   **T**   **F**

9. A handheld computer can enable you to synchronize data with a desktop computer.   **T**   **F**

10. A laptop computer is usually less portable than a desktop computer.   **T**   **F**

B. Meeting the Public

Directions: Items A–J contain some commonsense rules for meeting the public. Statements 1–10 violate one or more of these rules. In the space provided next to each statement, write the letter of the rule or rules that were violated.

Rules:

A. Give prompt attention to all customers.
B. Greet customers pleasantly, with a smile and/or an appropriate greeting.
C. Don't let personal business interfere with greeting the public.
D. If the person whom a customer wants to see or speak to is busy, let the customer know how long he or she will have to wait.
E. Be courteous and respectful at all times.
F. Do not reveal company secrets.
G. Avoid being intrusive.
H. Make refusals politely.
I. Show eagerness to assist the customer.
J. When saying good-bye, thank the customer.

Statements:

1. "There is no way Mr. Odubu will see you without an appointment." _____

2. "Ms. Sanchez can't talk to you now. She's in a meeting with a client from Montana." _____

3. "It's not my job to look up information for customers." _____

4. "You should receive a brochure in the mail this week. Good-bye." _____

5. "I'll be with you as soon as I finish making an appointment with my mechanic." _____

6. "Mr. Ang is meeting with investors to secure financing for a huge downtown construction project." _____

7. "I know your birthday's coming up. How old will you be?" _____

8. "Mr. Torres is not having a good day. I wouldn't want to bother him right now." _____

9. "I can't help you until later in the week." _____

10. "Look, I'm kind of busy making plans for my vacation. Can you call back later?" _____

C. Maintaining Customer Contact

Directions: Ruby Tobolka has been a sales representative for Austin Medical Supplies for eight months. She personally calls on her customers at least once every three weeks. Most of the supplies she sells can be bought from her competitors. Thus, she strives to maintain an excellent level of customer service as her competitive edge. What should Ruby do in each of the following situations to maintain customer contact?

1. While Ruby is traveling, she receives an E-mail message from her home office telling her that her most important client wants to talk with her about supplies she needs to receive within two days. It is 3:30 p.m., and Ruby is about an hour's drive from the client and an hour's drive from her hotel. She is very tired and wants to go to the hotel and rest. What should she do?

_____

_____

_____

_____

_____

_____

2. Ruby called one of her clients, Mr. Tyler, early this morning. Mr. Tyler's assistant told Ruby that he was at the hospital with his wife who was delivering their first child. Ruby's company has a policy against expensive gifts, but she feels that she should acknowledge the birth in some way. What should Ruby do?

_____

_____

_____

_____

_____

_____

3. Ruby received an E-mail message from a customer who buys very few supplies from her each month. The customer asked if Austin Medical Supplies would contribute a door prize for his company's upcoming employee health fair. Ruby has never had this particular type of situation arise before. What should she do?

_____

_____

_____

_____

_____

_____

_____

4. When Ruby checked her voice mail, she had a message from a new client canceling his appointment that afternoon due to a death in his family. The customer had previously indicated that he would place his first order with Ruby this afternoon. What should Ruby do?

_____

_____

_____

_____

_____

_____

5. When Ruby returned a telephone call to a customer, the customer told Ruby that the supplies that she'd shipped for next day delivery had not arrived. The package should have arrived by 2 p.m., and it is now 3 p.m. What should Ruby do?

_____

_____

_____

_____

_____

_____

D. Proofreading Practice

Directions: Proofread the following paragraphs from an E-mail message. Underline any errors and write your corrections in the space provided. For each line that has no error, write *OK*.

Dear Ms. Carelli: _____

Thank you for registering you new Speedy Browser software. As   _____
a registered user, you have access to our tecknical support staff   _____
24 hours a day, seven days a weak.   _____

You may reach us by telephone at 1-800-555-3435 or through   _____
our Web cite at http://www.speedybrowser.com. You may also   _____
E-mail our customer service representatives in   _____
customersvc@speedybrowser.com.   _____

IN addition to technical support, all registered users will recieve   _____
notices of new products and services that Speedy Browser offers.   _____
If you do not wish to receive these notices, please reply to that   _____
message and indicate "No Notices" in the header.   _____

If you have any questions, please contact at this E-mail address   _____
or call the toll-free number. Insuring customer satisfraction   _____
is our goal.   _____

Sincerely,   _____

Yolanda Lexington   _____

Section 13.3 Improving Contact With Customers

A. Key Points

Directions: After reviewing Section 13.3 in your textbook, answer the following questions.

1. How can continuing customer contacts enhance your business?

_____

_____

_____

2. What are three procedures to keep in mind when initiating or continuing contact with customers?

_____

_____

_____

3. Which customers deserve friendly and courteous treatment?

_____

_____

_____

4. What should you do if a customer asks a question that you can't answer?

_____

_____

_____

B. Talking With Customers

Directions: Circle *T* if the statement is true and circle *F* if the statement is false.

1. Every employee has the opportunity to influence a customer's image of the firm.   **T**   **F**

2. Immediately greeting a customer is not necessary or expected when it's obvious you are busy.   **T**   **F**

continued ➡

3. If a customer treats you rudely, you should respond in the same way. **T**   **F**

4. If a customer is waiting for an employee of your business who is running late, you should not tell the client how long the wait will be. **T**   **F**

5. If a customer appears to be undistinguished, you should still treat him or her courteously and with respect. **T**   **F**

6. When transferring calls, you should (if possible) make sure the call is answered. **T**   **F**

7. Maintaining a respectful, courteous tone when speaking with customers can reduce problems such as customer frustration and hostility. **T**   **F**

8. You should avoid making conversation about company personnel. **T**   **F**

9. If a visitor asks your opinion about company business, you should offer it freely. **T**   **F**

10. When you make a commitment to a customer, you should follow through on it promptly. **T**   **F**

C. Responding to Customers

Directions: Reword the following unprofessional responses to telephone calls. Make sure they convey a positive image of you, your supervisor, and your organization.

1. Mr. Brandon has been out of the office for over three hours. His appointment with the lending company took longer than he thought it would.

_____

_____

2. Mr. Brandon isn't answering his phone. I don't know where he is, but I know he's here today, because I saw him by the copier this morning.

_____

_____

3. Mr. Brandon isn't back from lunch yet, but he should be back soon, since he's been gone for almost two hours.

_____

_____

4. Mr. Brandon hasn't arrived in the office yet. Usually, he tells me when he's going to be late.

_____

_____

5. Mr. Brandon is running behind in his appointments this morning, so he asked me to hold all his calls. I don't know when you should call back.

_____

_____

_____

D. Using Your Electronic Thesaurus

Directions: Use the thesaurus on your computer to find one synonym and one antonym for each of the following words.

	SYNONYM	ANTONYM
1. initial	_____	_____
2. courteous	_____	_____
3. immediately	_____	_____
4. undistinguished	_____	_____
5. privacy	_____	_____
6. astute	_____	_____
7. discreet	_____	_____
8. conscientious	_____	_____
9. consideration	_____	_____
10. speed	_____	_____

Section 13.4 Responding to Customer Service Needs

A. Key Points

Directions: After reviewing Section 13.4 in your textbook, define the following Key Terms.

1. auto responder

_____

_____

2. FAQ

_____

_____

3. order confirmation function

_____

_____

4. E-whining

_____

_____

B. Creating a Company Policy

Directions: You work for Apple Appliances, a company that sells and repairs small kitchen appliances such as, toasters, coffee makers, and food processors. Your company is experiencing a large volume of returned merchandise. Most of the merchandise wasn't defective when purchased but has been damaged by carelessness and improper use. Often, the warranty has expired. Write a company policy for returning merchandise.

Apple Appliances: Return and Repair Policy

_____

_____

_____

_____

_____

_____

_____

_____

_____

_____

_____

_____

_____

_____

C. Customer Service Representative

Directions: Describe five characteristics that a customer service representative should exhibit in responding to dissatisfied customers in person, by E-mail, by telephone, and by letter. Use complete sentences.

1. _____

_____

_____

2. _____

_____

_____

3. _____

_____

_____

4. _____

_____

_____

5. _____

_____

_____

D. Handling a Customer Complaint

As the manager of the Customer Service Department at Metropolis Power Company, you received a letter from a customer complaining about the way repairs to his electrical system were handled.

In his letter, the customer related that the electrical meter that monitors electricity usage attached to the back of his house crackled and shot sparks, resulting in a power outage.

The customer called the Metropolis Power Company's customer service number and got the following response: "If you are using a touch-tone phone, press 1 now. If this call is about a bill, press 2 now. If this call is about establishing service, press 3 now. If this is an emergency, press 4 now."

Concerned that the electrical system might start a fire, the caller pressed 4 and heard the following message: "All of our lines are currently busy. Please hold. Your call will be answered in the order in which it was received." A Metropolis employee took the call five minutes later and stated that a service crew would arrive at his house within half an hour. The service crew did not arrive until two hours after the call was placed. The customer's electric meter was repaired and electricity restored an additional two hours later.

As manager of the Customer Service Department, you feel that the customer's call was not handled properly, and you want to prevent this type of incident from recurring. Upon investigating the incident, you discover that there were no other emergencies at the time and that the service crew members were making routine checks on their service route and had their cell phones turned off. In addition, the service crew forgot to check their cell phone messages during their lunch break, which delayed their receiving the customer's calls for at least an hour.

Directions: List at least five suggestions for improving the way this call was handled.

1. _____

_____

2. _____

_____

3. _____

_____

4. _____

_____

5. _____

_____

_____

E. Responding to Customers

1. A bank customer went through the drive-through window of her local bank after 5 p.m. on a Friday and made a deposit of $1,000. Early Monday morning she needed $200 in cash and went to an ATM to withdraw money, but she found she didn't have sufficient funds in her checking account.

When she spoke to the teller through the intercom, the teller replied, "Ms. Rousseau, my computer shows that there aren't enough funds in your account."

Ms. Rousseau realized immediately what had happened: her deposit made late Friday had not yet been posted to her account. However, she was offended by the teller's response. What should the teller have said to Ms. Rousseau?

_____

_____

_____

_____

_____

_____

_____

_____

_____

_____

_____

_____

continued ➻

2. Mr. Arnold received his monthly credit card statement and noticed that his balance showed a credit of $25, which was $40 more than what he owed the credit card company. He immediately called the credit card company and said, "You've made a mistake on my account statement."

The customer service representative took offense at Mr. Arnold's statement and replied, "Our system is fully automated, and we rarely make mistakes."

Mr. Arnold then replied, "Fine, then I'll keep the extra 40 bucks. Thanks!" Later, an apologetic customer service representative called back Mr. Arnold to tell him that they'd mistakenly credited his account instead of another customer's whose account number differed from his by two digits.

What should the customer service representative's response have been to Mr. Arnold's statement?

_____

_____

_____

_____

_____

_____

_____

_____

_____

_____

_____

_____

_____

_____

_____

_____

_____

_____

_____

_____

CHAPTER 14 Developing Presentation Skills

Section 14.1 Basics of Oral Communication

A. Outgoing Voice Mail Messages

Directions: For each of the following situations, write an appropriate message to be recorded as your outgoing voice mail message for incoming calls. Remember to avoid informing callers that your business will be closed for an extended period of time or that you will be out of town.

1. You are the office manager for a medical clinic. Write a voice mail greeting that can be used to handle general incoming calls. In your greeting, you should identify the business and suggest that the caller telephone during regular business hours. Remember to identify the regular business hours that the clinic is open and to include an after-hours number for medical emergencies.

   _____

   _____

   _____

   _____

   _____

   _____

2. You are the owner of Murphy's Upholstery Repair. As the sole employee of your business, you're often away from the office, picking up or delivering furniture or giving estimates. You rely on voice mail to check messages and stay in touch with customers. This week, you are out of town on vacation, but you are still checking messages and returning telephone calls promptly. Write a greeting that asks callers to leave their names and telephone numbers, so that their calls can be returned.

   _____

   _____

   _____

   _____

   _____

   _____

continued ➡

3. You are the owner of Bug-Out Pest Control, a business you started three months ago. You use voice mail after hours and during the business day when you are out on calls. You run the business from your home and gladly return calls 24 hours a day. Write a message telling the caller that you will return calls within an hour.

_____

_____

_____

_____

_____

_____

B. Enunciation Practice

Directions: The following multi-syllabic words can sound indistinct when speakers do not articulate each word part correctly. Practice enunciating each word correctly. Then, on the lines provided, write a sentence using each word. Be prepared to read your sentences aloud correctly in class.

1. adequate

_____

_____

2. aluminum

_____

_____

3. library

_____

_____

4. interesting

_____

_____

5. treasurer

_____

_____

6. developing

_____

_____

7. promotion

_____

_____

8. different

_____

_____

C. Pronunciation Practice

Directions: When saying the following words, speakers often add letters or change the sound of the existing letters. On the lines provided, write the dictionary pronunciation for each word. Then practice pronouncing each word and write a sentence using the word. Be prepared to read the sentences aloud correctly in class.

1. suggest _____

_____

_____

2. per diem _____

_____

_____

3. per capita _____

_____

_____

4. actual _____

_____

_____

5. corporation _____

_____

_____

continued ➵

6. cooperation _____

_____

_____

7. humble _____

_____

_____

8. honorarium _____

_____

_____

9. aesthetic _____

_____

_____

10. recognize _____

_____

_____

D. Word Wizard

Directions: Learning new words increases your ability to communicate. Below are some words and their corresponding definitions. Match the definition with its word by writing the appropriate letter beside each numbered item.

1. incapable of error	**a.** defer	**1.** _____
2. persistence	**b.** exempt	**2.** _____
3. to arrange according to a definite scheme	**c.** infallible	**3.** _____
4. the rising and falling of voice pitch	**d.** remiss	**4.** _____
5. to release from liability	**e.** systematize	**5.** _____
6. negligent in the performance of duty	**f.** tedious	**6.** _____
7. to put off until a later time	**g.** intonation	**7.** _____
8. tiresome and boring	**h.** eloquence	**8.** _____
9. clear and articulate expression	**i.** diligence	**9.** _____
10. sincere or honest	**j.** genuine	**10.** _____

E. States and Capitals

Directions: Underline each incorrectly spelled state or state capital. Write the correction in the space provided. Write *OK* in the space if all five items in the group are spelled correctly.

1. Bismarck, North Dakota
   Carson City, Nevada
   Atlanta, Georgia
   Denver, Colorado
   Piere, South Dakota   _____

2. Raleigh, North Carolina
   Austen, Texas
   Boise, Idaho
   Jackson, Mississippi
   Nashville, Tennessee   _____

3. Indianapolis, Indiana
   Lansing, Michigan
   Columbia, South Carolina
   Jefferson City, Missouri
   Mountpelier, Vermont   _____

4. Baton Roudge, Louisiana
   St. Paul, Minnesota
   Boston, Massachusetts
   Richmond, Virginia
   Charleston, West Virginia   _____

5. Phenix, Arizona
   Montgomery, Alabama
   Salem, Oregon
   Helena, Montana
   Madison, Wisconsin   _____

6. Lincoln, Nebraska
   Harrisburg, Pennsylvania
   Oklahoma City, Oklahoma
   Concord, New Hamshire
   Cheyenne, Wyoming   _____

continued ●→

7. Columbus, Ohio
   Augusta, Maine
   Montgumery, Alabama
   Annapolis, Maryland
   Trenton, New Jersey   _____

8. Little Rock, Arkansaw
   Des Moines, Iowa
   Juneau, Alaska
   Albany, New York
   Olympia, Washington   _____

9. Springfield, Illinois
   Salt Lake City, Utah
   Sacramento, California
   Providence, Rhode Island
   Tallahassee, Florida   _____

10. Honolulu, Hawaii
    Topeka, Kansas
    Frankfort, Kentucky
    Hartford, Connectticut
    Dover, Delaware   _____

Section 14.2 Communicating in Groups, Teams, and Meetings

A. Role Playing a Meeting

Directions: You can learn a lot from negative examples. For this fun exercise the class will be divided into committees of three to six members each. Choose a job-related or campus-related issue as a topic for your committee meeting. Select a committee member to chair the meeting. The committee chair is responsible for keeping the meeting on track.

The committee chair will ask each of the other committee members to play one or more of the following obnoxious characters. Use as many of the characters as feasible for your chosen committee meeting. Write enough of the role-play skit to enable each member to grasp the general direction of the committee meeting and his or her contribution to the meeting. *Remember*: This exercise demonstrates behaviors that you should not use in the real world.

Information Hog:	The Information Hog knows all the details but will not tell the group. "The boss told me the answer to that question, but I cannot release that information."
Time/Date Bug:	The Time/Date Bug keeps interrupting with insignificant details related to times or dates. "Did you talk with Mr. Starns at 9 a.m. or 10 a.m.? What time will the meeting be over?"
Fidget Master:	The Fidget Master has annoying habits such as playing with keys or coins, tapping fingers, sitting restlessly, shaking his or her watch to make sure it is still running, and so on.
Topic Changer:	The Topic Changer asks questions or makes comments that have little or no relevance to the topic being discussed. "Did you see the movie on Channel 18 last night?"

continued ▶▶

Mr. (or Ms.) Negative: Mr. (or Ms.) Negative is critical of every suggestion made. "That will never work; it will cost too much; management will never approve it; we tried it two years ago and it didn't work then."

Millie (or Willie) Giggler: This character thinks everything is funny.

Repeat Pete (or Rita):   Repeat Pete (or Rita) doesn't have an original idea but repeats what he (she) has heard from others.

Thunder Boomer: Thunder Boomer always talks too loud.

Whisper Wallflower: Whisper Wallflower speaks only when asked a question. This character's voice is barely audible, and another committee member always has to ask that his or her comments be repeated.

STUDENT NAME   **CHARACTERS**

_____   _____

_____   _____

_____   _____

_____   _____

_____   _____

_____   _____

_____   _____

COMMITTEE MEETING TOPIC

_____

_____

_____

_____

_____

_____

_____

_____

_____

_____

GENERAL DIRECTION OF SKIT

_____

_____

_____

_____

_____

_____

_____

_____

_____

_____

_____

_____

_____

_____

_____

SUGGESTIONS FOR IMPROVING THE MEETING

_____

_____

_____

_____

_____

_____

_____

_____

_____

_____

_____

_____

_____

_____

_____

_____

B. Preparing Agendas

Directions: An agenda is a list of topics to be discussed in a specific meeting. Prepare a five-item agenda for each of the following proposed meetings. Make up details as needed. You may want to refer to the sample agenda (Figure 14.3) on page 591 of your textbook as a guide.

1. *Organization:* Ever-Safe Parking Lots
   Meeting topic: increasing parking lot security
   Date and time: Monday at 10:00 a.m.
   Place: conference room 308

   _____

   _____

   _____

   _____

   _____

2. *Organization:* Matchbook Publishers
   Meeting topic: planning for the annual picnic
   Date and time: April 4, 2002 at 3:00 p.m.
   Place: employee break room

   _____

   _____

   _____

   _____

   _____

3. *Organization:* Armistice Farms Organic Frozen Foods
   Meeting topic: proposal for on-site day care center
   Date and time: Friday at 2:30 p.m.
   Place: conference room 22

   _____

   _____

   _____

   _____

   _____

C. Diplomacy for Group Progress

Directions: From each of the following pairs of statements, select the statement that better contributes to group progress. Write the letter identifying the better statement in the space provided.

1. a. That's a ridiculous idea.

  b. Your idea is interesting. Could you explain how it will apply to this situation? _____

2. a. Let's discuss the cost of implementation.

  b. That proposal is too expensive to consider. _____

3. a. Put me on the committee where I can be the most useful.

  b. I should really be in charge of committee selection, since I know the most. _____

4. a. I'd be happy to explain the new procedures again in detail.

  b. We don't really have time to go over the plans. Just do it. _____

5. a. You should have said something about that sooner. We're out of time now, and we still have to discuss plan B.

  b. That's a great idea, but we have to wrap up now. Let's put it on the agenda as the first item for the next meeting. _____

D. Enhancing Group Discussion

Directions: The following statements were made during an ad hoc committee meeting of the Fuzzy Puzzle Company. Rewrite each statement so that it will enhance group discussion rather than detract from it.

1. The executive committee would never endorse your proposal.

_____

_____

_____

continued ➡

2. I'm getting tired of listening to the same people talk all the time.

_____

_____

_____

3. Your ideas are so far-fetched that no one else understands them.

_____

_____

_____

4. I really don't care if you agree with me; I want to see this project green-lighted.

_____

_____

_____

5. I don't understand the difference between the proposed distribution tracking software and the old one, so let's move on to a different topic.

_____

_____

_____

6. What was on the agenda for today's discussion?

_____

_____

_____

7. Since everybody rejected my ideas, I don't care what you do.

_____

_____

_____

8. Let me make it clear: I disagree with you.

_____

_____

_____

9. There's no way this plan will work; it failed completely the
last time we tried it.

_____

_____

_____

10. You're looking really bored, Drew. Try to pay attention.

_____

_____

_____

E. Participating Effectively in Meetings

Directions: On the lines provided, write the six basic rules for participating effectively in
meetings. Then, choose two of these rules and explain in your own words
why this rule can enhance your effectiveness in a meeting.

_____

_____

_____

_____

_____

_____

_____

_____

_____

_____

_____

_____

_____

_____

_____

_____

_____

Section 14.3 Formal and Informal Presentations

A. Speech Topics and Purposes

Directions: List five topics that would be appropriate for a short, informal speech to be presented to your classmates. For each topic, write the purpose of the speech in the space provided.

TOPIC	PURPOSE
_____	_____
_____	_____
_____	_____
_____	_____
_____	_____

B. Impromptu Speaking Exercise

Directions: Take the five speech topics you listed in Exercise A and write each topic on a separate index card. Place your cards in a pile along with the cards of your classmates. Then, select three cards from the pile. From the three topics on the cards, choose one to give a short speech about. In the space provided, write five sentences about the topic that you could use in a two-minute impromptu speech on the topic.

_____

_____

_____

_____

_____

_____

_____

_____

C. Analyzing Your Audience

Directions: Prepare to give a five-minute speech to your classmates. Choose another topic from the pile of topics from Exercise B for your speech. Then answer the following questions about your audience.

1. How many people are in your audience?

_____

_____

2. What are the age range, gender composition, and occupations of your audience?

_____

_____

3. How much does this audience know about your topic?

_____

_____

4. Will this audience respond to a more formal or a more casual presentation?

_____

_____

D. Developing Your Speech

Directions: For the topic you selected in Exercise C, write points to keep in mind to develop your speech in terms of its content, clarity, treatment, and humor. You may want to review the guidelines for developing your speech on pages 587–589 of your textbook.

TOPIC:

_____

_____

_____

_____

_____

_____

_____

continued ◆▸

Student _____ Class _____ Instructor _____

Date Assigned _____ Date Completed _____

CONTENT:

_____

_____

_____

_____

_____

_____

CLARITY:

_____

_____

_____

_____

_____

_____

TREATMENT:

_____

_____

_____

_____

_____

_____

HUMOR:

_____

_____

_____

_____

_____

_____

_____

Student _____ Class _____ Instructor _____

Date Assigned _____ Date Completed _____

E. Rating Sheet for Speakers

Directions: The following chart is to be used either with preceding exercise D or with Practical Application C at the end of Section 8.4 in the textbook. Prepare a short speech on one of the topics in those exercises. Before making your presentation, give this chart to your instructor. Your instructor will give the chart to one of your classmates. Your classmate will rate your speech anonymously. Then your instructor will return the chart to you.

PRESENTATION EVALUATION

NAME: _____   GRADE: _____

TOPIC: _____   CLASS: _____

CONTENT (SCALE OF 1–25 POINTS)   _____

Related to Topic   Adequate Coverage
Clearly Expressed   Preparation/Research Evident
Organized Logically   Language Usage

DELIVERY (SCALE OF 1–25 POINTS)   _____

Professional Appearance   Gestures
Eye Contact   Grooming
Attire   Posture

PRESENTATION DYNAMICS (SCALE OF 1–20 POINTS)   _____

Composure   Volume
Pace   Expression
Pronunciation/Enunciation   Audience Rapport
Demeanor   Audience Attentiveness
Timing

VISUAL AIDS (SCALE OF 1–20 POINTS)   _____

Appropriate Type (slides, overheads, and so on)
Suitable Quality
Integration into Presentation
Conveyance of Ideas/Information

QUESTION/ANSWER SESSION (SCALE of 1–10 POINTS)   _____

Adequate Response   Language Usage

Student _____ Class _____ Instructor _____

Date Assigned _____ Date Completed _____

F. Reading Articles on Presentations

Directions: Read an article in a business publication that deals with presentations. List three to five suggestions covered in the article that would help you and your classmates become better presenters.

TITLE OF ARTICLE _____

MAGAZINE OR JOURNAL _____

PUBLISHER _____

DATE OF PUBLICATION _____

PAGE NUMBER _____

SUGGESTIONS FOR MAKING EFFECTIVE PRESENTATIONS:

1. _____
   _____

2. _____
   _____

3. _____
   _____

4. _____
   _____

5. _____
   _____

G. Annoying Speaker Attributes

Directions: By becoming aware of speaker attributes that interfere with your concentration during a presentation, you can develop a list of things not to do while presenting. Think about speakers you have heard recently either in person or on television or radio. Without identifying any of the speakers, list any speech qualities or non-verbal gestures that distracted you from the content of their messages.

_____
_____
_____
_____
_____

_____

_____

_____

_____

_____

_____

_____

_____

_____

H. Introducing a Speaker

Directions: Select a person whom you know (an instructor, parent, colleague, or friend). Write a three-paragraph introduction that would be appropriate to use if you were introducing that person as a speaker at a campus event. Be prepared to rehearse your introduction before your class. You may want to review the guidelines for introducing a speaker on page 585 of your textbook.

_____

_____

_____

_____

_____

_____

_____

_____

_____

_____

_____

_____

_____

_____

_____

_____

_____

I. Sound Alikes

Directions: Choose the word in parentheses that correctly completes each sentence. Write the word in the space provided.

1. You should be able to (adapt, adept) your speech to fit the needs of your audience.
   _____

2. By the end of your presentation, your message should be (plane, plain) to everyone.
   _____

3. It's a good idea to (write, right) down key points that you want to cover on index cards.
   _____

4. Remember to leave (some, sum) time for questions and answers after giving your speech.
   _____

5. This chapter will help you (devise, device) strategies for giving different types of speeches.
   _____

6. It's also prudent to practice reading your speech (aloud, allowed) several times.
   _____

7. Most people are (liable, libel) to get nervous before presenting.
   _____

8. The human resources (personal, personnel) can help you find background information on that speaker.
   _____

9. Dr. Dumas' speech included details about the fund's performance during the last (fiscal, physical) year.
   _____

10. During her talk, Ms. Hall (waived, waved) her arms to emphasize a point.
    _____

Student _____ Class _____ Instructor _____

Date Assigned _____ Date Completed _____

J. Attention-Getting Openings and Closings

Directions: Assume that you are speaking to a group of students at your alma mater. The purpose of your speech is to convey to these students some of the basic educational requirements for the field in which you have been working for over a year. (Select the field of your choice.) Suggest three different attention-getting ways to open your talk and three different ways to close your talk.

1. Opening:

_____

_____

_____

Closing:

_____

_____

_____

2. Opening:

_____

_____

_____

Closing:

_____

_____

_____

3. Opening:

_____

_____

_____

Closing:

_____

_____

_____

Section 14.4 Using Visual Aids and Technology

A. Using Visual Aids Appropriately

Directions: For each of the following types of visual aids, describe a situation in which that visual aid would be appropriate for presenting the material.

1. handouts

_____

_____

_____

2. posters

_____

_____

_____

3. document camera

_____

_____

_____

4. presentation software

_____

_____

_____

5. model of a human skeleton

_____

_____

_____

B. Creating a Visual Aid

Directions: Brainstorm a presentation topic and write the topic on an index card. Also, describe the audience and the location of the presentation. Place your card in a pile along with the cards of your classmates. Then, select a card from the pile. In the space provided, design a visual aid that you could use to help you present your topic. You may draw the visual aid, describe it in words, or use a combination of words and images to convey your design. You should identify the kind of visual aid you are designing.

C. Anticipating Technological Problems

Directions: For each of the following situations, describe what you can do to anticipate the problem and to be prepared with a solution that enables you to deliver your presentation in an effective manner.

1. The presentation software you brought to the conference is incompatible with the computer in the conference's media center.

_____

_____

_____

_____

continued ●▶

2. The bulb burns out in your overhead projector during a meeting at your office.

_____

_____

_____

_____

3. Your handouts are lost in transit to the university where you are giving a speech.

_____

_____

_____

_____

4. There is a power outage while you are pointing out features of a new product on your laptop.

_____

_____

_____

_____

D. Editing Practice

Directions: Underline any errors in the following sentences and write your corrections
on the lines provided. Write *OK* for any sentence that is correct.

1. Despite price increases, unit sales dropped off in the first
quarter, furthermore, sales dollars also decreased.   _____

2. The visual aids were developed by the graphic design house
Ship, & Sign.   _____

3. "Do you have any questions about the new customer service
procedures," asked Helen?   _____

4. According to the chart, each box should contain 5 grams of
potassium and should cost $.95.   _____

5. Ms. Sizemore plans to retire soon, she will then move to
Florida.   _____

6. By Mon. or Tues., the prices for travel packages will be
posted on the Web site.   _____

7. The keynote speaker is delayed at the airport; therefore we will adjust the schedule so he can speak later in the day. _____

8. For our May 15th conference, Mr. Elroy has invited Senator Jock to give the keynote address. _____

9. More information is available see the blue handout pages for those who wish to know more about the topic. _____

10. Rosemary would like to register for the afternoon sessions, at she is already familiar with the material in the morning sessions. _____

11. Ms. O'Neil, a former accountant with our Company, now manages her own firm. _____

12. Do you know whether Dr. Cortez has announced whom is to speak at the holiday awards banquet? _____

13. Either Bettina or Thomas have been assigned to lead discussion during Malcolm's absence. _____

14. As you know Mr. Barbarino is in Boston signing a contract for their ad campaign. _____

15. The reason the shipment was delayed, is that we didn't have three of the five items that were ordered. _____

16. The customers with whom I spoke are satisfied with the updated software. _____

17. Because we'd ordered more than 50 baskets we received an additional discount of 5 percent. _____

18. The hotel cleaning staff threw away the notes I left on the balcony. _____

19. Yes Mr. Milligan, I charged the batteries for your cellular phone and for your laptop. _____

20. Sean has already spoke with us about his ideas for renovating the warehouse. _____

CHAPTER 15 Searching for Jobs

Section 15.1 Job Search Skills

A. Analyzing Yourself and the Job

Directions: In the left-hand column, describe your career goals, education skills, experience, and personal characteristics. Then locate a specific job opening that interests you. In the right-hand column, describe the education, skills, experience, and personal characteristics required for the job. Decide whether the two columns match.

My Career Goals

_____

_____

_____

_____

_____

_____

_____

Job Openings

_____

_____

_____

_____

_____

_____

_____

My Education Thus Far

_____

_____

_____

_____

_____

_____

Education Required

_____

_____

_____

_____

_____

_____

Degree/Expected Graduation Date

_____

_____

My Skills

_____
_____
_____
_____
_____
_____
_____
_____

My Experience

_____
_____
_____
_____
_____
_____
_____

My Personal Characteristics

_____
_____
_____
_____
_____
_____
_____
_____

Skills Needed

_____
_____
_____
_____
_____
_____
_____
_____

Experience Required

_____
_____
_____
_____
_____
_____
_____

Personal Characteristics Required

_____
_____
_____
_____
_____
_____
_____
_____

B. Considering Job Factors

Directions: Circle the factor or factors in each group that would be most important for your ideal job. On the blanks provided, explain why the factor, or factors, is import to you.

1. Company

small	national
medium	international
large	values
local	purpose—goods or services

_____

_____

_____

_____

_____

2. Location

large city	willing to relocate within 500 miles of home
small community	willing to relocate within 1,000 miles of home
rural setting	willing to relocate within the United States
easy commute from home	willing to relocate internationally
accessible by public transportation	

_____

_____

_____

_____

_____

3. Job Content

variety of tasks	limited amount of responsibility
limited number of tasks	work directly with customers, clients, and the public
high degree of responsibility	limited interaction with customers, clients, and the public

_____

_____

_____

_____

_____

continued ➡

4. **Supervision**

close   democratic
minimal   supportive
authoritarian

_____

_____

_____

_____

_____

5. **Work Area**

office   noisy
outdoors   private
quiet   open

_____

_____

_____

_____

_____

6. **Schedule**

flexible hours   days
regular hours   nights
full-time   job share
part-time

_____

_____

_____

_____

_____

7. Rewards

financials   level of challenge
fringe benefits   opportunity to use skills and talents
opportunity for advancement   sense of helping others
sense of accomplishment   additional education and training provided

_____

_____

_____

_____

_____

8. Fringe Benefits

health insurance   child care
dental insurance   paid vacation
vision insurance   stock options
disability insurance   company car
retirement package   parking space

_____

_____

_____

_____

_____

9. Co-workers

work closely with others   develop friendships outside of work
work independently   limited social interaction with co-workers
develop friendships with co-workers

_____

_____

_____

_____

_____

continued ➤

10. **Work-Related Travel**

local (none overnight)

national

international

overnight travel—several nights per week but home on weekends

moderate overnight travel, up to five nights per week

extensive travel—traveling two or three weeks at a time including weekends

_____

_____

_____

_____

_____

C. Assessing the Job Market

Directions: List specific sources of information in your community you can use to find out about job opportunities. Include people, agencies, newspapers, and journals.

1. _____

2. _____

3. _____

4. _____

5. _____

6. _____

7. _____

8. _____

D. Classified Advertisements

Directions: Search the Internet or the Classified Ads section of the newspaper for job listings that interest you. Choose a job listing that you would respond to and attach it to this page. Think about the requirements listed for the job. Then, in the spaces provided, write what you would say about yourself in terms of education, experience, and personal qualifications in an application for this job.

Advertisement:

_____

_____

_____

_____

_____

_____

Education:

_____

_____

_____

_____

_____

Experience:

_____

_____

_____

_____

_____

Personal qualifications:

_____

_____

_____

_____

_____

E. Describing Job Experience

Directions: Write a description of your most recent or your current job. Use at least four of
the action verbs that appear on page 620 of your textbook.

_____

_____

_____

_____

_____

_____

_____

_____

_____

_____

F. Online Employment Search

Directions: Search the Internet for a job posting in your career area. You may want to use
a search engine to find Web sites that list jobs in your specific field, at a specific organization, or in your region. Or, you may want to search for job listings at one of the sites listed under the Online Searching for Employment section on pages 615–616 of your textbook. Select a job posting that interests you
and attach it to this page. Include the name of the Web site and the address
for the site where you found the job listing.

Web site: _____

Address or URL: _____

Advertisement:

G. Assessing Employment Search Methods

Directions: Assess the success of your various methods of searching for employment in the previous exercises. In the space provided, state which search methods were most helpful in finding job listings that appealed to you: newspaper ads, online searches, or another method. Then explain why you think this method was effective in helping you locate the job you wanted. Be prepared to discuss your findings with the class.

_____

_____

_____

_____

_____

_____

_____

_____

_____

_____

_____

_____

_____

_____

_____

_____

_____

_____

_____

_____

_____

_____

_____

_____

_____

Section 15.2 Chronological and Functional (Skills) Résumés

A. Reviewing Key Points

Directions: To review what you have learned about résumés in Section 15.2 from your textbook, answer each of the following questions.

1. When seeking employment, what four items can you prepare to present your qualifications?

_____

_____

_____

2. What kind of information should be included in your résumé?

_____

_____

_____

3. What personal information does federal law protect?

_____

_____

_____

4. If a person has not yet received a degree, what should he or she include in a résumé?

_____

_____

_____

5. When listing work experience, what information should be included?

_____

_____

_____

6. What categories are optional on a résumé?

_____

_____

_____

7. What is a chronological résumé?

_____

_____

_____

8. When is a functional (skills) résumé preferred over a chronological résumé?

_____

_____

_____

9. Why is it important to proofread your résumé?

_____

_____

_____

10. How can a person make his or her résumé stand apart from others?

_____

_____

_____

B. Formatting Your Résumé

Directions: In the circle provided, check *Yes* for each guideline that is appropriate for a résumé. Check *No* if the guideline is not appropriate.

	YES	NO
1. Font size on a résumé should be no smaller than 10-point size and should not exceed 14-point type.	◯	◯
2. Headings, bold-faced letters, and italics should be avoided.	◯	◯
3. Résumé, application letters, and envelopes should ideally be on the same color stationery.	◯	◯
4. A résumé should make use of the white space on the paper, making it easy to read.	◯	◯
5. Colored paper, such as pink, blue, and yellow, is acceptable for résumé in certain fields.	◯	◯
6. A résumé should be limited to two pages.	◯	◯

C. Preparing a List of References

Directions: On the lines provided, write the names of six people you could possibly use for references. Include each person's address, home phone number and work number, and their title. Include people you have worked with as well as personal references. Do not use family members. Make sure that the person is willing to speak on your behalf.

1. _____

   _____

   _____

   _____

   _____

   _____

   _____

2. _____

   _____

   _____

   _____

   _____

   _____

   _____

3. _____

   _____

   _____

   _____

   _____

   _____

   _____

4. _____
_____
_____
_____
_____
_____
_____
_____

5. _____
_____
_____
_____
_____
_____
_____
_____

6. _____
_____
_____
_____
_____
_____
_____
_____

D. Creating Phrases for a Résumé

Directions: To practice using action verbs in your résumé, write a specific description for each of the following work descriptions, using action words and phrases.

1. Rosa worked weekends at a veterinarian clinic. Sometimes she worked the front desk, answering phone calls, taking messages, and checking in patients. Occasionally, she helped in the kennels with feeding and walking boarders.

   _____

   _____

   _____

   _____

2. Charlie attends a junior college part time and works evenings at a local restaurant. He helps the chef keep inventory and prepares order forms that are sent out the following morning. Charlie is also responsible for making soups and sauces. When necessary, Charlie trains new kitchen hires.

   _____

   _____

   _____

   _____

3. Beatrice has worked in a flower shop for a year. She has learned to make floral arrangements with both traditional and exotic flowers. Besides making bouquets for individuals, she also has experience making arrangements for large functions. She also took the initiative to begin creating balloon arrangements for younger customers.

   _____

   _____

   _____

   _____

4. Mark works part-time at a small engineering firm, assisting certified engineers. He inputs data about jobs that contractors will use to propose a bid. Mark is a computer whiz and has solved several technical problems in the firm.

   _____

   _____

   _____

   _____

Section 15.3 Scannable Résumés

A. Reviewing Key Points

Directions: Circle *T* if the statement is true and circle *F* is the statement is false.

1. A scannable résumé should be double-spaced.	**T**	**F**
2. Important headings should be bulleted.	**T**	**F**
3. Font size on a scannable résumé should not exceed 14 points	**T**	**F**
4. Because the résumé is being scanned, the color of ink used is not important.	**T**	**F**
5. Abbreviations should be used sparingly.	**T**	**F**
6. The first line of text should be your name, followed by your career objective.	**T**	**F**
7. Avoid folding your résumé or using staples.	**T**	**F**
8. Copies of your original résumé are acceptable for scanning.	**T**	**F**
9. Text should be flush left; tabs and indents should be avoided.	**T**	**F**
10. Action verbs are preferable over keywords to describe related experience.	**T**	**F**

B. Using Keywords

Directions: Computers that scan résumés look for keywords and nouns associated with the specific positions within the organization. Rewrite the action phrases listed below in phrases that are more suitable for a scannable résumé.

1. Developed and implemented the new mentoring program.

_____

_____

2. Interviewed, hired, and scheduled summer interns.

_____

_____

3. Presented training programs.

_____

_____

4. Researched programs to reduce overhead costs.

_____

_____

C. Writing Clear Sentences

Directions: Rewrite each of the following sentences to make sure they communicate clearly.

1. Submitting my résumé to human resources, I realized that I had misspelled several words.

_____

_____

_____

2. When told about an opening at Dell, it was too late to apply.

_____

_____

_____

3. To use the Internet, the instructor held a special class in the computer lab.

_____

_____

_____

4. To enter the field of biochemistry, years of study and research are necessary.

_____

_____

_____

5. Frank went to the job fair to speak with potential employers and to submit his résumé with his sister.

_____

_____

_____

D. Preparing a Scannable Résumé

Directions: Using keywords listed in the following job posting, prepare a scannable résumé. You may attach the résumé to the back of this page.

Clean Up! America! (CUA) is a national environmental public education organization. Our mission statement: Through programs, involvement and education, Clean Up! America! directs our nation to conserve and enhance our natural resources.

Clean Up! America! (CUA) is a governmental organization committed to conservation and waste reduction. CUA produces a variety of newsletters and pamphlets, operates a hotline, and conducts educational programs.

Job Description

Candidate will assist in preparing a free environmental resource packet that is mailed to middle schools and high schools nationwide. Duties include making contact with other environmental agencies; writing, proofreading, and data entry of our monthly newsletter; assisting staff in devising an outreach program for schools and community centers to expand the existing energy education program.

Student _____ Class _____ Instructor _____ Glencoe/McGraw-Hill

Date Assigned _____ Date Completed _____

Section 15.4 Application Letter and Application Form

A. Writing an Introduction

Directions: Your application letter should begin with a statement of your intent of the position for which you are applying. The following advertisement was placed on the Web site for *The Mapleton Tribunal*. On the lines provided, write a brief introductory paragraph of an application letter that states your intent.

Growing law firm seeks a highly motivated, energetic person for administrative assistant position. Multi-task, pleasant telephone manner is essential, computer skills are a must. Proficient in Windows, knowledge of Excel, typing, analytical skills, and well-organized. Mail résumé to Vintage Legal Firm, 600 Holland Avenue, San Rafael, California, 94903.

_____

_____

_____

_____

_____

_____

_____

_____

_____

_____

_____

B. Highlighting Your Experience

Directions: The body of the application letter should show the employer how your experience and qualifications perfectly match the position. Using the advertisement above, write a paragraph that emphasizes your education and training in relation to the opening.

_____

_____

_____

_____

continued ●▶

_____

_____

_____

_____

_____

_____

_____

_____

C. Making a Final Impression

Directions: The last paragraph of the application letter should be an invitation for an interview. Remind the employer how to reach you. On the lines provided, write a final paragraph for the application letter you have completed for Exercises A and B.

_____

_____

_____

_____

_____

_____

_____

_____

_____

_____

_____

D. Completing an Application Form

Directions: Complete the application form on the next page. Read and follow all directions carefully.

Satellite Communications Company
An Equal Opportunity Employer

Personal Data

Company Use Only

Date_____
Interviewer_____

Applying for Position As _____ Salary Desired _____ Date Available _____

Date Applied _____

Name _____
              (Last)   (First)   (Middle)

Address _____
           (Street)   (City)   (State)   (Zip Code)

Telephone No. _____ Social Security No._____ U.S. Citizen? _____
        (Area Code)

Who referred you to us? _____

Educational Data

SCHOOLS	NAME OF INSTITUTION	ADDRESS	MAJOR	COURSES TAKEN	No. Yrs. Attended	Yr. Grad.	Degree
High School or Equivalent							
College							
Other							
Other							

Employment Data

NAME OF COMPANY	ADDRESS	YOUR POSITION and DUTIES	Dates	Salary Received	Supervisor's Name	Reason for Leaving
			From	Start $		
			To	Finish $		
			From	Start $		
			To	Finish $		

References

NAME	ADDRESS	TELEPHONE NUMBER

E. Reviewing Key Points

Directions: Circle *T* if the statement is true and circle *F* is the statement is false.

1. It is not appropriate to address an application letter to a specific person.   **T**   **F**

2. How you complete the form can reveal if you have organized work habits.   **T**   **F**

3. It is acceptable to use red ink to complete an application form.   **T**   **F**

4. Leaving blank areas may reveal that you cannot follow directions.   **T**   **F**

5. Because some forms must be completed within the organization's office, spelling errors are overlooked.   **T**   **F**

6. Unsolicited application letters should not specify a specific position.   **T**   **F**

Section 15.5 Employment Portfolio

A. Analyzing Contents for Your Portfolio

Directions: In the left-hand column, describe the current state of completion for items that may be included in your portfolio. In the right-hand column, list activities that you can do to prepare these items for placement in your portfolio. You might, for example, need to have your résumé proofread or print it on high quality paper; or your references may be incomplete.

Current Standing   **What I Need to Do**

Résumé:

_____   _____

_____   _____

_____   _____

References:

_____   _____

_____   _____

_____   _____

Diplomas and certificates (copies):

_____   _____

_____   _____

_____   _____

Transcripts:

_____   _____

_____   _____

_____   _____

Certificates and Awards:

_____   _____

_____   _____

_____   _____

continued ➡

Document/Writing examples:

_____   _____

_____   _____

_____   _____

Special software examples:

_____   _____

_____   _____

_____   _____

Photos:

_____   _____

_____   _____

_____   _____

Other:

_____   _____

_____   _____

_____   _____

_____   _____

_____   _____

B. Presenting Your Portfolio

Directions: Preparing the contents of your portfolio is a process that will continue over time. Even in its early stages, you must be ready to present it during an interview. On the lines provided, list five situations in which you might introduce your portfolio.

1. _____

2. _____

3. _____

4. _____

5. _____

C. Word Power

Directions: Learning new words and incorporating them into your vocabulary increases your ability to communicate. A well-spoken interviewee can make a positive impression on an employer. Match the definition on the left with its word in the right-hand column. Write the appropriate letter beside each numbered item.

1. a failure to observe a law or promise   **a.** prerogative   _____

2. a large number, countless   **b.** incentive   _____

3. a occurring by good luck   **c.** consolidate   _____

4. to merge or unite   **d.** breach   _____

5. a right or privilege   **e.** tribute   _____

6. something that makes one work harder   **f.** fortuitous   _____

7. an honor or acknowledgement   **g.** myriad   _____

D. Polishing Your Speech

Directions: Which of the six Cs of communication (clear, complete, concise, consistent, correct, or courteous) is violated in each of the following sentences?

1. Your interview is scheduled for Monday, May 19.

_____

2. One of my former employers have agreed to write a letter of recommendation.

_____

3. After the receptionist introduced me to the manager, she asked if I wanted something to drink.

_____

4. I insist that you call me at home.

_____

5. I would like to take this opportunity to assure you that I am proficient in Excel.

_____

6. My classes this spring are on Monday, Friday, and Wednesday.

_____

CHAPTER 16 Interviewing and Employment Issues

Section 16.1 Preparing for the Interview

A. Researching a Prospective Employer

Directions: Select a company in your locale for which you would like to work. After researching the organization, answer the following questions. You may want to call the company for information, go to its Web site, search for articles that mention the company, and/or speak with people who are familiar with the organization.

1. Is the company publicly or privately owned?

_____

_____

2. What are the main products or services that the company provides?

_____

_____

3. When was the company established?

_____

_____

4. Where is its home office?

_____

_____

5. How many branches or subsidiaries does it have? Where are the other offices (if any)?

_____

_____

6. How many people are employed at the local office?

_____

_____

continued ➡

7. Does it have offices outside the United States? If so, where?

_____

_____

8. Who are the firm's chief competitors?

_____

_____

9. Is the company involved with the community? If so, how?

_____

_____

10. From what sources did you find this information?

_____

_____

B. Preparing Questions to Ask the Interviewer

Directions: You have been invited to interview for a position with the company you
identified in Exercise A. Based on the information you compiled in Exercise A,
prepare three questions to ask the interviewer.

1. _____

_____

_____

2. _____

_____

_____

3. _____

_____

_____

C. Anticipating Interview Questions

Directions: To prepare for a job interview, develop answers to the following questions that are often asked at interviews.

1. What are your strongest points?

_____

_____

_____

_____

_____

2. What are your weakest points?

_____

_____

_____

_____

_____

3. Why did you select this particular course of study?

_____

_____

_____

_____

_____

4. Why would you be a good candidate for this position?

_____

_____

_____

_____

_____

Student _____ Class _____ Instructor _____

Date Assigned _____ Date Completed _____

D. Interview Quiz

Directions: Circle *T* if the statement is true and *F* if the statement is false.

1. Effective interview planning begins many days before the interview.   **T**   **F**

2. You should confirm your appointment for an interview beforehand.   **T**   **F**

3. You should not ask for directions to the company location, because it makes you look uninformed.   **T**   **F**

4. Job applicants who have researched the company they interview with are better able to discuss how their experiences match the company's needs.   **T**   **F**

5. You should prepare a list of questions and take them to the interview with you.   **T**   **F**

6. A goal of a job interview is to find out if the job fits your career plans.   **T**   **F**

7. Chewing gum during the interview is acceptable to make sure that your breath is pleasant.   **T**   **F**

8. You should bring at least three copies of your résumé to an interview.   **T**   **F**

9. Preparing a résumé takes the place of completing an application form.   **T**   **F**

10. You should get eight to ten hours of sleep the night before the interview.   **T**   **F**

11. During the interview, it is appropriate to ask what your primary responsibilities will be if you get the job.   **T**   **F**

12. You should act like you don't know anything about the company in order to get more information during the interview.   **T**   **F**

13. The best time to negotiate for salary and benefits is during the interview.   **T**   **F**

14. You should take notes during an interview.   **T**   **F**

15. Being qualified for a job guarantees that you will get it.   **T**   **F**

Copyright © Glencoe/McGraw-Hill

E. Becoming Knowledgeable About Industry Trends

Directions: Search the Internet and print media such as the local newspaper for information about current events that affect the industry in which you want to work. In the space provided, describe three issues or events that currently affect your prospective field.

_____

_____

_____

_____

_____

_____

_____

_____

_____

_____

_____

_____

_____

_____

_____

_____

_____

_____

_____

_____

_____

_____

_____

_____

_____

_____

_____

_____

_____

_____

_____

_____

Student _____ Class _____ Instructor _____

Date Assigned _____ Date Completed _____

F. International Countries and Cities

Directions: In the space provided, write the correct spelling of each international country or city that is misspelled. If the item is correct, write *OK* in the space.

1. Switserland; Rome; Stockholm; Haiti _____

2. Florence; Berlin; Uruguay; Israel _____

3. Jamaica; Estonia; Beijing; Phillipines _____

4. Montreal; Johannesburg; Vienna; Tokeyo _____

5. Eygpt; Cologne; Mexicali; Portugal _____

6. Peru; Barsellona; Tanzania; Latvia _____

7. Frankfurt; Honduras; Grease; Kyoto _____

8. Turkey; Cairo; Bogotá; Bolivia _____

9. Edinburg; Munich; Toronto; Moscow _____

10. Ireland; Jerusalem; Brussels; Kenya _____

11. Ontario; Casablanca; Paraguay; Ukrain _____

12. Pakistan; Dominican Republic; Calcuta; Afghanistan _____

13. Mongolia; Thayland; Nagasaki; Guatemala _____

14. Hanoi; Perth; Malaysia; Australea _____

15. Winnipeg; Greenland; Panima; Buenos Aires _____

16. Dublin; Sweden; Helsinki; Austria _____

17. Manchester; Romania; Seyria; Nigeria _____

18. New Guinea; Bangladesh; Amman; Poleland _____

19. Venezuela; Budapest; Jordan; Algeria _____

20. Argentina; Warsaw; Luxemburg; Seoul _____

G. Proofreading Practice

Directions: Underline any errors in the following letter and write your corrections on the lines provided. Write *OK* for any line that is correct.

Ms. Irena Diaz   _____

Editorial Directer   _____

Best Word Productions, Inc.   _____

2000 Multimedia Dr.   _____

Austin, TX 78733   _____

Dear Ms. Diaz   _____

Thank you for meeting with me to discuss the assistant editor   _____

position yesterday. It was a pleasure to greet you, and I   _____

appreciate you're taking the time to conduct the interview.   _____

I feel confident that I can make a effective contribution to Best   _____

Word as an assistant Editor and have enclosed the contact   _____

information for the references we discussed during the intrview.   _____

Please let meknow if you would like any further information   _____

from me. Thanks again for meeting with me. I look forward to   _____

hereing from you son.   _____

Sincerely,   _____

Student _____ Class _____ Instructor _____

Date Assigned _____ Date Completed _____

Section 16.2 Interviews and Interview Questions

A. Types of Interviews

Directions: Identify the type of interview technique being implemented for each of the following situations: screening, one-on-one, panel or committee, group, stress, unstructured, interview, or situational.

1. When you arrive for an interview, you find yourself in a room with four other applicants. The interviewer asks that each of you introduce yourself.   _____

2. You are introduced to the department manager. After introductions are made, the manager asks you to talk about yourself. She asks if you have any questions, then sees you to the door.   _____

3. After you submit your résumé and application form to the human resource department, you are invited in to speak with one of the human resource employees. He reviews your résumé and application with you.   _____

4. You interviewed with the principal of a high school for a position in the history department. Then, you are scheduled for a second interview. When you arrive, you walk into a conference room with six people from different departments. Each person has a copy of your résumé, and they take turns asking questions.   _____

5. After you cover highlights of your education and work experience, the interviewer asks that you describe how you have handled dissatisfied customers in your previous position.   _____

6. During the interview, the interviewer states that it is common for employees to encounter customers who may be physically or mentally challenged. She then asks how you would handle such a customer.   _____

7. About ten minutes into the interview, the interviewer asks, "How would you react if I told you that your interview was terrible?"   _____

8. Human resources has scheduled an interview for you and the supervisor of the opened position. The supervisor spends an hour speaking to you about your prior work experience and specific skills related to the opening. _____

9. You receive a telephone call from a company, and the person asks a few general questions regarding your résumé. _____

10. The position for which you applied is with a team of six other members. After interviewing with the team leader, you are scheduled for an interview with the other five members. _____

B. Anticipating Interview Questions

Directions: To prepare for a job interview, you should develop answers to questions that are frequently asked at interviews. On the lines provided, write a response to each question. Your responses should be clear, concise, and courteous.

1. How did you do in school?

_____

_____

_____

2. How has your college experience prepared you for a business (or other) career?

_____

_____

_____

3. What qualifications do you have that make you think you would be successful in this business?

_____

_____

_____

4. How do you evaluate success?

_____

_____

_____

continued ➡

5. What was the last book you read? How did it affect you?

_____

_____

_____

6. How do you get along with other people?

_____

_____

_____

7. What are your strongest points?

_____

_____

_____

8. What have you learned from your mistakes?

_____

_____

_____

9. What are your biggest accomplishments?

_____

_____

_____

10. How would you deal with a supervisor who was difficult to work with?

_____

_____

_____

11. What would you do if you disagreed with your supervisor's opinion about an important matter?

_____

_____

_____

12. How do you work under pressure?

_____

_____

_____

13. How would you describe yourself?

_____

_____

_____

14. Rate yourself on a scale of one to ten.

_____

_____

_____

15. Tell me a funny story.

_____

_____

_____

C. Proofreading Practice

Directions: Read the following paragraph from a memo to find any spelling or
grammatical errors. Write your corrections in the space provided.

It has come to my attencion that you have an opening in the   _____

editorial department. As you are most familar with the day-to-day   _____

responsabilities of the job, I think it would be best if you wrote a   _____

brief job description to submit to human resources. I also   _____

understand that you are oferring three internship this summer. Of   _____

the three openings, which will be the more demanding? I have a   _____

wonderful aplicant who comes highly reccomended.   _____

Section 16.3 Communication Skills During the Interview

A. Making a Positive First Impression

Directions: In the space provided, write five actions you can take to ensure that you make a positive first impression at an interview.

_____

_____

_____

_____

_____

_____

_____

_____

B. Interview Quiz

Directions: Circle *T* if the statement is true and *F* if the statement is false.

1. Most interviewers want to establish a positive rapport with the interviewee. **T** **F**

2. Punctuality and appearance contribute to the impression you make during an interview. **T** **F**

3. It's acceptable to be late to an interview due to unforeseen traffic problems. **T** **F**

4. You should avoid wild colors when dressing for an interview. **T** **F**

5. Solid preparation will help you feel confident during an interview. **T** **F**

6. You should sit down as soon as you walk into the interviewer's office. **T** **F**

7. You should speak slowly and directly to the interviewer. **T** **F**

8. When asked by an interviewer about hobbies or leisure activities, it's a good idea to mention ones that are physically active, such as, swimming.
    T   **F**

9. When lunch or dinner is over, you can assume that the interview has concluded.
    T   **F**

10. When your interviewer rises, it's a signal that the interview is over.
    T   **F**

C. Creating an Interview Checklist

Directions: In the space provided, write a ten-point list of things you should check to do before arriving at an interview. You may want to refer to this list before you interview for your next job.

1. _____

2. _____

3. _____

4. _____

5. _____

6. _____

7. _____

8. _____

9. _____

10. _____

D. Assessing Your Interviewing Skills

Directions: On the bar below, circle the number that corresponds to how comfortable you
feel about interviewing for a job. (The number 1 indicates that you are very
uncomfortable interviewing and the number 10 indicates that you are very
comfortable interviewing.) Then, describe why you feel as comfortable as you
do and what you can do to feel more at ease while interviewing.

| 1 | 2 | 3 | 4 | 5 | 6 | 7 | 8 | 9 | 10 |

_____

_____

_____

_____

_____

_____

_____

_____

_____

_____

_____

_____

_____

_____

_____

_____

_____

_____

E. Editing Practice

Directions: Underline any errors in the following sentences and write your corrections on the lines provided. Write *OK* for any sentence that is correct.

1. Most interviewers have three standard goals for an interview.   _____

2. A skilled interviwer will try to put an applicant at easy.   _____

3. Being late to an interview can cuase you to feel stress and frustration.   _____

4. It is important to look look your best at an interview.   _____

5. You should carry you're essentials in a briefcase.   _____

6. If in doubt, dress more conservatively than you usually do.   _____

7. You are perfcctly capable of expressing confidence during an interview.   _____

8. Remember to take a few deep breaths while wading for the interview to begin.   _____

9. You may want to think about how your educasion has prepared you for a job.   _____

10. Usually; the interviewer will let you know when the interview is concluding.   _____

Section 16.4 **After the Interview**

A. Accepting a Job Offer

Directions: You have received a letter from MARIAH Financial Services offering you a position as a financial consultant. The letter outlines your terms of employment and specifies that you will begin work three weeks from today (current date) when training for new consultants begins.

Write a letter to be faxed or E-mailed to Mr. Alex Parsons, Human Resources Director, accepting the position and confirming your first day of employment. The address of the company is: 800 Palm Street, Lincoln, NE, 68502. Use the current date and your own return address, as well as the block-letter style with standard punctuation. Compose the letter on a computer if possible and print and paste it in the space provided.

B. Declining a Job Offer

Directions: You recently accepted employment as a graphic designer with Sharp Graphics, Inc., but two days later you received a better offer with a higher salary, better benefits, and more opportunity for advancement from Superior Graphics, Inc.

Write a tactful letter to be mailed or E-mailed to Ms. Ruth Liner, President of Sharp Graphics, Inc., letting her know that you have accepted another job. The address is: 300 Ball Court, Newland, KY 41071. Use the block-letter style with open punctuation, the current date, and your own address. Type and print the letter from a computer and paste it in the space provided.

C. Writing an Interview Follow-Up Letter

Directions: You applied today for the position of administrative assistant to Ms. Amy Tyler, the plant manager of Tyler Manufacturing Corp. Ms. Tyler interviewed you personally because she needs to fill the job as soon as possible. You want the job and can begin work immediately.

Write Ms. Tyler an interview follow-up letter using the modified-block style with indented paragraphs and standard punctuation. The corporation's address is: 1800 Tyler Avenue, Beaver Creek, OR 97214. Use the current date and your own return address. Type and print the letter from a computer and paste it in the space provided.

D. Writing a Thank-you Letter to Others

Directions: After searching for a job for five months, you met a former classmate, Blaine Nelson. He used to work at Logan's Insurance Agency and suggested you apply there. He also agreed to be a reference for you. A week later you were offered the job.

Write a thank-you letter to Blaine using the modified-block style with block paragraphs and standard punctuation. His address is 900 Brown Street, El Paso, Texas, 79925. Use the current date and your own return address. Type the letter on a computer, print it, and paste it in the space provided.

Section 16.5 Requesting a Promotion or a Compensation Increase

A. Researching Salary Trends

Directions: Identify two or three specific job titles in the industry in which you want to work. Using the Internet, your school career offices, the Chamber of Commerce, and local businesses, find out what the salary range is for those positions. As some of the information may be aimed at specific geographic areas, make sure you adjust the figures to the cost of living in your area. Write the results of your survey on the lines provided.

_____

_____

_____

_____

_____

_____

_____

_____

_____

B. Building a Case

Directions: For each of the following cases, write notes that could be used to ask for a pay raise or alternate compensation. Once you have written your notes, choose a partner and present your case to him or her verbally.

1. Beverly Wooten is a real estate agent for Homefinders, Inc. She has worked with this company for five years. She has not received a pay raise, as the owners believe she is compensated by her sales. She recently proposed a system that allows agents to take time off during the weekends, and she helped train two new agents.

_____

_____

_____

_____

_____

2. Bryan Wilmington works at GoldenEye Productions. This past year, he enrolled in night classes, focusing on technical equipment used in his office. He also has been assisting the lead technician in formatting Web sites and editing videotapes. Bryan always receives good evaluations and gets the usual cost-of-living increase. However, he feels that he should be awarded an eight percent raise.

_____

_____

_____

_____

_____

_____

3. Frank Mendoza is a chef at Mezaluna. He has been written up in several food magazines as one of the most creative chefs of the area. The restaurant owner has already rewarded Frank monetarily. However, Frank has a new baby, and he wants to spend more time at home, especially on the weekends.

_____

_____

_____

_____

_____

_____

4. Deanna Vickers works at a daycare center. She has been there seven years. She rarely calls in sick and is quite punctual. She volunteers to work overtime when other daycare providers must leave, and she initiated the Children's Science Fair Week. Deanna is shy and does not like confrontations, but she wants to buy a house and feels she deserves a raise.

_____

_____

_____

_____

_____

_____

C. Avoiding Disaster

Directions: There are certain dos and don'ts when asking for a raise or promotion. List five things that you should never do when asking for a compensation increase.

1. _____

2. _____

3. _____

4. _____

5. _____

D. Editing for Courtesy

Directions: On the lines provided, rewrite each of the following sentences to improve the tone.

1. I can't find your name in our computer, so I can't let you in.

_____

_____

2. Why don't you pay attention when I explain something to you the first time?

_____

_____

3. This memo is awful; you need to rewrite it.

_____

_____

4. I think your evaluation of me is wrong, and I intend to fight this assessment.

_____

_____

5. There's no way I can work tonight. I have tickets to the Yankees game.

_____

_____

Section 16.6 Leaving a Position

A. Reviewing Key Points

Directions: Review the key points covered in Section 16.6. Circle *T* if the statement is true and *F* if the statement is false.

1. Before leaving an organization, you should leave a list of instructions or suggestions that may be helpful to your replacement.　　　　　T　　　　　F

2. It is acceptable to provide your employer with a three-day notice that you are leaving.　　　　　T　　　　　F

3. Your supervisor should be the last person to know about your resignation.　　　　　T　　　　　F

4. You should state your reason for leaving a position in a positive manner, even if your employment experience was negative.　　　　　T　　　　　F

5. It is your responsibility to make sure your paper work is up to date before leaving a position.　　　　　T　　　　　F

6. If you lose your job, you should ask friends and family for emotional support.　　　　　T　　　　　F

7. It does not matter if you thank the company for the experience gained in an exit interview or in your letter of resignation.　　　　　T　　　　　F

8. You should maintain a positive relationship with your former employers.　　　　　T　　　　　F

9. If you are laid off due to downsizing, you should demand severance pay.　　　　　T　　　　　F

10. Letting others know that you are out of work is a hindrance, and you should keep that information confidential.　　　　　T　　　　　F

B. Writing a Letter of Resignation

Directions: You have been an office assistant at Big House Real Estate for two years and have been attending night school. Graduation is in two weeks. You have been offered and have accepted the position of office manager at Metro Regional Clinic at a significant increase in income and responsibility. One of your career goals is to get a master's degree in business administration, and Metro Regional has offered to pay for your tuition while you are working on this degree.

Write a letter of resignation using the modified-block style with block paragraphs and standard punctuation to Mrs. Adrianna Tomlin, Executive Director, Big House Real Estate, 222 Butternut Ridge, Appleview, SC 29611. You and Adrianna are personal friends. Address her by her first name in the salutation, and specify that you are giving three weeks notice of departure. Use the current date and your own return address. Type the letter on a computer, print it, and paste it in the space provided.

C. Punctuation Check

Directions: For each of the following sentences, correct any punctuation errors. Write *OK* if a sentence has no error.

1. Kim was offered a position at our Orlando offices, however she wants to stay in Phoenix.

   _____

   _____

   _____

2. Unfortunately I must seek employment elsewhere.

   _____

   _____

3. Although I will be leaving Sports Unlimited, I will remember the wonderful friends I made.

   _____

   _____

   _____

4. My supervisor, Kathryn Holloway has been promoted, and will be leaving our department.

   _____

   _____

   _____

5. Our company was forced to lay off several employees, because our sales have been slow.

   _____

   _____

   _____

D. Updating Vocabulary

Directions: On the lines provided, rewrite each of the following sentences, replacing outdated words and expressions.

1. I would like to schedule my exit interview at your earliest convenience.

   _____

   _____

   _____

2. Kindly advise Malcolm that his presence is required at our annual budget meeting.

   _____

   _____

   _____

3. At the present time, we have no openings in your field.

   _____

   _____

   _____

4. In the event that a replacement has not been found, I am willing to stay another week if necessary.

   _____

   _____

   _____

5. Your letter of resignation is duly noted.

   _____

   _____

   _____